P9-DWH-011

"In an appealing narrative style, Bob Keck offers a personal and social history of the transformation of medicine from being totally materialistic and mechanistic to becoming comprehensive, holistic, and integrated. He provides scientific data and a rational basis for accepting the irrational, emotional, and spiritual aspects of the healing process. Although the book is aimed primarily at the individual, religious communities as a whole could profit from paying attention to what Keck has to say about developing an appreciation of the sacred in the quest for physical health."

THE REVEREND JAMES R. ADAMS, PRESIDENT
The Center for Progressive Christianity

"Dr. Keck's prescription for healing as a sacred path opens up vast new vistas. . . . There is an awakening logic presented in this book that demands listening to, as matters of faith and science must now include the healing powers of both our spirit and body. . . . Bob has a succinct way of organizing and presenting a growing body of knowledge so as to make sense of these evolving/revolutionary concepts, a call to action for both lay people, scientist/physicians, and theologians. . . . Keck's concepts . . . can enrich and deepen our experience . . . while bringing ever more clarity to our concept of healing."

JAY COONAN, M.D.
Associate Professor of Clinical Medicine
University of Colorado Health Sciences Center

"*Healing as a Sacred Path* gives us reason to believe that the long-awaited paradigm shift in medicine has indeed begun. Taking us beyond the old medical model of fixing to the new paradigm of healing, this remarkable book of personal transformation will illuminate the path for any courageous soul wanting to heal and willing to take charge of the miraculous healing process. I will be recommending this book to a lot of people. Thank you, Robert Keck."

CATHERINE FESTE, AUTHOR
The Physician Within and *Meditations on Diabetes*

"*Healing as a Sacred Path* challenges our thinking about the spiritual messages inherent in our own experiences of illness and healing and provides thought-provoking suggestions for using these experiences as tools to develop deeper meaning in our lives."

SUSAN FRAMPTON, PH.D.
Executive Director, The Planetree Alliance

"What a privilege it has been to read Dr. Bob Keck's book *Healing as a Sacred Path*. It is an inspiring book . . . a 'must read' for anyone who is on their own journey for healing and wholeness."

TREY KUHNE, M.DIV., PH.D.
Medical spirituality consultant

"Bob Keck is an extraordinary individual—in his willingness to share a very personal story in service to others so they may find their way through the valley experiences of life to new heights of spiritual, emotional, and physical healing; and in his exceptional range of exploration, understanding and insightful analysis of the broad range of inner and outer resources available."

THE REVEREND GLENN R. MOSLEY, PH.D.
President and CEO, Association of Unity Churches

"This book is a very timely discussion of the current chaos in medicine and religion. Medical science without the mind can no longer claim to have all the answers to illness. Also, spirituality has surpassed religion. Bob Keck, with his personal journey and his study of the causes of this fragmentation, gives us an incredible opportunity to regain and maintain our health in a holistic manner combining Mind, Body, and Spirit. I heartily endorse this book for anyone wanting better health and healing."

THEODORE C. NING, JR., M.D., CLINICAL PROFESSOR
Department of Surgery (Urology)
University of Colorado Health Sciences Center

"Robert Keck's *Healing as a Sacred Path* opens up important questions of illness and healing for doctors, clergy, and people of faith. Inclusive and nondogmatic in spirit, Keck details his own story of suffering severe and chronic pain for years before availing himself of the inner resources of healing available to him and everyone. . . . He shows us how to take responsibility for our own healing while also using the resources of conventional medicine. . . . Keck's knowledge of the field is impressive."

THE REVEREND ROBERT A. RAINES, PH.D. (RETIRED)

"Dr. Keck leads us on a journey of self-discovery, using the vehicle of his own story. His wonderful words, images, and vision enable us to understand the power when both spiritual and medical converge to promote healing in us all. The miracle of *Healing as a Sacred Path* deserves attention by all who seek a deeper appreciation of the human condition, and our strivings to transform ourselves and the world in which we live."

DAVID S. WAHL, M.D.
Associate Clinical Professor of Psychiatry
University of Colorado Health Sciences Center

HEALING *as a* SACRED PATH

HEALING *as a* SACRED PATH

A Story of Personal, Medical, and Spiritual Transformation

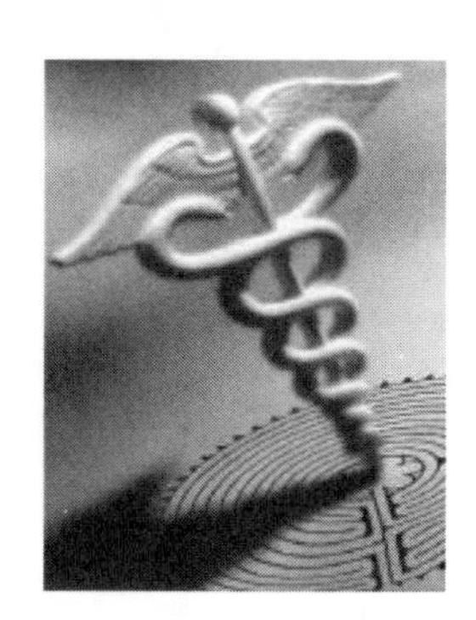

L. ROBERT KECK, PH.D.

Chrysalis Books

Library of Congress Cataloging-in-Publication Data

Keck, L. Robert. 1935–
Healing as a sacred path : a story of personal, medical, and spiritual transformation / by L. Robert Keck.
p. cm.
Includes bibliographical references and index.
ISBN 0-87785-389-4
1. Healing—Religious aspects. 2. Keck, L. Robert, 1935– I. Title.
BL65.M4 K34 2002
291.3'1—dc21

2002006505

Credits:

Material on pp. 191–192 from *Speak the Language of Healing: Living with Breast Cancer without Going to War* by Susan Kuner, Carol Matzkin Orsborn, Linda Quigley, and Karen Leigh Stroup appears by permission of Conari Press, Berkeley, California.

"Now I Become Myself" from *Collected Poems 1930–1993* by May Sarton. Copyright © 1993, 1988, 1984, 1974 by May Sarton. Used by permission of W. W. Norton & Company, Inc.

Excerpt of poem on p. 289 from "Enough" in *Where Many Rivers Meet* by David Whyte. Copyright © 1990 by David Whyte. Reprinted by permission of Many Rivers Press, Langley, Washington.

The poem "I Will Not Die an Unlived Life" from the book *I Will Not Die an Unlived Life: Reclaiming Purpose and Passion* (Conari Press, 2000) is reprinted by permission of Dawna Markova, Ph.D., www.ptpinc.org.

Material on pp. 284–285 from Murray Stein, *Transformation: Emergence of the Self* is quoted by permission of Texas A & M University Press.

Edited by Mary Lou Bertucci
Cover design by Karen Connor
Interior design by Sans Serif, Inc., Saline, Michigan
Set in Giovanni by Sans Serif, Inc.
Printed in the United States of America.

Chrysalis Books is an imprint of the Swedenborg Foundation, Inc. For more information, contact:
Swedenborg Foundation Publishers
320 North Church Street
West Chester, PA 19380
or
http://www.swedenborg.com.

To

Roger and Frances Keck

(In memoriam)

My parents spent "many years in heaven before they died," to borrow a phrase that Alice Walker used when speaking of her mother. Through the extraordinary power of their love, they brought many of us into that heaven with them. It was being surrounded by that love that enabled me to believe in and to eventually be open and receptive to miraculous healings.

And

Diana

Wife, partner, lover, and soul-mate

As we grow towards thirty years of marriage, I am more convinced with each passing day that she is the most powerful healing force to grace my life. Her incarnation of loving power has deeply blessed any and all of us who are privileged to be in her life—whether as husband, friend, indoor or outdoor animal companion, or clients who come to her for psychotherapy. If we want healing, she has the loving power that can facilitate miracles in our own inner capacity for health and wholeness. I only wish that everybody in the entire world could experience, in their own lives and with those with whom they are in relationship, such transforming and miraculous love. The world would be such a better place within which to live.

CONTENTS

An INVITATION

Physical pain has no voice,
but when it at last finds a voice,
it begins to tell a story . . . .

ELAINE SCARRY
The Body in Pain

This book is an invitation to explore with me the role that spirituality can play in health promotion, in disease prevention, and in the processes of healing. Spirituality is, I will be suggesting, a vast untapped resource for experiencing healings that we previously thought impossible.

We will be exploring healing as a sacred path through three stories. First of all, I will share some of my own story. For me, physical pain always has had a voice, and it has been a central theme in my life's story. Mine is a story about a descent into hell—polio, broken back, excessively severe chronic pain, and crippling. It is about the medical culture's impotence in helping me get out of that hell, official paralysis when confronted by the challenge my body was presenting, and hope-destroying pessimistic pronouncements from the experts—predictions that the rest of my life would be defined by severe pain, strong drugs, and permanent confinement to a wheelchair.

Fortunately, that was not all there was to my story. An inexplicable exit from that hell into a heavenly "miracle healing" changed both the direction and content of my life. Pain was, and still is, a frequent companion for me, but now it has a different story to tell. Both passion and compassion changed the story—an intellectual passion for trying to understand how such a healing could occur when all the medical experts said it was impossible and a spiritual compassion for all the other people suffering their own versions of hell. My story, therefore, is both very personal and public, a search for how the more general theoretical, philosophical, medical, and spiritual implications can be of help to other people.

For reasons I am still trying to understand, I have had a lifetime of health/illness confrontations—almost seven decades of navigating the challenging rapids of illness, the whirlpools of confusion, the backwaters of depression and despair, and the thrill of finding myself still above the water line, reflecting on the lessons and enjoying the view.

When I have delved deeply into my experiences, I have found myself searching for extreme language to express the profundity I felt—heavenly feelings of joy, exuberance, zest, a lot of laughter, and a deep sense of my life's being blessed. At the same time, however, in the same life story, other extremes have been experienced, such as the hell of physical and emotional torture, the severe agony of interminable suffering, and the slow agonizing deaths of what I have come to describe as "soul-selves." A soul-self, as I will discuss throughout this book, is our deepest and most consuming identity at any particular time of our lives, our singular container of meaning and purpose. I discovered that both the dying of old soul-selves and the birthing of new ones play prominent roles in illness and in healing.

As will become evident, I had a series of health challenges long before I understood, or had any interest in, the spiritual theme that was to become so prominent with later reflection. After being to hell and back several times, a powerful dream predicted, perhaps releasing energy for, a dramatic healing that carried with it a strong sense of "call"—of a mission and a purpose, an attempt to understand the larger context, the deeper insights, and the broader principles that can have meaning for others. The redirection of life led not only to career changes but to an academic doctorate and a professional career of teaching, consulting, speaking, and writing. All in all, it has not only contributed to my experience of greater health and well-being, but it has also given wonderful meaning and purpose to my life along the way.

The second story we will explore will be that of the changing medical history regarding the role of spirituality in healing. At first spirituality was in medical exile, but now it is being embraced. It is a fascinating evolutionary story, within which we will try to look carefully at how the text and texture of our personal stories of health and illness are influenced by the context of the larger cultural and medical paradigm.

The third story is about what I perceive to be the future direction of healthcare—a profoundly promising and catalytic synergy between medicine and spirituality. It will be a future in which the concept of healing as a sacred path can open new vistas and new possibilities, for physicians and for the general public. It is an invitation for you, the reader, to "author-ize" your own story, possibly finding within these pages some insights that will enrich, inform, educate, and inspire your own miraculous healings.

The Labyrinth and the Caduceus

The jacket cover of the book that you hold in your hands depicts the symbols of that projected cooperation between medicine and spirituality. The labyrinth is the ancient symbol of spiritual seekers, inviting a walking meditation that takes one within, facilitates the encounter with sacred power, and then returns one to the world to live and share that power. It is both a symbol and an activity that is creating quite a growing movement throughout the world. Its widespread appeal, in my opinion, is that it transcends the exclusivity of any one religion, which speaks to the ecumenical soul of our time, and synthesizes bodily movement and the sacred journey into our spiritual depths.

Although the caduceus has been accepted as the symbol of the medical profession, it has a mythological and esoteric history. There is actually a varied and somewhat confusing history to the caduceus, but in one sense, that is what gives it its magic. Asclepius, the Greek god of medicine, is often pictured with his staff, around which is entwined a single snake, the symbol of transformation. Asclepius is said to have instigated rituals of dream incubation, wherein people slept in the temple so as to have the gods appear in their dreams and prescribe cures for their illnesses. The caduceus, however, is typically associated in Greek mythology with Hermes (in Roman mythology, Mercury), the messenger of the gods. Hermes had winged sandals and a winged hat, and his magic wand was entwined with two snakes and with two wings mounted on the top. As you get into the first three chapters of this book, you will see why it has some meaning for me that, in classical art, Hermes was depicted as an athletic youth. Hermes was also said to have power over dreams.

The word *caduceus* is Latin, derived from the Greek and means simply "a herald's wand." In this respect, and for this book, it is heralding a new medicine and a new spirituality that together are creating a liberation of latent, underutilized, and in that respect "new" potential for miraculous healing. This book heralds what I believe to be a message from the divinity within each of us, that we can approach healing as a sacred path and can find healing treasures we never imagined.

If you have a labyrinth available to you, I encourage you to take your own healing agenda into that walking meditation—perhaps even throughout your reading of this book. Take each insight that you may find in this book and may feel is important to your own healing into the center of the labyrinth, meditate, and discover its relevance to your own life. You will emerge having taken a significant step in your own sacred path towards healing.

Definitions

It is important to clarify what I mean by a few key words, for their definitions are crucial to understanding some of the central themes of this book.

"God"

I do not use the term *God* to refer to "a Being" who, by definition, is separate from humanity. Rather, I use *God* to refer to the divine "Ground of Being," or, as the theologian Paul Tillich put it, "Being itself." Whereas God as "a Being" leads to either/or categorizations and separations between the divine and the human, thinking of divinity as the Ground of Being leads us into a holistic both/and. This also throws out any notion of a God of only one gender. But more importantly to the theme of this book, it is the major shift that opens the floodgates for letting the "supernatural" become "natural," for bringing heaven to earth, for democratizing the Incarnation, and for releasing the many miracle healings that await us.

Theologically speaking, it means that I am defining God from a "panentheistic" perspective, as opposed to either theistic or pantheistic. Panentheism—the *en* in the middle is important—is the word that points to God's being *in* everything and everything being *in* God. It is a holistic synthesis of divine and human, immanence and transcendence. It is, in my opinion, the theology of the future.

In her poetic yet down-to-earth manner, Maya Angelou describes panentheism in common language, a sentiment also expressed biblically in Psalm 139, John 14:10, and Ephesians 4:6—it just took us several thousand years to recognize it. Maya Angelou, however, speaks to our time in history, when she writes, "I believe that Spirit is one and everywhere present. That it never leaves me. That in my ignorance I may withdraw from it, but I can realize its presence the instant I return to my senses. . . . I cannot separate what I conceive as spirit from my concept of God."[1]

"Prayer"

Given the concept of God just explained, I don't regard prayer as a conversation with some separate, distinct, grandfatherly Being up in "his" heaven. Prayer is not a spiritual version of satellite technology—we send a request up to God, and God, if it is "his" will, zaps a favor back down to earth. Rather, prayer is the intentional communion and communication with the divine energy of the universe—the divine within the depths of you and me, in our "in-betweenness," and throughout all creation. It is an immanent and intimate relationship with the transcendent—that which transcends my capacity to understand and also transcends the singular "me" to connect me with other incarnations of the divine and with the entire marvelous, mysterious, and magnanimous universe.

"Miracle"

It follows, therefore, that "miracles," the "miraculous," and/or "miracle healings" are not some supernatural intervention into human reality by an external God. Rather, miracle healings are quite natural because the divine is naturally within us. Miracle healings are, therefore, the manifestations of the possibilities that have been created within us naturally but which have been beyond or outside our purview and our paradigm. Because they represent what we *thought* was impossible, we assigned them to the "supernatural," projecting them onto an external God. All of that, however, says more about our lack of understanding human nature than it does about the nature of God.

"Healing" and "Curing"

To understand the theme of this book, it is also important that we clarify the difference between healing and curing:

- *Healing* involves the process of one's total body/mind/spirit moving towards health, wholeness, and holiness. It involves an escalation of meaning and purpose, growth and development. It is an appreciation of mystery and an experience of the miraculous.

- *Curing,* on the other hand, is a medical term for the prolonged absence of a particular physical disease diagnosis.

Healing may lead to curing, but it is also possible to have healing without curing. One may grow into a high state of wellness, wholeness, and holiness, while still living with the physical challenges that are medically defined as a disease. The flip side of that coin, of course, is that we sometimes confuse the cure of a disease with the notion that we have become more whole, more healed, more in touch with the holy. It ain't necessarily so!

I want to make clear throughout this book that I value the best of scientific medicine *as well as* the anecdotal experiences of unique individuals. As much as I will affirm the former, I will reject the trivialization and marginalization that the medical paradigm has given the latter. The special-case individual incarnation of spirit, along with its unique healing potential, has been too long overlooked, ignored, denigrated, and disempowered. Mind-boggling, paradigm-busting, and soul-quaking miracles are available when we challenge and change traditionally held beliefs.

By implication, then, there is no one way, no common path, no external absolutes, no expert gurus for describing your way into miraculous healing. I share my story, therefore, not as any superior model, not even as a model per se. Nor in any way do I suggest that you should or even could walk the same precise path as have I. We can learn from one another, as we can be nourished by supportive spirits and similar experiences. We can be stimulated, motivated, and inspired by other people's stories, and frequently are. Hopefully, the severity of my challenges and the desperation I felt for finding some meaningful solutions may uncover some insights that you might find helpful. It would be wonderful if some of my discoveries enabled some of your own. But, in the final analysis, the path by which any of us finds true miracles is uncommonly and singularly ours and ours alone. The divine is incarnate, and often incognito, within each of us—in special and unique ways.

In this book, I will be "pushing the envelope" for both medicine and religion, exploring the innovative frontiers of both. Everyone has a sleeping giant of healing potential within, and that is something we will emphasize in these pages. Conventional medicine and traditional religions have often disempowered our inner healing capacities. If, however, we affirm and awaken that sleeping giant, we will grow a life in which "miracle healings" and "spontaneous remissions" have a chance to become commonplace. Miracles, in other words, will and are becoming democratized.

The Jungian therapist and author Jean Shinoda Bolen has said, "Every writer who has transformed his personal experience into universal experience helps people connect with their own experience. . . ."[2]

It is my invitation to you, therefore, and my fervent hope that in the following stories you will find ways that enable you to affirm and awaken your inner healer and to author-ize your own story of miraculous healing.

PART I

A Personal Story: To Hell and Back

CHAPTER ONE

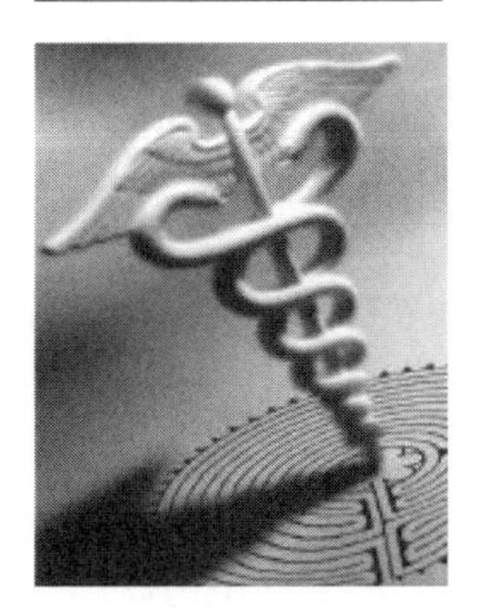

The SOUL *of an* ATHLETE *in the* MAKING

Man has no body distinct from his Soul:
for that called Body is a portion of Soul discern'd
by the five senses, the chief inlets of Soul in this age.

WILLIAM BLAKE

Ninety percent of baseball is mental.
The other half is physical.

YOGI BERRA

I grew up in the Middle-American heaven called Iowa, geographically and spiritually just a few miles from Kevin Costner's "Field of Dreams," in an idyllic family that could have been the model for a Norman Rockwell painting. The "script" of my family's life was a bit more interesting than the TV show *Ozzie and Harriet* but in the same genre. My father was an ethical, hard-working, truck-driver-turned-entrepreneur. My mother, a conscientious stay-at-home-mom who primarily determined the quality of our home life, had an extraordinarily loving heart and a sharp and exceedingly able mind. Mine was primarily a normal, ordinary, 1940s and '50s version of family life in which my older brother John, my younger brother Bill, and my younger sister Judy shared in the weekly activities of school, music lessons, playground activities, and the church youth group, as well as the annual one-week vacation at the YMCA "Family Camp."

There was one oddball in the family, however—me! All outward appearances would suggest that I fit well within this family, but internally I was convinced that I must have been adopted and my parents were just not admitting it. They loved me thoroughly, totally, unconditionally, and I loved them; but down deep inside, I knew that there was a fundamental incongruence. They were Iowa folk, and I was from a very different "state of mind." They were an Ozzie-and-Harriet family, and I was an incognito Jimmy Dean. They were extraordinarily nice, while I was a passionate rebel, temper-proned, and not always nice. Nevertheless, they were so wonderful and so mature in their capacity to love that they thoroughly accepted and affirmed even the maverick in the family.

I first became aware of how different I was at a very early age. Unlike my brothers and other friends who just liked sports, I was totally and completely an athlete. My earliest childhood memories were of wanting to play ball—every minute of every day. When other little boys were dreaming of becoming a fireman, a policeman, or some other logical projection into adulthood, the first and only goal I had as a child was to become an All-American football player. Period. Exclamation point! In fact, it is not even accurate to call it a dream or a goal. It was a strong premonition, an absolute knowing—my destiny, written indelibly on life's ultimate oracle of meaning and purpose. I could hardly wait for my fate to unfold. That would be as good as it gets.

When all the other boys and girls were doing what children

ordinarily do, I had an almost adult kind of clarity and commitment to my life's calling. My meaning and purpose, indeed, my experience of soul was most clear when I was able to express myself physically in athletic activity. The holy trinity that I worshiped was football, basketball, and baseball.

I was about three or four years old when I insisted that my parents buy me the helmet and shoulder pads that would be the outer trappings of my inner identity. I badgered my older brother John and his friends into letting me play football with them because the level of competition was better than with my peers.

I was incensed when my mother would call me out of a football game to take my regular afternoon nap. How humiliating! What a waste of time! Leaving a football game in order to take a nap? How ridiculous! What a lousy way for a future All-American to be treated! Although obedient, the inner rebel protested. One time, I agreed to take my nap, but I refused to take off my football uniform. As you might imagine, that nap, while in the claustrophobic wrap of helmet and shoulder pads, produced a mighty scary nightmare.

I was stubbornly beholden to any and all preparation necessary to become that All-American football player. In the early years of elementary school, I scoured the sports pages in the daily newspapers to see if I could find any great football player whose name was "Robert." I could not. Not a single one. There were, however, great football players named "Bob" or "Bobby." So—you guessed it—I insisted that everyone stop calling me "Robert" and begin to call me by my athletic identity, "Bob" or "Bobby."

The name change did not exactly rise to the spiritual level of a Cassius Clay's becoming Muhammad Ali or the biblical Saul's becoming Paul, but in my eight-year-old mind, "Robert" becoming "Bob" was a serious matter, an absolute necessity if I were to achieve my destiny of becoming an All-American football player.

My obsession with and love for sports, however, was not limited to football. As mentioned above, my "holy trinity" was football, basketball, and baseball, and I was ready, willing, and able to worship whichever deity was in season.

Having a brother four years ahead of me in school, who was also a talented athlete, facilitated my athletic development in several ways. Not only could I play in the summer sandlot games with his friends and him—both my interest and talent generally exceeded those of my own age—but I could rely on him to teach me some of the skills and techniques. Dad and John even built a pitcher's mound, home plate, and backstop in our back yard so that I could practice my pitching; and John, as a generous and attentive brother, would spend hours catching for me.

My father also erected a basketball hoop off the driveway behind the house where I would spend hours upon hours practicing. At night, when it would be too dark to see the basket, I would go into the house, up to the second-floor "loft" that overlooked the basketball area, move a couple of tables over to the window and lay a floor lamp on its side on top of the tables, sticking the top third of it out the window so as to illuminate the basketball area and enable a few more hours of practice.

Although my parents totally supported all of us children in pursuing our interests and dreams, they understandably became a bit concerned at how preoccupied—obsessed—I was with athletics, and at such a young age. They expressed the observation that I seemed to be going a bit overboard with sports—the kind of observation, in the particular manner and tone, that means your parents not only want you to *observe* such-and-such, but strongly prefer that you *change* such-and-such. Since I tended not to be quite as nice and gentle as the rest of my family, I would generally respond, in a loud and indignant tone, "So?" I cannot stress this point enough: sports were my deepest feeling of soul, my greatest enjoyment. I was, therefore, uncompromising, unrepentant, unapologetic, and unchanging. I had to be what I was meant to be!

It was not that playing athletics was a favorite activity of young

Bob Keck. It *was* Bob Keck. I was not a child interested in athletics—I was an athlete. How could I, therefore, stop being me?

It soon became apparent that my early soul-level identity of and enjoyment in athletics was matched by above-average abilities. That, of course, created a powerful synergy: my love of sports was fed by success, and the success expanded my love. Being innately gifted, combined with success among my peers, led to a robust self-confidence and an ego that knew no fear.

Such an immature ego, however, is bound to meet its comeuppance. Mine was inevitable, given that I had an older brother who was much bigger and stronger that I. In a story that has become family legend, when I was a twelve-year-old and John was a fifteen-year-old, I challenged John to a football contest.

I insisted that we go out into the front yard, that he take the football under his arm and try to run right through me. I was going to show him a thing or two about tackling. I had no concern about his superior size, speed, and skill—my big brother was about to get decked!

John, as I mentioned before, was always a bit kinder and gentler than I. So he came running right at me until I was braced to make the tackle, and then he slipped in a finesse move and ran around me. I did not lay a hand on him.

I was angry. John had not gone along with the plan. I wanted him to try to run right through me, so I could dump him on his backside. Finesse was not supposed to be part of this context. "Get back there and do it again and this time, don't try to avoid the contact," I demanded, as if his deft move was more an act of cowardice than skill. I was determined to show my big brother who was really superior at football. One on one! Man to man!

Once again, John ran to the other end of our yard, some forty or fifty feet in front of me, tucked the football under his arm, and came running full-tilt right at me. I prepared myself mentally and physically for the collision. And just as I was about to demonstrate superior strength, power, and determination, just as I was braced for the clarifying confrontation, John did it again! He faked as if he were going to run right into me but, at the last moment, slipped in another finesse move, ran around me, and left me grasping empty air.

Now I was *really* angry. I called him every insulting name in the book. Was he afraid to confront his little brother head on? Had he no pride? No guts? Was he a total wimp? A complete chicken? A coward? "Do it again," I insisted, "and this time, do it right!"

By this time, John had had it with his little brother's arrogance and insults. It was time to teach me a lesson. So, once again, John went to the far side of the front lawn, tucked the football under his arm, and came running right at me with, I might add, considerably more speed. This time there was, indeed, a collision. At some point thereafter, after the tweeting birds, the flickering stars, and the ringing in my ears ceased, I regained consciousness and found myself lying flat on my back, somewhere, it seemed, in Missouri or points further south. My body felt as if it had just been run over by a truck.

You would think that such experiences would humble me. You would be wrong. By this time evidence was beginning to accumulate that, when it came to athletics, my IQ slipped into the single digits. Consequently, the defeat at the hand of my older brother made me more determined to develop the skills so that he could not do that to me again. But he did, and I kept practicing and kept insisting on a rematch. Basically the same scenario was repeated over and over. Again and again. Throughout the years of my being in junior high and his being in high school, he was always bigger and stronger than I, always kinder than I, but would eventually give in to my insults and challenges, and he would again and again batter my body. My ego, however, with single-digit intelligence firmly in place, was slow to learn any humility. With every defeat at the hands of my brother, I simply got more determined. Such was the tenacious training for the All-American wannabe.

My obsession with football resulted in, as a seventh-grader, my learning all the offensive plays of the Roosevelt High School football team, for which John was the starting quarterback. Consequently, I was invited by the coach to be on the sidelines during all the games, keeping a log of each play—position on the field, down and yards to go, the play John called, and the resulting loss or gain. Keep in mind that this was a time when the quarterback called all his own plays on the field, so that I would have to recognize which play it was while it was in process. With this log, the coaches and quarterbacks could then analyze, at half-times as well as between games, what plays were working, under which circumstances, etc.

Oddly enough, football stories notwithstanding, my athletic talent emerged earliest and most strongly in basketball. As a twelve-year-old seventh grader, I was so obsessed with playing basketball that I researched extensively all the various youth basketball leagues in Des Moines—church leagues, YMCA leagues, Jewish Community Center leagues, etc.—to see when they played their games, so that I could play in several leagues all at once. I was talented enough to make any team and generally became the leading scorer in any league I could get in, even those including older eighth- and ninth-graders.

When I look back from the perspective of six decades and survey the development of meaning and purpose in those first twelve or thirteen years of my life, I see a remarkable singularity of focus, a clarity of dreams and ambitions, and the early experience of heavenly joy and zestful exuberance in being an athlete. I felt a deep sense of being who I truly was meant to be when I was throwing or hitting a baseball, dribbling, passing, or shooting a basketball, or running, kicking, or passing a football. No one had to tell me about the integrated and holistic reality of body, mind, and spirit, for I knew it at a deep organic level. I loved it, and I lived it.

I did not think or talk in terms of my soul's purpose back then, or speak of what God was calling me to be and do—no such lofty spiritual consciousness. Yet, there was an amazing clarity, at that early phase of my life, that I was destined to be an athlete. And that essential identity loved the change of athletic seasons in the same way I now, as an adult, look forward to the special qualities of nature's seasonal changes. Back then, it was the joy of expressing myself all spring and summer with a baseball, all fall with a football, and all winter with a basketball. That was the diversity and breadth of expression that nourished my childhood soul. It was a heavenly experience that held no premonition of the hell that I was about to experience.

My First Descent into Hell—Polio

It was the summer of 1948; I was a thirteen-year-old about to enter the eighth grade at Roosevelt Junior High School. As usual, I was playing baseball every day, and for as much of every day as was possible.

By itself, a simple headache did not, at first, portend my involvement in one of history's great scourges—a disease that paralyzed or killed an estimated 500,000 people a year, leaving some twenty million with irreversible paralysis, prior to the introduction of effective vaccines in the mid-1950s. In 1948, however, not much was known about polio.

My simple headache quickly got worse. Much worse. I told my buddies that I was feeling so bad I would have to drop out of the baseball game. I went home, not thinking about polio, but just knowing that the pain was getting so bad that I could hardly stand it. Simple walking made my head throb. Light, any slight glimmer of light, felt like a dagger cutting right through my eyes and into my brain.

When I walked in the front door of our home, my mother could tell with one glimpse how bad I was feeling. She helped me move gingerly up the stairs to my bedroom in the southwest corner of the second floor of our home. I laid down on the bed and asked her to pull down all the window shades, making the room as dark as possible. I closed my eyes and tried to endure the pain. I heard my mother go into the bathroom and soak a washcloth in cold water, which she then placed gently over my eyes and forehead. Her loving attention comforted me, and the cool washcloth felt good, but the pain was all-consuming.

My mother knew something was seriously wrong. She was also aware, of course, of the larger cultural trauma surrounding polio. Without hesitation, she called our family doctor.

Dr. Standifer knew our family well. He lived just two houses from us and was also the father of my close friend Jim. So it was the tall, familiar, angular family friend who entered my bedroom with the obligatory physician's black bag. Among other rituals of examination, Dr. Standifer put his hand behind my head and gently tried to lift it to see if I could touch my chin to my chest. I could not. My neck was extremely stiff, and even the doctor's slow and gentle attempt to raise my head sent excruciating pain down my spine.

Although my pain was virtually all-consuming, to the extent of barely hearing any conversation in the room, I faintly heard Dr. Standifer say to my concerned parents, "We've got to get this boy down to the hospital for a spinal tap." There was a tone of urgency in his voice, but no further explanation that I can remember.

The trip to the hospital was horribly painful and the spinal tap more so. The physical pain paled in comparison, however, with the psychological, emotional, and spiritual pain that I was about to face.

My mother, father, and I were alone in the small examination room, awaiting the test results. I was so consumed with the pain of the severe headache that I was oblivious to the fear and concern that my parents were feeling, their imaginations stressed by the prospects of their son's having contracted the dreaded polio myelitis acute viral disease.

A gentle tap on the examination room door preceded Dr. Standifer's entrance. The look on his face gave us the news even before he announced, with sympathetic feelings yet with a tone of finality, "Bob has polio."

Unless you lived through that period in medical history, it may be difficult to grasp the sense of hopelessness and fear that such an announcement sent through every fiber of our being—probably similar to what people feel today when they receive the diagnosis of cancer or AIDS. Since no cure for polio was known, there was a profound sense of foreboding and despair in such a diagnosis. My soul shuttered, for it felt as if Dr. Standifer had just pronounced its death sentence.

I could see the agony on my mother's and father's faces, although they were trying to hide it from me. After all, we knew other children who had died from polio, some of them close friends, and others who lived but were paralyzed by the disease.

Questions immediately flowed forth, of course, even though the soul-quake of the polio diagnosis continued to send aftershocks throughout my entire being—shock waves of the sort that made it virtually impossible to hear or retain much of what was being said. Nevertheless, I desperately needed to know. What does this mean? What is going to happen to me? At a visceral level, my question was clear and precise. Am I, the athlete, going to survive?

The questions and the answers among my parents and Dr. Standifer were drowned out by my internal spasms of soul and the severe headache. Their discussion was like background noise that I wanted to hear and understand but couldn't. My thirteen-year-old athletic soul was being ripped apart, piece by agonizing piece.

I was in a state of shock as they admitted me into the hospital. Just before I was to be wheeled off into an isolation polio ward, I had a few moments where I tried to gain some clarity in my understanding of what was happening. My parents assured me of what Dr. Standifer had been saying: I apparently did not have the kind of polio that would be life-threatening, the kind that one of my football buddies died of when it paralyzed his capacity to breathe. But what they could not know was the degree to which the next phrase was, for me, essentially life-threatening: it threatened the core of who I was, the only part of life that was meaningful to me. "Dr. Standifer tells us that you have a 50-50 chance of becoming paralyzed, but we will not know for several days whether or not this turns into paralysis. And if you do become paralyzed, you have a 50-50 chance of recovering most of your physical capabilities."

The 50-50 stuff struck me as little more than wild guesses—too easy a number to pick out of the air when little was actually known. Even the possibility of paralysis, however, was like driving a stake through my heart or amputating my soul. It would kill my most essential sense of self. In fact, for the thirteen-year-old Bob Keck, paralysis would be worse than death.

The excruciating pain and despair I was experiencing physically, emotionally, and spiritually was made worse by the prescribed treatment—isolation, confinement, and the torture of scalding hot-packs placed periodically on the muscles of my body. For two weeks, I was confined to a bed in the isolation wing of the hospital, sharing a room with three other polio patients. Not only was I isolated physically, due to the infectious nature of the disease, I was isolated emotionally from my family and friends, my entire emotional support system—able to see them only through the distant hospital window, as they stood outside to show their love, to wave, to smile, as they tried to lift my spirits, while blowing me kisses.

"In torture," writes Elaine Scarry, "the world is reduced to a single room."[1] From an adult, larger, and more mature worldview or objective perspective, my torturous two weeks of waiting to see if I would be permanently paralyzed certainly does not compare to the torture that others have endured throughout the world. But, for me, faced with the greatest torture I had confronted in my thirteen years, there was no larger or more mature point of view. My very soul was being tortured and my entire world was reduced to that single room in the isolation ward.

For the first couple of days I was still struggling with the physical pain of the headache. But as the headache subsided, the soul-level torture of a potentially impending death of my athletic life came to the forefront. It came with considerable power, the most vicious, violent, and unrelenting trial-by-fire in my life up to that time. Day and night, there was the constant, and maddeningly repetitious and eerie breathing sounds the iron-lung would make from across the room as it tried to keep my roommate alive. I felt really sorry for that guy, knowing that he was certainly worse off than I; but my own trauma kept drawing me deep within, and the iron lung's maniacal mechanical sounds of sucking and belching air seemed at some level to represent the ebb and flow of my own emotional battle between depression and hope.

Night, of course, was the worse time of all. So lonely. So interminably lonely. Was this agonizing wait to see if I am going to be paralyzed, tantamount to awaiting execution? Or was this a tough test, a depressing downtime that would, in essence, simply be a brief timeout? Would the ball game, and my life as an athlete, soon resume?

It was my first experience with a theme that I will return to several times throughout this book—namely, the level of pain associated with the apparent death of one's primary identity. As mentioned earlier, I was not just a person with an interest in athletics, I was an athlete—totally and completely.

Consequently, isolated in body, mind, and spirit, I felt that the possibility of paralysis was not a matter of ceasing a given hobby or activity but one of personal extinction. Later on, I'll ruminate more about how throughout life, the death of a perceived soul-self, the loss of a primary identity, is a powerful ingredient in the experience of pain, particularly severe chronic pain. But, for now, back to my story of being a thirteen-year-old facing identity extinction.

The Comeback Kid

My first escape from hell, my gradual awareness that my life as an athlete just might continue, actually began while I was still in the hospital. Although the doctors said that we would not know my fate regarding potential paralysis, at least for certain, until the full two weeks of isolation had expired, I had personally decided after one week that I was feeling better and that there was little likelihood of paralysis. So, it was none too soon to begin getting back into athletic shape.

The official medical advice was that I was supposed to remain physically quiet and passive. I was told not to move unless it was absolutely necessary, and I was forbidden to get out of bed.

My athletically honed mind and independent personality, however, had a different strategy. I never knew passivity, submission, or surrender to win a ball game. So, I figured, I'll try a more aggressive approach. I will sleep some during the day, and then at night, when the nurses rarely come around, I will begin a physical fitness and strength-recovery regimen.

After gaining the commitment of a conspiracy of silence from my roommates, I began nighttime chin-ups on the bar that supported the glass partition between our beds and slipped out of bed to do my push-ups and sit-ups on the floor.

During the last week in the hospital and during the two following weeks of isolation at home, I gradually increased my fitness and conditioning so that I would be ready—as soon as I would be released from "solitary confinement"—to resume my soul-full athletic enjoyment and what I assumed would be an automatic ascendancy into stardom. After all, my thirteen-year-old mind reasoned, I had just gained a total victory over the medical scourge of my time. Now, nothing could stop me from my athletic destiny. Or so I thought.

None of my doctors told me about the so-called "late effects of polio," or what now has become known as "post-polio syndrome." As I said earlier, not much was known about the disease back then. We all thought the consequences of polio were clear-cut, black or white—you either lived or died, became paralyzed or did not. If you lived and were not paralyzed, then polio was behind you, and life could go on as before. Little did we know.

As I resumed my athletic activity, I soon discovered that polio had left my body with a rather significant challenge of muscular fatigue and cramping. No matter how hard I tried to increase my conditioning, I would tire more rapidly than did my fellow athletes. And after virtually every athletic contest, I would spend the night with severe leg cramps. There were many nights when a sudden and extreme cramping of a hamstring would yank my heel up to my butt, accompanied by excruciating pain. With my inability to straighten the leg out by myself, thus stretching and relieving the cramping muscle, I would have to yell for my father, waking him up in the middle of the night, requiring his substantial strength to straighten my leg out, apply hot-packs, to get the hamstring muscle to relax. He and I spent many an agonizing night that way.

My preoccupation once again, however, was athletics. In spite of the bothersome muscular fatigue and cramping, my primary identity, my soul-self sense of being an athlete, came back to the forefront. Throughout my high-school years, that identity was fed and strengthened, not only by the increasing development of my natural talent but by the equally increasing external success and recognition.

At any time in life, but particularly in the ego-developing teenage years, affirmation, admiration, and adulation are addictive. I was having so much fun sipping the elixir of athletic success that the periodic sour taste of muscular fatigue and cramping was simply a bothersome hassle to be endured.

It did not take me long to rise from the hell of polio back into the athletic heavens. By the time I was fifteen-years-old, I had become only the second sophomore in the history of Des Moines athletics to be selected to the basketball All-City First Team. By my junior and senior seasons, I had attained All-City and All-State honors in my "holy trinity"—football, basketball, and baseball.

The Second Descent into Hell—A Misdiagnosis

Suddenly, and without warning, during my junior year in high school, I was thrust down into hell once again. We were two-thirds the way through the basketball season. I was the leading scorer in the city, always taking on the challenge of guarding the other team's star player, and our team was optimistic about our chances in the upcoming state tournament.

In the midst of all this, all the team members were given a routine physical exam. A few days later, my parents received an urgent telephone call: "There is a problem with Bob's blood test."

After arriving at the doctor's office, another blood test was taken. Again, a soft knock on the examining room door preceded the entry of a somber-faced doctor. Contrary to the earlier time when Dr. Standifer talked primarily to my parents, this doctor talked directly to me. I was now a seventeen-year-old, and he was a basketball fan enamored with my athletic talent.

"I'm so very sorry to tell you this, Bob," the doctor said, with a nervousness in his voice that betrayed his professional role. "You have a very serious case of acute hepatitis, which is an inflammation of your liver. You will have to stop your basketball activity immediately and begin complete bed rest. I see no reason that you can't do this at home, but it is crucial that you cease any and all physical activity and stay in bed. We'll take more blood tests in two weeks and see where we go from there."

This made no sense at all. I felt fine. I had no symptoms. I was right in the middle of a great basketball season. I was having an enormous amount of fun, and I was nourishing my athletic soul. Reluctantly, I went along with the medical diagnosis and complied with the doctor's orders. I could not imagine, however, that I would not be released from this horrendous interruption in two weeks and would not be able to return to the team in time for the post-season tournament.

My parents set me up with a bed in the loft—a 1950s version of a "family room"—where I could watch some of the programming on our new television set—the very loft, incidentally, in which, up to that point in time, I would rig up the floor lamp lying horizontally on some tables and sticking out the window, to practice basketball into the night. Now all I could do was to lie in bed, all day every day for two weeks, looking longingly through that window at the basketball hoop, wanting to be out there practicing. It was pure agony to listen to my team on the radio play its next several games. But, I figured, this was just a temporary hassle. Right? Wrong!

After two weeks, more blood tests. Same conclusion. The doctors reiterated that I had a very severe case of acute hepatitis. Prescription: two more weeks of complete bed rest.

My girlfriend, Caroline Brown, and other friends brought school work by the house for me and would sit and visit with me. My fellow athletes would stop by after practice, and we would replay the previous game in our conversations.

Two weeks later, more blood tests. Same results. Bed rest prescribed again for another two weeks.

This confinement was now beginning to get to me. Was this really only going to be temporary, I wondered? If so, why am I not getting well? I went into that "sick bed" feeling perfectly fine and had my usual zest, enthusiasm, and vigor for life in general and sports in particular. But after lying in bed for four straight weeks, after repeated blood tests that indicated I was sick, I began to feel weak and actually started believing the doctors that I was very ill.

Two more weeks. More blood tests. Once again, the tests indicated that I was still deathly ill with a severe case of acute hepatitis. By this time, however, the doctors were beginning to admit that they were mystified by my condition. They could not figure out why I was getting neither better nor worse. The tests were precisely the same every time.

The only thing that helped during the following week was the fact that I was again selected to the All-City basketball team. The other First-Team All-Stars, along with the newspaper photographer, came out to my home so as to have me included in the picture that would appear in the *Des Moines Register* the next morning. The other four guys surrounded my "sick bed." I felt a confusing mixture of honor and humiliation. Once again I was recognized as among the best at the sport, but I was getting weak and becoming convinced by the doctors that I was deathly ill. I felt a deep incongruity between being selected for this honor and lying in bed for the all-star picture!

The regular season was now over, the post-season tournament was about to begin, and I was still confined to bed. I embraced the radio as I listened intently—with a competitive intensity mixed with a deep sadness—as my teammates fought gallantly but eventually lost the game and were eliminated from the tournament. Later that night, after friends had gone to their homes and my family members were all asleep, I cried. I cried long and hard. I think I cried all night, in part because I felt that I could have helped my teammates win that game and in part because I felt that my very identity was facing extinction.

Two more weeks went by, and the next round of blood tests produced precisely the same results. There was now a growing confusion on the part of my doctors, matched only by my deepening depression.

This went on for a total of ten weeks. Ten weeks! By this time I was physically very weak and totally convinced that my life as an athlete was over. The doctors told my parents that they should take me to The Mayo Clinic in Rochester, Minnesota, for more extensive diagnostic work. My case totally baffled them.

The general feeling in Middle America was that if your doctor recommends that you go to The Mayo Clinic, you must be *really* sick. So it was not a happy trip as my parents and I drove the some two hundred miles up to Rochester. Nor did it raise our spirits when, after some preliminary testing, the physicians at The Mayo Clinic informed us that we needed to consult "the best liver specialist in the world." And he, they said, is not at The Mayo Clinic but at the University of Minnesota in Minneapolis.

So our journey in search of medical clarity and of a healing continued. There was not a lot of conversation during that relatively short drive to Minneapolis. I don't know what was going through the minds of my mother and father—they were trying to keep my spirits up and did not speculate on the potential negatives—but clouding my mind was the thick fog of wondering how sick I must be for the prestigious and celebrated Mayo Clinic also to give up on me. I wondered how far up the medical mountain we must climb in order to reach the pinnacle of understanding of what was going on in my body.

Following the inevitable and extensive testing, the now-familiar visit with the doctor followed. This time, however, it was not in the usual small examining room. A meeting was arranged with the "best liver specialist in the world" in his office. I had a knot in my stomach and a mixture of fear and wondering raced through my mind, as we sat down, knowing that he was about to give us his conclusions.

"This is quite an unusual case," the "best liver specialist in the world" said as an opening. "I've never seen one quite like it."

I did not express my feelings aloud, but I was getting really irritated by this time. I was neither a "case" nor an "it." I was an athlete whose very soul was being tortured and torn apart. I did not like the feeling of being so physically weak—not one bit! So, I was thinking, "Don't give me these generalities. You are supposed to be the greatest. Just tell me when I will be well and when I can get back to my athletic activity."

Unlike the citizens of Des Moines, this physician did not know that I was a star athlete, that I was an important person in my own right. He only saw a kid in front of him so, naturally, he talked to my parents rather than to me. "The conclusion we have reached," the physician continued, "judging from all the testing, is that Robert does not now have, nor has he ever had, acute hepatitis. He is actually not sick at all. He has what we call a 'constitutional hepatic dysfunction.'"

"What the hell is that?" I blurted out. My voice, and my intensity, escalated. "What do you mean I don't have acute hepatitis? You mean to tell me that I have been in bed for ten weeks and I'm not sick? You mean I missed the state tournament for no reason at all? And what the hell is a 'constitutional hepatic dysfunction?'"

The doctor was actually pretty cool in response to my outburst, his calm demeanor not in the slightest ruffled by this angry teenager yelling in his face. All of which, of course, frustrated me all the more because it seemed to underline the feeling that nobody really knew how much I was hurting inside.

"A constitutional hepatic dysfunction," the doctor continued, in a very detached clinical manner, but at least he was now talking directly to me, "means that your liver, operating normally for you, is outside the range of normality for anyone else. It is, therefore, understandable that your doctors in Des Moines thought that you had a severe illness. Your test results indicated that to them. But as it turns out, you have actually never had hepatitis. You are fine. You can now go home and resume your regular activities."

Down deep inside I was enraged. I knew it wasn't appropriate to be angry at this doctor who was, in fact, giving me good news. I also felt it was not quite right to be angry at my doctors in Des Moines, for they had simply made a reasonable diagnosis given my test results. Nevertheless, I was angry at the general circumstance, enraged at having gone through the physical, mental, and spiritual torture and all the physical and energetic deterioration of those ten weeks in hell.

My rage, however, was soon channeled into the challenge that now faced me—getting back into athletic shape after ten weeks of total inactivity. After all, the deity de jour—baseball—was quite capable of transforming my rage into focused discipline and practice.

Comeback No. 2

After ten weeks of being confined to bed, it was particularly difficult to quickly recover the arm strength necessary for my role as a pitcher and left-fielder on the baseball team. Arm strength had been one of my primary assets, whether on the mound or in the outfield. However, after spending over two months lying in a bed with very little use of my arm muscles, arm strength and throwing velocity, when combined with the polio propensity for muscle fatigue, were the last things to return in my athletic reconditioning. Fielding and batting were more quickly recoverable, so, it was not a totally lost season.

My senior year in high school was another joyful romp through the star-studded heavens of athletic success—with the singular and serious exception of the long night of despair and embarrassment I spent after I single-handedly lost the football city championship for our team when I threw an interception at a crucial time late in the game. But the quick transition from football season into basketball season, the fact that I scored 25 and 27 points in the first two games, respectively, and jumped out into the scoring leadership among the metropolitan area schools, a position I never relinquished, enabled me to put that particular football game's failure quickly into the background and to feel once again that I was contributing to my team's success. Success or failure in any sport was quickly forgotten when the seasons changed, another sports deity ascended into prominence, and my persona as well as my focus of "worship" was totally transformed.

The basketball state championships in my senior year, however, revealed both the level of skill I had attained and the burden I carried regarding the lingering effects of polio, an ongoing mixture of heaven and hell, as it were.

Following the regular season, our basketball team made it into the so-called "Sweet Sixteen," the final teams that qualified for the state championships to be held in the University of Iowa Field House in Iowa City. It was a big deal. Massive numbers from our large high school made the pilgrimage to the festive event. Many of the student's families went, and mine did as well. The press was there in full force. Like high-school championships in virtually any state, this was a major happening!

Our first game was highly publicized, what many suggested would be, in essence, the state championship game, pitting the two best teams in the entire tournament field—Corpus Christi of Fort Dodge and Roosevelt of Des Moines. Corpus Christi was ranked number 1 in the state, had been all year, and for good reasons. They had an amazing season record of thirty wins and no losses, with an even more amazing thirty-point average victory margin. What made Corpus Christi so overwhelming was a defensive innovation generally unheard of at that time—a full-court zone press for the entire game. With incredibly well-conditioned athletes, the team was "in your face" for the entire length of the court and for the entire game. Superbly coached with zone defensive techniques that none of us had confronted before, Corpus Christi baffled, confused, and outplayed all its opponents, usually stealing the ball or causing a turnover before the opposing team could even get the ball across mid-court.

The Corpus Christi athletes were so good, so quick and well conditioned, that they usually caused panic and errant passes from their opponents. All this made Corpus Christi the clear favorite—not only to beat us, but to take home the state championship. Few of the pundits, coaches, spectators, or sportswriters gave Roosevelt High School, or anyone else, more than a very slight chance of beating what seemed to be clearly an unbeatable team.

The media, however, perhaps simply trying to create some drama for a game that seemed to have a foregone conclusion, were trying to make the case that Roosevelt of Des Moines had the best chance of beating the odds-on favorite, Corpus Christi. The hype, therefore, was on.

Within a few days of our scheduled confrontation with this apparently insurmountable foe, coach Al Comito called me aside. "I want to try a strategy that no one will expect," he said. "As you know, conventional wisdom would have it that we can beat a zone press only by good, quick, and effective passing. Every team has tried that against Corpus Christi, and every team has failed. What I want to try is to have us inbound the ball to you, have our other players spread out to give you plenty of room, and let you single-handedly dribble through the zone press to get the ball into the front court. Once you have it into the front court, you can create some movement to either shoot the ball yourself or to find an open teammate to pass it to. It means, however, that to make it even to half-court, you will sometimes have two or even three players rapidly trying to close in on you, to trap you and to cause you to throw an errant pass. It will be a tough challenge, but I think you can do it. What do you think? Are you up to it?"

Coach Comito knew me well enough to know that there was no way I would turn down such a challenge. He had been both my baseball and basketball coach throughout my entire high school career. "Doggone right, I am up to it," I said, brimming with self-confidence, loving the opportunity of having the team's fate in my hand and absolutely certain that I could succeed at the task that had been given to me. I could hardly wait for the game to start.

The strategy worked! I was able to "break" their zone press, dribbling the ball through the maze of the Corpus Christi athletes who were coming at me from seemingly every angle trying to get the ball away from me. And once I got the ball into the front court, I had a great cadre of teammates who were able to sink the shots, make the passes, and grab the rebounds that were necessary to win. We defeated the team that was practically handed the state championship on a platter before the tournament began. We beat the ostensibly unbeatable! We had accomplished the seemingly impossible.

There was an incredibly celebrative mood permeating all the Roosevelt players, friends, and families. We were all ecstatic. Members of the media were hounding us for interviews. Most of us players were so caught up in thrill of victory that we could hardly hear Coach Comito's warning us to get a good night's sleep, for we had round-two tomorrow afternoon against Clinton High School. "Enjoy the moment," Comito said, "but don't forget—we have only won round-one, and round-two is tomorrow."

For me, however, all the celebration was compromised by a deep foreboding about how my body would make it through the night. I joined in with the celebrative feeling that all my teammates had, but I knew secretly that a good night's sleep was probably not in the cards for me. I was thrilled with the team's victory and my personal success in breaking the vaunted zone press. To accomplish that, however, I had pushed my body to its limit. I was, deeply, thoroughly, and completely exhausted. I was on top of the world emotionally, but I had pressed my body to such an extreme limit that I was sure to pay a severe price in leg cramps all night and cramps plus exhaustion the next day.

My private premonitions came true. I was up all night with severe leg cramps. The morning, of course, eventually dawned, although the night seemed interminable to me. I began the new day with an already exhausted body, now even more debilitated by lack of sleep. My leg muscles ached profusely.

Everyone around me was still on a "high" with our victory the night before. The general assumption was that we could now march right through all the rest of the competition to our destiny—state champions. Clinton High School, our second-round opponent, simply represented the next stepping stone to our eventual grasp of the coveted trophy.

I did not tell anyone about my miserable sleepless night, for I did not want to diminish the celebrative mood nor dampen the high hopes for the rest of the tournament. But down deep, I was struggling with a concern that was destined to revisit my soul periodically throughout the rest of my life. How do I balance, manage, deal appropriately with two very opposite, very conflicting, very powerful forces within me? On the one hand, I had an indomitable spirit and a self-confidence that I could meet virtually any challenge and accomplish any goal before me. On the other hand, my body seemed frequently unable to rise to the level of my spirit. My essence felt indefatigable, but my body was too easily fatigued. My spirit could run any marathon, but my leg muscles cramped up after a brief sprint. Why, I often wondered, was there such a gulf between my talent and spiritual zest for athletics and my physical limitations in expressing it?

There were times when my body and soul were at one flying with the eagles, able to surmount the highest mountain of a challenge. Then there were the times when my soul still wanted to fly into the heavens, but my body seemed to be dragging me down into hell. There are profound and ongoing spiritual lessons in a lifetime of that conflict, and I will revisit that issue from time to time throughout this book. But that would be getting ahead of the story. So, let's remain in 1953 and how, as an eighteen-year-old, I experienced that conflict.

The immediate challenge before our team was the game that afternoon with Clinton High School as our second-round opponent in the state tournament. The challenge before me personally was that secret question and that private concern: would my body cooperate with my ability and desire?

Most of the time I could overwhelm my body with my mental and spiritual determination and motivation, if there was a particular need to do so. This, I figured, was such a time. I tried my best to psych myself up for the game. I tried to call on any and all physical and mental reserves that I could muster.

The intensity of being in the state tournament helped. The psych-up began in the locker room. The team energy coalesced and was catapulted to enormous heights as we ran out onto the court to the sounds of a huge cheering crowd and the blaring pep band. Personally, I could feel the surge of pride with the attention from the media and the crowd in light of my performance the night before. Under those circumstances, it was easy to enable my will-power and my enthusiasm to blot out my deep physical exhaustion. It worked, however, only for a short while.

The game started, and I hit my first five shots. By the end of the first quarter, Roosevelt was in the lead, bolstered by a truckload of confidence that we were heading for another victory.

I can remember virtually nothing about the rest of the game. Shortly after the second quarter started, my body gave out, and my mind was in an energy-depleted fog. I tried to continue and, in fact, I did play on. But the score sheet after the game revealed that I had not scored a single point after the first quarter. We lost the game and were eliminated from the tournament.

I had experienced both heaven and hell within one twenty-four-hour period. I had gone from the heights of exceptional performance to the depths of total physical, mental, emotional, and spiritual exhaustion. As a team, we had gone from accomplishing the impossible and gaining the expectations of a state championship, to packing our bags, heading for home, and sadly leaving the glory to others.

You might be wondering—and quite logically—why, after such experiences, would I not simply give up athletics and devote myself to something a bit less physically challenging. The consequences of polio would seem to make it a very clear and reasonable choice—move on into something less physically exhausting. But that choice at that time in my life was not possible. To consider giving up athletics was tantamount to changing myself at the deepest and most fundamental level, and I was not ready for that. Being an athlete was simply being myself at a very deep integral level. The pain, fatigue, and cramping were substantial, but polio did not change who I was—it just made the process of my being me a bit more challenging.

It also became apparent that, in the minds of college coaches and professional scouts, my talents overshadowed any concern they might have had regarding my endurance limitations. Keep in mind, however, that my athletic talent was showcased in the light of day and in the spotlight of media attention, whereas no college or university coach, no professional scout—in fact, virtually nobody else—saw the hell I went through during the night following a ball game.

Consequently, throughout my senior year of high school, I was inundated with letters, telephone calls, and visits from coaches stopping by the house to entice me to enroll in their school and to play for their teams. My major problem with the recruitment process, however, was that they all wanted me to concentrate on one sport, whereas I still worshiped the "holy trinity" and wanted to play all three sports at the collegiate level.

Iowa, Oklahoma, Northwestern, and Notre Dame, for instance, were among those recruiting me as a football quarterback. On the other hand, Kansas, UCLA, Ohio State, and Kentucky were among those recruiting me for basketball. At the same time, the New York Yankees sent a scout out to try to talk me into bypassing college altogether, and get an early start on what they thought would be a promising baseball career. Even my high-school football and basketball coaches thought that my abilities probably had me best suited for professional baseball. I chose, however, to go on for higher education and delayed the professional decision until after my collegiate career. Keep in mind, my dream ever since I was about three years old was to be a collegiate All-American—in football.

Some combination of my love for playing all three sports,

uncertainty as to which sport I would want to pursue professionally, an individualistic and maverick spirit, and perhaps a nod to my family's value system that gave education the priority (I tried to believe that, but usually did not!) led to the seemingly inexplicable choice of turning away from the prestigious and lucrative offers from the larger universities, and the temptation of fame and fortune in professional baseball to attend a small college where I could play all three sports while still getting a quality education—the choice was Cornell College in Mt. Vernon, Iowa, the school from which my older brother John was about to graduate.

But before I could get to college there would, once again, be hell to pay.

The Third Descent into Hell—A Broken Back

I decided to take the summer months as a brief time-out from the sports that had consumed all my days, all year, every year—a brief three-month respite prior to getting started on my collegiate athletic career. Through friends of my family, I was offered a job working as a guide for canoe trips out of Ely, Minnesota, in the wonderful, wondrous wilderness called the "boundary waters" along the Canadian–American border.

If you have ever been there, you know what a gorgeous and idyllic experience it is, out on those Minnesota and Canadian lakes—the azure-blue pure waters of those pristine lakes lapping against the side of the canoe as you drift in a 1950s kind of leisurely pace towards the far shore while watching the eagles soar overhead, spotting a fish now and then breaking the water's surface to gulp a few insects, and listening to the plaintive call of the loon that would then dive before surfacing an unexpected distance away. The relaxed mind could get totally preoccupied with trying to guess where the loon would resurface.

Half-way through the summer I had enough experience and knew the trails, maps, and process well enough to be be given the longer and tougher trips. On this one particular trip, we had already enjoyed three days of those beautiful lakes, undertook several brief portages, discovered more pristine lakes, and set up camp during the late afternoon along a shoreline, pitching our tents, fixing meals over the open campfire that have that very special, now nostalgic, aroma, and then bedding down and falling asleep to the sounds of the wilderness that, among the other marvelous messages, seemed to be telling you how lucky you were to be there. It was a beautiful, grand, exhilarating experience.

Each new day began the entire wondrous experience all over again for the three married couples I was guiding on a seven-day camping trip. My eighteen-year-old mind imagined them to be "middle-age," but looking back on it now, I suspect they were in their mid-to-late thirties. In that environment, age meant little. I had the expertise they needed to relax and have some fun on their camping trip, and the process itself necessitated cooperation and mutual enjoyment. This group, in particular, was a very compatible group, and we were all enjoying the wilderness experience together.

The fourth day began like the first three—breakfast of bacon and dried, packaged, scrambled eggs that smelled and tasted better than you might imagine, packing up the tents and all the gear, and heading out for the new morning's venture into heaven's bliss of tree-lined lakes and the feeling of being on top of the world without a single worry to interrupt the leisurely experience of beauty. The beginning of the day was like all the others and gave no indication that hell was waiting for me just beyond the far shore.

We had paddled through three interconnected lakes and needed to negotiate a brief portage across a rather difficult but not long stretch of land that separated us from the next series of azure-blue pristine lakes.

We reached the shore, stepped out and pulled the canoes up

onto dry land. In the usual routine, I, like the others, lifted my heavy pack onto my back. Then, in what had become a quick, easy, coordinated move, I flipped the canoe up on top of my shoulders and was ready for the portage. I made sure that all the others were set and then led the way. We started off having to negotiate a rather steep incline, after which there was no more than about fifty or sixty feet of rather level ground, before we confronted the steep decline down to the next lake. As I approached the descent, I swung my body and the canoe on my shoulders around so that I could be talking directly to the others following me. "Be really careful coming down this descent to the lake," I warned. "It looks a bit slippery."

I should have paid more attention to my own warning. I was about half-way down the steep descent when my left foot slipped. When I tried to catch myself with a quick move of my right foot, I tripped on an exposed root. Before I knew it, I was hurtling headfirst down the steep incline. I tried to right myself but was only partially successful before I crash-landed in a kneeling position, landing on a big stone, my back vertical, but with the heavy pack and canoe on top of me. I heard some load cracks and pops before I felt the sharp excruciating pain in my lower back, pain that was shooting down my legs as if miniature razor blades were racing internally from my hips to my knees. I fell forward, face-down in the water with the canoe and my backpack trapping me underwater.

The others, who had witnessed my entire descent into disaster, came quickly to my aid, lifting the canoe and backpack off me, and getting my head out of the water. The level of pain let me know that my back had sustained some severe damage, and I asked the men to help get me onto dry land where I could lie for a few moments and try to assess just how serious the damage actually was.

It did not take long, however, to realize that this was not going to be simply a brief interruption of our journey or that the pain was just a temporary nuisance. I was in deep trouble! I wasn't certain precisely what the damage was, but I knew it was serious, that the canoe trip was over and that I needed to get back to medical attention as soon as possible. Keep in mind that this was before the days of cell phones, pagers, etc. We were a good distance into the wilderness, and we were alone. I mean, *really* alone. Our little first-aid kits were equipped to take care of cuts and burns, but nothing this serious.

Once again, I experienced how severe pain narrows one's awareness. In this case, the room of torture became very small indeed. So narrow and constricted was my awareness that I remember virtually nothing about how those six good people got me back to Ely. I have quite simple and focused memories of how excruciating the pain was when they lifted me in and out of the canoe, using the paddles as splints under my back, onto and out of the various portages, but I cannot remember any of the other details. I can't even remember the names of those six heroes who had their vacation shortened and who somehow managed to get me back to civilization. I was in a world of pain—a very small, self-centered world of pain—and that world remained constricted and virtually out-of-touch with a larger world of awareness for some time.

Once they got me back into Ely, I remember a doctor telling me that he had my parents on the telephone. I tried to assure my parents that I would be fine, but I wasn't at all sure of that. I don't remember much else until I was being prepared for surgery back in Des Moines. The entire experience of severe pain was to become an all-too-familiar phenomenon in my life—the way in which severe pain can totally obliterate the memory of what is going on around you, while the memory of the pain itself can be chiseled into your soul in a way that nothing can obliterate.

The next thing I remember was Dr. George, in Des Moines, showing my parents and me the X-rays. Those hazy gray images told us that my back was broken in two places, at the forth and fifth lumbar vertebrae and that the impact had driven my spine almost an inch down inside my pelvis. Dr. George speculated that the polio contracted during the growing years of my early teens might have weakened my spine, making it more susceptible to this kind of fracture.

Fortunately, my spinal cord was not severed, but the vertebrae needed major work. I was taken immediately into surgery. Bone chips and four large screws were strategically placed to stabilize my spine, making it permanently rigid up to the third lumbar vertebrae.

On the physical side of the matter, the severity of the pain was more than I had ever encountered. The night after surgery, as if to put an exclamation point on what I was in for, the muscles in my lower back that had been involved in the surgery went into severe cramping, thanks to post-polio syndrome. It was the most horrendous night of pain I had ever experienced.

The daily physical therapy I was undergoing in Des Moines, for the few weeks that remained of the summer, was intense and extremely painful. I was, however, making relatively good progress on the physical side of things and was able to start my freshman year classes at Cornell on time. At the time, I thought that my challenge was basically physical. I also thought that I had already experienced the deepest hell and was now, although going through a painful process, on the rise. I was wrong on both accounts.

The physical challenge was substantial, but I was not prepared for the emotional avalanche that started at the top, swooped up all the pieces of my life, and threw me down into the "valley of the shadow of death." At the very time my body was getting better, I began to sink into the depths emotionally.

Intellectually I reasoned that I had made comebacks before, so why not again? Deeper parts of my psyche, however, made a very different contribution. Even though I was gaining ground on the physical rehabilitation, inexplicably I began to sink deeper and deeper into a grief and despair that my athletic soul-self might not be recoverable. For the first time since I had contracted polio, I began to wonder seriously if my deepest and most essential identity was dying. I felt a profound foreboding that I might not be able to resuscitate once again that soul-self that had been my touchstone all my life. The physical pain of trying to get to and from classes and to endure the rehabilitation was now combined with a deep fear that my athletic dreams and goals might never be realized.

For the first time I began to appreciate how physical pain can be intensified by one's emotional state. Depression, grief, anger, and loneliness—as I mentioned before, severe pain increases the sense of loneliness, in spite of the fact that one has loving family and friends.

It began to take on the semblance of an eighteen-year-old's version of living the life of Job. My soul-level identity was dying, I was experiencing an excruciatingly painful physical rehab, and then Carolyn, my high school-sweetheart who had enrolled at Stanford University, fell in love with another guy, and sent me a "Dear John" letter. I sank deeper and deeper, could not bring myself to study, began flunking classes right and left, and was put on academic probation.

I was experiencing severe pain, I was being rejected, the very existence of my soul-self was being threatened, and I was on the brink of flunking out of college. My life was in the pits!

Comeback No. 3

The old cliche "time heals all wounds" has at least some truth to it. I also seemed to be blessed with a rather substantial "bounce-back" capability—it just is not my nature to remain depressed or in despair for very long.

The physical rehab continued to progress well, and by the first of November, I was throwing the football again. I began to feel confident that I could still realize my athletic dreams. I got over the rejection by my high-school sweetheart and on a blind date met a visiting high-school senior who would eventually become my first wife, Lee Colley Brown. With a broken heart and a broken back both healing, I was able to re-energize my passion for my athletic dreams and nourish my essential soul-self. Although academics, I must admit, were never the priority for me in college—football, basketball, and baseball were—I at least found the motivation and energy to get passing grades so that I would not be declared ineligible!

The ascension of my emotional state, as well as my physical conditioning, took place throughout my freshman year, in rather remarkable fashion. I was once again confident that I could achieve my athletic goals and was back to my obsession of throwing the football and studying films so as to gain a sophisticated understanding—to the extent that I was able—of offensive and defensive strategies of that era. Cornell's football coach Jim Dutcher had watched my progress carefully and announced to me that I would be the starting quarterback in the fall of my sophomore year. He so believed in my potential that he asked me to accompany him on a trip to Florida where I could get a couple weeks of tutoring by two of the leading professional quarterbacks of the time.

By my junior year I had set school and national pass-completion records that stood for a number of years. The premonition of that little preschooler's self identity, the one who refused to take off his helmet and shoulder pads when taking his afternoon nap, was finally realized—I was awarded All-America honors as a quarterback.

I had dated Lee from the moment she arrived on campus at the beginning of my sophomore year, and we were married just prior to my senior year. I was in love, and my deepest soul-level self-identity—that of being an athlete—was being fulfilled.

My senior year in college was more of the same. I was enjoying the early months of being married and had another successful football season. Although a three-year starter in basketball at Cornell, I did not have a professional level of talent in that sport, but that did not diminish my joy of the game.

As I neared graduation, life was good and getting better. The New York Yankees had returned in their attempt to persuade me to commit to a professional baseball career, and the Baltimore Colts were offering me a contract to play professional football.

I had scaled the mountain of my athletic soul-self, in spite of having a few Sisyphus-like set-backs. I was at the pinnacle of what I had wanted athletically to accomplish at the collegiate level. All that remained, before ascending into Bob Keck's version of heaven, was making the delicious decision—should I play professional baseball, in which some experts thought I had the most natural ability, or should I try professional football, which I personally loved the most?

As I sat at my desk on that spring morning in 1957, mulling over the offers from the Yankees and the Colts, trying to imagine which would be the most fulfilling, I had absolutely no clue, no hint, no warning, as to how the next forty-eight hours would change my life.

CHAPTER TWO

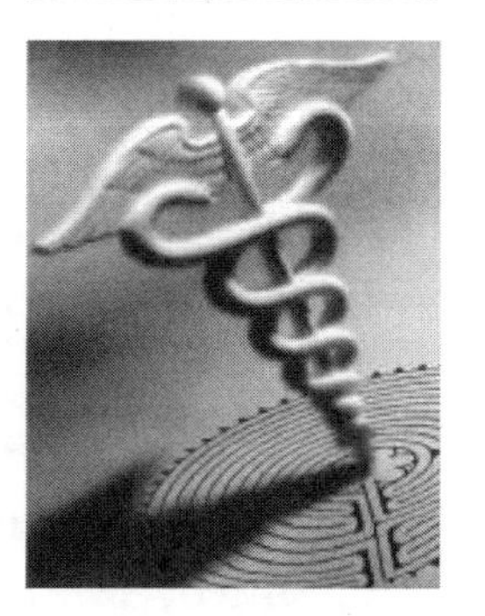

A SOUL-QUAKE *of* MAXIMUM MAGNITUDE*

The secret of alchemy was . . . the transformation of personality through the blending and fusion of the noble with the base components, of the differentiated with the inferior functions, of the conscious with the unconscious.

C. G. JUNG

Cornell College had a "Religion in Life Week" during the spring of each year, involving lectures and sermons by and meetings and discussions with a particularly gifted or prestigious individual. The featured speaker in 1957 was Dr. James S.

* Although I have told portions of this story in my previous books, it needs to be retold here because of its influence on how I have approached the health challenges that this book is all about and because it highlights two particular aspects of what I have come to believe are central to miraculous healing. In all likelihood, had I not experienced this dramatic soul-quake in the particular way that I describe here, I would not now be living or writing about healing as a sacred path.

Thomas, an executive of the Methodist Board of Education in Nashville.

I had little interest in either the schedule of activities for the "Religion in Life Week" in general or in Dr. Thomas in particular. After all, I was preoccupied with the most delightful decision in my life and the importance of choosing the direction of my future—would it be the Yankees or the Colts? So, as I mentioned at the close of the previous chapter, I was at my desk mulling over that decision.

Lee was across the room, at the kitchen table, doing some of her own class work. "Bob," she said, "I'm going over to the library for a few minutes and then will be picking up the groceries for tonight's supper. Do you have any preference regarding the appetizer?"

"Appetizer? What's that all about?" I asked.

"Don't you remember," Lee said, "that we agreed to host a supper tonight with Dr. Thomas and some of the other married couples, so that those of us not living in the dorms could have some informal fellowship time with him?"

"Oh, that's right," I responded, obviously revealing that I had, indeed, forgotten, and, "No, I don't care what the appetizer is. You choose." I was preoccupied—Yankees or Colts?

There were relatively few married couples on campus at that time, and because we had a fairly large apartment, we had been asked to host this gathering between Dr. Thomas and the other married students. I had no reason to object, but my mind and heart were not in it. I was "elsewhere"—New York or Baltimore, Yankees or Colts?

As supper time neared, the other married students began arriving. One of the couples picked up Dr. Thomas and brought him to the gathering. When they came and I was introduced to our guest, I remember being pleasantly surprised, having an immediate sense that this was a very interesting guy.

Dr. Thomas was an ordained Methodist minister, with a doctorate in sociology, employed at that time by the Methodist Board of

Education. Physically, he was an imposing figure—a tall, handsome, powerfully built African-American, in his late thirties, with a captivating mixture of a soft and humble manner combined with an obvious spiritual and intellectual power. He had a magnetism that would not let my attention return to—you know—Yankees or Colts. I actually forgot about that decision for a couple of hours.

For the entire evening, I was fascinated with and curious about this man, Dr. James Thomas. I watched him respond to questions from other students with a quiet confidence, a marvelous sense of humor, and a gentle attentiveness to each and every person. He clearly embodied a high level of physical, spiritual, and intellectual power, while at the same time giving the impression of extraordinary integrity, humility, gentleness, and an almost childlike delight at having a good laugh. And with his powerful, deep, baritone voice, his laughter was both hearty and infectious.

After he and the others left that evening, Lee and I talked about what an extraordinary man he was and what a privilege it felt like to be in his company. It was a great evening; but I, of course, had a preoccupation to nurture, a decision to make, and the rest of my life to set in motion.

The next day was more of the same joy and delight about where my life was at that time, mulling over the various pros and cons of the two optional choices that would decide the next phase of my life. That evening, Lee and I went to the worship service in the Cornell chapel, where Dr. Thomas would be preaching. As far as I was concerned, I was going more out of a sense of an obligatory courtesy to our previous evening's supper guest than any particular desire to go to a worship service. I had usually found worship services to be rather boring, although I was a bit curious as to how the man I visited with the night before would handle the formality of a worship service and preaching. In other words, my body was going into the chapel out of a sense of obligation, my mind was somewhat curious about Dr. Thomas, but my spirit was still 100 percent preoccupied with my expression of soul: would it be a football heaven or a baseball heaven?

The chapel was beginning to fill as Lee and I entered. About halfway down the center aisle, Lee slipped into a row on our right, and I ended up sitting at the end of the row with my left elbow propped up on the end of the pew. Along with a few general and light conversations and greetings, several friends stopped on their way to their seats to ask if I had made a decision as yet. "No," I responded, "not yet. I'm still working on it."

The worship service began and proceeded through all the typical parts of a worship service, but a very small portion of my mind was involved. Even while going through the motions of a worship service, my mind kept running over the "what-ifs" and the various scenarios were I to choose one sport over the other. I would imagine myself becoming part of the storied history of the New York Yankees. (*Everybody's standing . . . must be time to sing a hymn.*) Then I would shift to scenarios of what it would feel like getting full time into the delightful process of strategizing offensive maneuvers against the upcoming opponent, were I to play with the Baltimore Colts. *(Judging from everyone around me, I guess I should act as if I am praying.)*

Dr. Thomas eventually began his sermon, and because of the previous evening, I gave *some* portion of my attention to hear what he was saying. A skilled speaker, I thought. He is presenting some interesting ideas. Although I was impressed, I now have absolutely no recollection of what he actually said. I was interested, but everything seemed quite normal—nothing gave me any warning or hint to the fact that my life was about to be changed dramatically.

Then it happened! In a split-second, in a moment that will forever defy complete understanding or explanation, my life was totally changed. In the previous instant, I was Bob Keck the athlete, just as I had been for the twenty-two previous years of my life—in the next instant I had an overwhelming knowing—absolutely, completely, and without any doubt—that I was not going to be a professional athlete. My life was totally redirected, and the closest I can come to explaining the feeling of the "new me" is that I had experienced having every cell of my being infused with divine love and I was now committed to the service of that love. It was not like making a decision. It was more as if I was totally changed in an instant, and the new me was simply, and naturally, heading in a very different direction.

There were no visions, no voice calling me to do this or that, no bells or whistles, no lightning bolts, no trumpets! Nothing like what we have all come to believe is part of a dramatic mystical experience. The mystical, magical, and mysterious soul-quake occurred totally without warning, completely personal and internal, without engaging any of the usual physical senses, and certainly without my bidding or permission. There were no real specifics about what all this meant. It was just a wonderful, total feeling of integrity in the experience—absolutely knowing that love was the priority, everything else was relativized, and that I would eventually discover where it would lead me.

I can only grasp for language, like virtually anyone throughout history who has had a powerful mystical experience, language that seems to point to "being one with the universe" or "being absorbed in God" or whatever. Language and concepts fail—again, the feeling was just that of knowing that love was the priority, the All, and that my life had been completely changed, and powerfully dedicated.

What did *not* happen was about as fascinating as what *did* happen. I immediately looked around to see how long my inner transformation took, or if I had made any noises or exclamations in the process, and whether or not Dr. Thomas was still speaking. To my amazement, it seemed like everything that had happened to me had taken place during a temporary "freeze-frame" in the motion picture taking place that night in the Cornell Chapel. As life started up again, nobody seemed to have any idea as to what just happened inside me. I looked at Lee, and she was still watching and listening to Dr. Thomas. Dr. Thomas was clearly still in the midst of his sermon, but I wasn't hearing a word. Nothing externally, it appeared, had changed. But everything within me had changed completely.

Also surprising was the fact that there was no explicit way that I felt Dr. Thomas was involved, yet it doesn't make sense to say that he wasn't. I don't think it had anything to do with anything he was saying—again, I literally cannot remember a word he said. I certainly felt no sense of being "called" to be a disciple of Dr. Thomas—definitely the last thing that he would have wanted. But the spiritual and intellectual power I sensed in that man the night before and the fact that this took place precisely while he was preaching—it all adds up to a suggestion that, in some way, he was an enabler of what happened to me. There is enormous magnetism in the personification of spiritual maturity and power. Could it be that, at an unconscious level, my soul recognized in Jim Thomas what I was being called to? Understandably, therefore, I feel an enormous sense of gratitude for Jim Thomas' simply being Jim Thomas and for his coming into and somehow facilitating the most phenomenal transformational moment of my life.

I continue to be impressed by how far that experience transcended any conventional concepts or explanations. No language nor means of expression seem to capture what happened. I can speak in analogies and metaphors, but even they fall short of anything that feels like adequate description. It was like a flood of reality—a tsunami would be more like it—that washed over my soul and rearranged everything. My life had been overpowered by the Divine, which had, previous to that moment, been dormant within me.

The Immediate Aftermath

The service ended. Everything appeared to be quite normal. Lee, my wife of six months, who came into that chapel service thinking she was married to a guy about to embark on a professional athletic career, had no idea what had just happened to me. How, I began to wonder, am I going to explain this to her? I felt so inadequate in understanding it myself; how could I explain it to anyone?

As we made our way out of the chapel, we were chatting with various friends, although I did not really want to be involved in superficial visiting. I had too much going on inside. Some friends also asked me about my professional decision, and I just shrugged it off as soon as I could. I needed to tell Lee first, and I needed to do that in private.

As soon as we were alone, I tried to share the experience with Lee. There was such an enormous gulf between the power of the experience and my ability to explain it that I probably sounded like a babbling idiot. About the only clarity, about the only thing I could explain, was that I knew I did not have a future in professional athletics. I knew absolutely that I would be saying *no* to both the Yankees and the Colts. It was crystal clear what I was *not* going to do—but it was remarkably vague as to what I *was* going to do.

To her everlasting credit, Lee was incredibly large spirited about all this. She had no apparent concerns about this radical turn of events. I recall absolutely no regret on her part about my turning my back on the potential fame and fortune of professional athletics. And if she secretly thought that I had lost my mind, she at least hid it very well. She affirmed and supported me in and through the entire process, as I worked my way through all the queries, questions, and the questing that followed.

The days that followed felt like the wonderful experience of living an entirely new life. I looked the same on the outside but felt that I was completely new on the inside. I could still throw the football as far and as accurately and could still play baseball as before. Nothing had changed physically, yet everything had changed spiritually. I now knew totally and completely, without a hint of doubt, that I was *not* going to be a professional athlete. To my amazement, there was never one iota of doubt—then, or in the forty-five years to date—no second-guessing, no regrets.

It was a strange feeling, having everyone I met during the succeeding days think that I was the Bob Keck they knew before but my knowing that everything inside had changed. I had experienced a spiritual power with which I had been previously unfamiliar, and it gave me a different map, a totally different vision, a transformed life, and a new commitment.

What seemed to be the logical path into this new commitment, the traditional way of serving love in the world, would be to go to graduate school in theology and enter the professional ministry. At least, that was the most reasonable scenario that I thought of, in middle America in the 1950s.

I set up a meeting the next day with Dr. Thomas, in the office that the school had provided him for personal consultations, shared with him my best understanding of the event of the evening before, and asked his help in thinking through what my next steps would be.

Needless to say, my dramatic change of plans came as quite a shock to all my friends, my coaches, as well as the Yankees and Colts. Everyone who knew me prior to that transforming moment was shocked at my radical and completely unexpected turnabout. Everyone that is, except my parents.

One of the most extraordinary revelations of my entire life was awaiting me as I drove back to Des Moines to share the news with my parents. I did not think it would be fair to give them such dramatic news over the telephone—I should do that in person. So I called to simply say that I was coming home so as to share with them some important news.

It was well into the evening by the time I turned into the driveway of the home on 44th Street in Des Moines, the home where all those practice hours had taken place on the basketball court, on the pitcher's mound out back, and on the front lawn where brother John had taught me so many hard lessons. Mom and dad met me at the door. To set their minds at ease, I greeted them with a big smile—I didn't want them to think that the news that I had come to share was bad in any way. We went into the living room, sat down, and I proceeded to tell them the entire story of my transforming experience and the subsequent change in professional plans. Instead of becoming a professional athlete, I said, I was now committed to the cause of love and justice. In terms of specifics, that probably meant obtaining a graduate degree in theology and entering the professional ministry.

I knew mom and dad would be loving and affirming—they always were. But I certainly expected them to be as surprised and shocked at my announcement as everyone else had been. After I finished and waited for their reaction, it was I who was shocked—shocked by the fact that they simply looked at each other, smiled, and simultaneously looked back at me and said, in unison, "That's wonderful, Bob."

"What do you mean, that's wonderful? Aren't you surprised? Aren't you shocked? Could you have ever imagined that I would be sitting here telling you this?"

They then shared with me a secret that they had held in their hearts for twenty-two years, a story that they had never before wanted to tell me, for fear that it might make me feel that I was letting them down or that I might think that they would be disappointed in whatever direction I chose to take in my life. The story, their long-held secret, had to do with what had happened to them just prior to my birth.

My family lived in rural northern Iowa when my mother became pregnant with me. The earlier births had been in their home; but because they had previously lost a child shortly after birth and medical science at that time could not tell them why—some years later, the deaths of that child and of a subsequent one were attributed ostensibly to my mother's myasthenia gravis—they went up to a small Mennonite hospital in Mountain Lake, Minnesota, for my birth with the hope that a hospital birth might give me a better chance for survival.

The night before my birth, my mother and father were in prayer together. They were accustomed to praying together, but this time my parents experienced a shared, and quite powerful, numinous entrainment with divine power. Feeling the presence of God, they committed themselves to raising me in such a way that I would know the love of God deeply and thoroughly, so that I would eventually dedicate my own life in loving service to the world.

I was speechless. What an astonishing experience. What an incredible commitment. And how in the world did they keep that wonder-filled and numinous experience a secret for twenty-two years—twenty-two years of my being a difficult child, to say the least? Twenty-two years of my having a single-minded commitment to athletics. Twenty-two years of my showing little interest in anything religious—in fact, constantly trivializing it in comparison to sports, even flatly rejecting the suggestion by our minister when I was in high school that I consider the ministry as a vocation, barely able to keep from laughing in his face. All through our growing-up years, they parented my siblings who were relatively good, behaved, obedient children, and then there was Bob, the rebel, the maverick, the nonconformist, the child obsessed with sports to the extent that it would have made ordinary parents think they had a pathological addict on their hands. They had twenty-two years of my giving them fits by not taking school seriously, throwing temper tantrums, even once in junior high having to be bailed out of jail in the middle of the night—actually, I was only playing a practical joke on a classmate, but his parents thought I was stealing his motor-bike and called the police!

There were many—indeed, many, many, many—instances throughout those twenty-two years when ordinary parents would have become completely frustrated with me, when ordinary parents would have bemoaned the fact that I appeared to be going in a direction very different from that of their deeply felt commitment. Yet they never tried to control my life. They never whined aloud, wondering, "Where did we go wrong in raising Bob." They never tried to lay a guilt-trip on me. They simply loved and supported me without judgment. They were, indeed, saints in the art of divinely inspired and unconditional love.

Needless to say, those few moments with my parents left my athletically honed self-confidence in a queasy, questioning quandary. Before the Cornell Chapel experience, I had always thought that I was in charge of my life; after that experience, I had to wonder. Now, this story my parents told underlined the doubts, the questions, and the quest. The Divine is evidently far more involved, and far more fascinating, than I had ever guessed. I found that I knew almost nothing for sure any more. Except for this—I knew that I had been extraordinarily blessed to have Roger and Frances Keck as my parents. They were, indeed, profound and powerful ambassadors of heaven on earth.

For me, the commitment was clear. But commitment does not equate with full understanding. Having the idea that love permeates all of reality is one thing; really "getting it" is another altogether. I realized then that love was the All; but I had a lifetime, and more, to begin to grasp and to live that reality fully. Commitment was simply the first step, and I still had many years ahead of me in which I would stumble and bumble my way into greater and greater understanding of how to live, give, and receive love. I have messed up a lot along the way and am quite sure that I will continue to do so. I also had more health challenges to face. But before leaving this portion of my story, I want to explore with you what I think are two important implications for the subject of healing as a sacred path.

The Relevance for Healing

The reason for sharing this personal experience, which at a superficial glance would not seem to be necessarily important to a book on healing, is that this profound life-changing experience in 1957 introduced me to two major themes that are critically and centrally involved in my current understanding of health promotion, disease prevention, and healing.

1. God, the divine energy of the universe, is within as well as without.

Prior to that transformative moment, I assumed, like most in the wider culture, that God was up and out somewhere, that humans were fundamentally separate from God, and that we needed to request favors. But to the best of my ability to understand what had happened to me in that life-changing moment, it was that the divine energy within me that knew my life's purpose was not to play either professional football or baseball—my soul's purpose was to invest my life, totally, in more important spiritual matters. I was about to make a major decision that was not aligned with my soul's purpose, and Divinity knew that I needed a major wake-up call.

The overwhelming power of the experience may have been necessary because I was a particularly thick-headed and stubborn guy, but the essential point is that it did not feel at all that it came from "above" or from the "outside." It felt like an inner resource of divine power that flared forth, for whatever reason, to "enlighten" and to "awaken" every aspect of my being, thus totally transforming me. It was time for me to be about that which was integral to my soul's purpose.

As I suggested in "An Invitation" at the beginning of this book, the theological term for this is *panentheism*, but whether we talk theologically or not, divine power and energy permeate every cell of our being. They are within us—sometimes apparently having a "mind of their own" and sometimes waiting for us to be attentive to them, to cultivate them, to nurture them—but whether we are awake or not, divinity is there! The grace of it all is that it is there whether we earn it or not. It is there available to us, without being brokered by any outside authority.

As I also said earlier, once we really explore this concept of the Divine, it completely changes our notions of "miraculous healing." Throughout the rest of this book, we will revisit in various ways the enormous potential that we all have within us. Old medical and religious paradigms have often distracted us from that reality—indeed, some trivializing, ignoring, or marginalizing it, while some actually tried to *forbid* us from exploring the Divine within. But I am convinced that the future potential of a synergy between spirituality and healing is in the direction of our awakening to the Divine within and of learning more about how we can facilitate tapping into that power.

2. *Even the most intransigent and stubborn soul-self can die, so that a new and more appropriate soul-self can emerge.*

An obvious theme of my personal story up to this point is that my primary identity for the first twenty-two years of my life, my deepest sense of a soul-self, was in being an athlete. This particular experience of transcending one soul-self for another had nothing to do with healing, per se, and it was not brought on by my willful intention. Nevertheless, it taught me that what I thought would be impossible—a Bob Keck who was *not* totally preoccupied with athletics—did, in fact, happen. Subsequent years have taught me that we can do this again and again, if necessary, and a new soul-self can open one to greater possibilities, including miraculous healings.

In more recent years, I have come to believe that this basic phenomenon—the transformation of soul from one identity to another—may, in some cases, be the most critical and important factor in promoting health, preventing disease, and facilitating the processes of healing.

Often, our self-identity plays a role in our propensity for getting sick, and the extent to which that is true is the extent to which a transformation of soul-self participates in preventing illness. Likewise, if being victimized is a prominent part of developing our current and deepest identity, then a "victim" soul-self can, in and of itself, prevent healing. As Marilyn Ferguson once put it, "Our past is not our potential."[1] If we want the potential of healing, we may have to question with all seriousness how much of the past is rooted in a particular soul-self.

As we will explore throughout this book, the very act of reinventing, revisioning, creating, innovating, and awakening to a new soul-self may be the most effective and most direct escape route out of the hell of suffering. Such transformations of the deepest soul-self may not cure a disease, although we should be prepared to be surprised once in a while, but they can definitely heal our lives, transform the experience of severe pain, and eliminate a great deal of suffering.

The relevancy at this particular stage in my life's story is not that I stopped enjoying athletics. Quite the contrary, I simply channeled my athletic passions into amateur handball and went on to win numerous city and state championships while in ministry in Iowa and Ohio. The point is that "athlete" was no longer my deepest soul-self, no longer my primary identity. It was, and continues to be, a fun recreational activity that still thrills my soul, but it no longer defines or describes who I am at the most fundamental level. Given who I was for the twenty-two years prior to that transformational instant, that is one whale of a miracle!

CHAPTER THREE

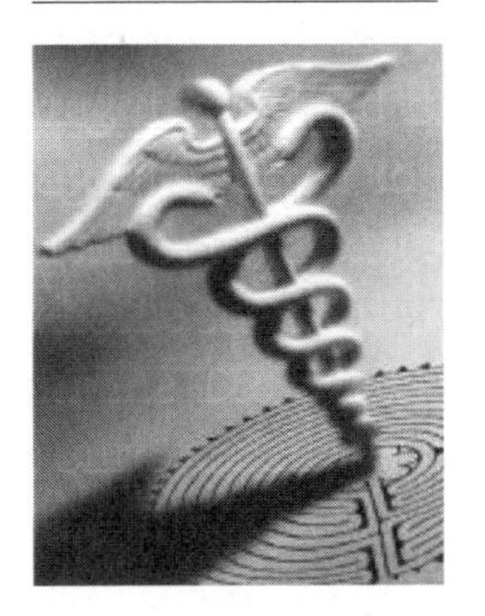

ANOTHER JOURNEY *to* HELL *and* BACK

Our soul wishes us to embark on the journey without knowing the destination. . . . Perhaps the path, a sincere striving to understand more, is the goal.

MARC IAN BARASCH

The healing path is not always smooth and direct, and mine apparently still had some additional dips and turns, highs and lows, as well as clarity and confusion yet to experience. Most critically, it seems that I had hell to pay, at least one more time.

After finishing three years of graduate theological education at Vanderbilt Divinity School, and a year's internship in the campus chaplaincy at Hamline University, Lee and I, along with our first child, two-month-old Lindsay, settled into life in Des Moines, where I became the minister at St. John's United Methodist Church. Soon thereafter, in 1962, our son Jim was born, and in 1965 our daughter Krista completed our family.

Being pastor of a congregation provides many wonderful as well as some tragic opportunities for a ministry of love and compassion. It is a profession that provides both the need and challenges of being both "pastoral" and "prophetic," expressing love in individual and social ways. Because all of us who enter the ministry have our own particular set of talents and skills, as well as personal philosophical and theological propensities, few of us are able to balance these two gargantuan challenges with perfection. Some of us are really good at sensing and giving loving attention to the individual pastoral needs of our congregation. Others of us tend to be more aware of the larger systemic issues of social injustice and feel the need to express love's demands for justice and equality.

My first incarnation of a soul-self dedicated to love tended to lean heavily towards the latter. A combination of a personal tendency to be aware of the larger context within which we live and the way in which historic and traditional social injustice was brought into the limelight in the 1960s fueled my passions. Lee's propensities were similar in this regard.

So, in addition to the regular activities of congregational life, Lee and I became deeply involved in and passionate about the social justice side of love—how people's lives can be constricted, restricted, and truncated because of poverty, bigotry, and discrimination, inadequate housing, racism in general and segregated schooling in particular. The socially charged1960s provided plenty of grist for the liberal activist's mill, and Lee and I were into it up to our eyeballs. Feeling that the Des Moines Public School Board provided an opportunity for some of that activism, I ran for and was elected to the board at age thirty.

During this very outward, professional, public, and political time throughout the decade of the 1960s, however, my body appeared to be headed for hell once again. The late effects of both the broken back and the polio, accentuated by the fact that Lee's and my marriage was becoming increasingly stressful, and the stress of being a public, political, and social activist were probably all contributing to the increasing experience of back pain.

As mentioned earlier, my love for the athletic expression of my body/mind/spirit unity was channeled into handball while in graduate school, and that became my primary recreational activity and periodic "time out" from the demands of my ministry. But because handball is such an extremely difficult and challenging sport on the body, it also became quite an obvious barometer of what was to be a downward slide into the hell of physical pain and suffering.

A defining moment of my descent in hell came on an otherwise lovely spring Sunday afternoon in the late 1960s. The Iowa State Handball Tournaments were always held in a very concentrated format over a weekend, so as to accommodate competitors coming in from across the state without unduly interfering with their weekday jobs. This schedule, although convenient for most people, was not user-friendly for the pastor of a church who had Sunday morning responsibilities.

This particular year's state tournament was being hosted by the YMCA in Cedar Rapids, some 135 miles away from Des Moines. The schedule was complicated even further in that I had a wedding scheduled on Saturday afternoon. What, in hindsight, seems like extraordinary, if not unbelievable, accommodation and graciousness, the tournament committee bent over backwards to schedule my matches around my church responsibilities, as I was the defending state champion.

I was also fortunate to have a friend, Dave Holmes, who piloted his own plane and offered to be of assistance in a rather crazy weekend schedule. The arrangements were made for Dave to fly me up to Cedar Rapids on Friday afternoon, accompanied by my good buddy, Cleo Murphy, who was going along to lend support.

The plan was that I would play my scheduled first-round match on Friday evening and, if victorious, would play my second-round match on Saturday morning. The tournament committee assumed that I would still be in the tournament after the second round, so I was scheduled for the quarter-finals on Saturday evening, which would give me the window I needed to fly back to Des Moines, conduct the wedding, and return to Cedar Rapids for my quarter-final match. They were equally accommodating for Sunday, holding off the semifinals until mid-afternoon, so that I had time to return from my morning's responsibilities in Des Moines. Then, if I won the semifinal match, I would play the championship match Sunday evening, after only a couple hours of rest.

It all went like clockwork. I won all my matches, conducted the Saturday wedding and the Sunday morning worship services, and defended my state championship title. The entire weekend's schedule, however, took an enormous toll on my body.

Cleo and I joined Dave aboard his plane for the flight back to Des Moines. As the minutes passed, as the intense psych-up and adrenalin rush decreased, as my intense will-power relaxed, I began to realize that I was in trouble. My muscles began cramping, and my entire body was sinking into a desperate feeling of over-exhaustion, that horrible feeling of being sucked into a quicksand of fatigue, with seemingly no ability to stop the process. The conversation on the way home between the three of us, the celebrative rehashing of the final match, all began to fade into the background, as the ringing in my ears got louder and more attention-consuming.

We landed at the Des Moines airport, and as I deplaned, I collapsed onto the tarmac and passed into unconsciousness. I vaguely remember Cleo's driving his car out to the plane and assisting me into the front passenger's seat. I was only partially conscious as he drove me home where he and Lee assisted me into bed. I spent the next two weeks in bed, with Dr. George, the same orthopedic surgeon who had previously performed the corrective surgery on my back, periodically stopping by to check on me. It was both a horrible ending and a horrendous beginning.

That was the end of my tournament handball—at the time, I

thought forever. It was the end of my joyous expression of soul when using my body athletically—at the time, I thought forever. It was also the beginning of my agonizing descent into a deeper hell than I had ever imagined.

In hindsight, we can now see how allowing myself to get so fatigued was counterproductive for my health and well-being vis-a-vis the late effects of polio. All during the years of increasing pain, I had been in consultation with my Des Moines physicians. They had consistently told me that handball should be no problem. They were, understandably, thinking primarily of my previously broken back; and since there was little chance of a major collision on the handball court and because the activity itself strengthened back and hip muscles, they encouraged me to continue. Neither they nor I knew anything about was was later diagnosed as "post-polio syndrome," or PPS.

It was discovered that somewhere between ten and forty years after contracting polio—the late 1960s were for me about twenty years after my experience with polio—the disease can reappear to cause considerable additional muscle fatigue and weakness, in addition to more extensive joint and muscle pain. The bad news for me was that PPS generally strikes those who had polio after age ten—I was thirteen. The good news for me, but certainly horrible news for others, is that PPS tends to be less severe for those who were not initially paralyzed, and worse for those who were—a double-dose of bad news for those who suffered the most initially. For some, PPS can be so severe as to mimic amyotrophic lateral sclerosis (ALS), or the so-called Lou Gehrig's disease. PPS, however, is rarely life-threatening. So it was fortunate for me that my initial experience with polio was relatively mild—certainly compared to the experience of some others—and that, presumably, my future difficulties would be relatively mild as well.

A brief venture into the more technical language of the National

Institute of Neurological Disorders and Stroke, describes post-polio syndrome as follows:

> PPS is caused by the death of individual nerve terminals in the motor units that remain after the initial attack of polio. This deterioration of individual nerve terminals might be an outcome of the recovery process from the acute polio attack. During this recovery process, in an effort to compensate for the loss of nerve cells (neurons), surviving motor neurons sprout new endings to restore function to muscles. This results in large motor units that may add stress to the neuronal cell body. As a result of this rejuvenation, the individual may have normal-functioning muscles for some time. But after a number of years, the motor neurons with excessive sprouting may not be able to maintain the metabolic demands of all their new sprouts, and a slow deterioration of the individual terminals may result.
>
> Restoration of nerve function may occur in some fibers a second time, but eventually nerve terminals are destroyed and permanent weakness occurs.[1]

In fairness to my physicians of the next several years, as well as to explain the reason I later returned to handball as a recreational activity, I want to stress that this is twenty-first century knowledge being projected back onto my experience in the middle to latter part of the twentieth century. Few of us back then had any knowledge of PPS.

Returning then to my desperate situation in the late 1960s, I was sinking deeper and deeper into a life of severe chronic pain and increasing crippling. My Des Moines physicians were unable to do anything to help me stem what seemed like an inevitable slide into a horrible and horrendous life of fighting severe chronic pain and depending upon strong drugs for pain management. Surgery, of course, was the orthopedic surgeon's primary paradigm, and my surgeons concluded that additional surgery would be of little help. All they could do, they said, was provide me with the strongest narcotics available to reduce the pain as much as possible.

That, I figured, was not a very pleasant future to look forward to, as I was only in my early thirties. I was desperate. I was going to go for the very best. I would call Dr. Ken Johnson, an orthopedic surgeon at what I called "Medical Mecca"—The Mayo Clinic.

Ken and I had become close friends beginning in the summers that we were both in graduate school and were serving on the staff of the YMCa Camp Olsen in northern Minnesota. In off hours we played handball together, turning the camp garage into a makeshift handball court. We proceeded to knock out some lightbulbs and windows, and the ball took some weird bounces off the uneven cement-block walls but had a great deal of fun and friendly competition (and we joyfully repaired the damage after we were done). Over the succeeding years, as Ken's doctoring and my ministering progressed, I would stop through Rochester from time to time, and we would revisit our fun in the handball court together and in the fellowship that followed.

"Ken," I said into the telephone, "I'm not calling about a handball game this time. Instead, I am calling for your help. I am in a great deal of constant pain, and I am beginning to get all crippled up." I proceeded to describe the whole range of physical difficulties that I had been experiencing, as well as what my Des Moines physicians had concluded. "Do you think some additional diagnostic work at The Mayo Clinic might be able to be of more help to me?"

Ken's response was both immediate and heartfelt. "Bob, you get your tail up here right now, and I will coordinate a thorough diagnostic examination of your condition. We've got to get you back on your feet, so that you can have fun on the handball court once again."

I was a bit embarrassed to ask, but I needed to know about the costs. A minister's salary did not exactly provide me with a lot of expendable income or a plush savings account. "Just come," Ken said with his usual athletic gusto and finality. "You can stay at my home, and I'll find some way to work you through the diagnostic process without its costing you anything." And with the customary male-buddy-kind-of-humor, he added, "When we play doubles together, I've always had to carry you anyway, so I'll just have to do it one more time!"

I arrived in Rochester looking very little like the strong athlete Ken had known. He appeared a bit shocked when he first saw me, but his compassion was extraordinary. I don't remember all the tests he put me through, nor all the hours he spent visiting with me. I do, however, remember his conclusions.

"It doesn't appear, Bob, that there is anything medically or surgically we can do for you. Because of what seems to be a mysterious and debilitating combination of the polio and the broken back, all we can do is give you stronger muscle relaxants for the cramping and stronger medication for the pain. I also need to tell you that you probably need to prepare yourself for what may be a lifetime of severe pain. You'll need to take strong prescribed medications. It is even a possibility that you might eventually face permanent confinement to a wheelchair. Bob, I'm so sorry to have to tell you this."

Despite Ken's compassion, the prognosis was devastating. The trip did not cost me financially, but the cost to my psyche was enormous. I was being tortured once again, and my deepest soul-self was back on death row with a terminal prognosis. Not only could I no longer be an athlete, but I would never be able to offer the kind service I was committed to or make the kind of contribution to love and social justice to which I felt spiritually called. The severity of my pain was making it difficult to give attention to anybody else's pain. Everything about me felt as if I was being sentenced to a permanent residence in hell and a slow, agonizing death.

In 1970, as my physical condition worsened, I was trying to meet the responsibilities of being the pastor of a congregation and to perform the duties of president of the school board. At the same time, two new professional offers surfaced. Friends and Democratic political activists wanted me to run for the office of city mayor when my school board presidency came to an end the next year. They felt that

I was the most electable liberal around. At the same time, I was being offered a church position in Columbus, Ohio.

Since I was still in the individualistic, tough-it-out, don't-share-your-feelings, masculine, athletic persona, few people knew how much pain I was in. And few knew how fearful I was of what felt like an interminable, unstoppable, damnable descent into a hell of pain, paralysis, and drugs. How could I possibly encourage people to raise money for and to work on my behalf in a mayoral race? Who knew how long I could even perform the duties of an elected official, let alone do it effectively? I also seemed to know, intuitively, that my healing journey would be aided if I took the Columbus job—perhaps, in part, because it was less prestigious and offered a much lower public profile.

The move to First Community Church in Columbus, however, did not stall my physical deterioration. It was an extremely unusual and delightful church in which to serve—a large, fascinating, and diverse staff of extraordinary professionals, an open and loving congregation in general, and some wonderful people in particular who became lifelong friends. But my inner turmoil grew more intense. The pain yelled louder into my already constantly ringing ears. The room that my consciousness occupied got smaller, the drugs got stronger, and the fog I was living in got thicker.

I could not sit still through staff or committee meetings and had to get up periodically and move around. At the same time, I had to take a stool into the pulpit to preach because I could not stand for fifteen or twenty minutes at a time. I was no longer able to hide my hell. It became increasingly obvious to anyone around me, as the pain began to interfere with normal walking, standing, or sitting activities. My world was getting fuzzier and fuzzier, as my total attention, by necessity, drew me more and more into myself. I increasingly became an inaccessible father to my three children, a lousy husband, and a mediocre minister. Much of that time, in fact, is simply a blur in my mind and a gap in my memory. I can only speculate, with great sadness, what I missed in those precious childhood years of Lindsay, Jim, and Krista.

A good friend at the church, Sally Davis, had recently undergone successful back surgery at The Ohio State University hospital. She strongly encouraged me to see some of her doctors, just to see if any new and helpful insights might have developed within medical circles since I was at The Mayo Clinic.

I followed her advice and, in the process, came to know a wonderful physician by the name of Dr. Ernie Johnson, who became involved in the diagnostic work being conducted on me and was later to play an important role in my healing. Unfortunately, however, my back situation was considered so unusual and so severe that I became a research project for an entire team of physicians, and Ernie was no longer in a primary role. As before, none of these physicians knew about post-polio syndrome—nor did I, which is why I was consulting orthopedics who were experts concerning broken backs—which only contributed to the difficulty of making an accurate diagnosis and prognosis.

To make a long, extensive, and difficult diagnostic process short—after all, you have already heard a similar story before from me—the conclusions were no different.

"You'll just have to accept your fate, Bob," the physician who was chosen to be the one to give me the news counseled. "There is no medical or surgical solution that would seem to be helpful to your pain. You will, in all likelihood, continue to have an escalation in your symptoms, probably spending the rest of your life in severe pain, needing to take strong medications. We predict that within a very few months, you will face permanent confinement to a wheelchair. I don't want to give you false hope, Bob. That is simply the facts as we see them. That is our best analysis."

But it was what he said next that was to boggle my mind, irritate my personality, churn in my gut, and catapult my soul into action. "We all feel that it is important that you stop your denial, Bob. You seem to be constantly thinking that you will find a solution to your pain and disability. But your medical history shows that three times you have been through major diagnostic work-ups on your condition, and three times the answer has always been the same. The prognosis is that you will be in pain, will have to take strong medicines, and in all likelihood, will be confined to a wheelchair for the rest of your life." And with an insensitive and arrogant air that seemed to be saying, "Now go home and quick bugging us," he quickly picked up his file, turned, walked out of the examination room, and left me sitting there stunned.

I had learned that it is very difficult for anyone, including physicians, to be very present, let alone sympathetic, when it comes to severe chronic pain—in part because of their medical training, in part because of the very nature of pain itself. Physicians are trained to respond to objective data—a high temperature, evidence on an x-ray or an MRI, a cut to be sutured, a burn to be treated, a cancer to be eradicated, a heart to be bypassed. But it is the very subjective nature of pain that makes it so difficult. As Elaine Scarry put it so accurately, "to have pain is to have certainty; to hear about pain is to have doubt."[2]

For the sufferer, pain cannot be denied, for anyone on the outside, it cannot be confirmed. It is, therefore, and quite understandably, hard to be believed and certainly difficult to generate genuine sympathy for.

The Dying of Another Soul-Self

Again, it is from the perspective of several decades of living and thinking deeply about these issues of health and illness that I can look back on my early 1970s descent into hell and begin to understand some of the dynamics involved.

I can now see how, although not quite as dramatic as the soul-self transformation in 1957, this descent into hell was involving two aspects of my deepest identity.

First of all, I came out of the first transformation of a soul-self with the commitment to love. My primary understanding or interpretation of that was focused upon external, political, and social activism, trying to bring education where there was ignorance, justice where there was injustice, equality and tolerance where there were bigotry and discrimination, and an integrated society where there was segregation. Now I found myself unable to devote energy or physical presence to those causes. I felt I was failing my calling, copping out on my commitment; instead of helping the world at large, my world was closing in on very self-centered agony. My existence was one of merely coping with pain and deterioration. I felt my "call was being invalidated, as I increasingly became an invalid.

The second invalidation had to do with my marriage to Lee. Our marriage was becoming increasingly stressful, and after many years of marriage and individual counseling, I became convinced that our differences were irreconciliable. I would not presume to speak for Lee or the children, but eventually I came to realize that I would never find a solution to my severe chronic pain if I continued down that same road. I struggled long and hard about the effect of a divorce on our three children—ages eight, ten, and twelve at the time. I came to believe, however, that it was best for all concerned, and we started divorce proceedings.

Although best for the long run, the immediate impact on my sense of a dying soul-self was to contribute to its demise. It is an extremely complex issue—beneficial for some reasons and hurtful for others—but I had never conceived myself as one who would get a divorce. Not only was I the first in my extended family to do so, but being a clergyman complicated this issue substantially.

Sinking deeper and deeper, I felt as if I were in a free-fall, spiraling from invalidation of my soul-self, to becoming more of an invalid, only to fall deeper into invalidation. My deepest sense of self was being killed, canceled, erased, wiped out, and obliterated!

In the Darkest Night of the Soul, a Healing Dream

Sometimes it is precisely when we think we are in hell, that heaven calls to us. Sometimes it is when our deepest soul-self feels obliterated that God introduces us to an even deeper, even more appropriate soul-self for our future, thus removing our sense of dying and moving us into the promise of becoming. And, so it was with me.

When I was experiencing my darkest version of what the Spanish mystic St. John of the Cross referred to as the "dark night of the soul," I had what Marc Ian Barasch calls a "Healing Dream."

> I have coined the term *Healing Dreams*, because they seem to have a singular intensity of purpose: to lead us to embrace the contradictions between flesh and spirit, self and other, shadow and light in the name of wholeness. The very word for "dream" in Hebrew—*chalom*—derives from the verb meaning "to be made healthy or strong." With remarkable consistency, such dreams tell us that we live on the merest outer shell of our potential, and that the light we seek can be found in the darkness of a yet-unknown portion of our being.[3]

Barasch seems to have been inside my soul when he wrote the sentences above. I have never run across anyone anywhere speaking more accurately to what I experienced in the dream that came to me in that dark night of my soul. It was a dream that has been the most healing dream I have ever had, yet it did not speak to healing directly. It spoke to wholeness, and it spoke to my untapped potential, the previously unknown portion of my being. In a dream that has continued to be both accurate in predicting the subsequent thirty years of my life and that has continued to reveal itself for that entire time, I dreamed . . .

> *I awoke one morning sick and stayed home in bed. The rest of the family was gone, so I believed that I was the only one in the house at the time. To my surprise, however, it gradually dawned on me that I was*

hearing voices down in my basement. Curious as to who could possibly be in my basement, I got out of bed and went down to investigate. To my amazement, I discovered an architect's office in my basement. How, I wondered, could I be oblivious to the fact that an architect had an office in my very own basement?

I got into a conversation with the architect who, by the way, seemed to know me very well and not be at all surprised to have me discover his office. He explained to me, in the tone of a gentle, compassionate teacher, that he not only was a designer of homes in general but that he had designed my home in particular. The punch line came when he informed me that he had designed many rooms in my house of which I was, to this point, totally unaware.

The rest of the dream consisted of the architect's giving me a tour of my house, showing me room after room that I had not known existed in my house. When the dream concluded, I was so changed by what the architect had shown me, in this much larger and much more wonderful home, that I decided not to go back to my former job, but began giving tours of the house.

Cultural anthropologist Angeles Arrien reminds us that indigenous peoples all around this planet of ours know that nighttime dreams are sacred stories with profound messages being offered for our journey. Even more importantly, indigenous peoples believe that you desacralize the story if you don't act on it, if you don't live it.

Although it was a long and gradual process of awakening for me, my Architect Dream was a powerful symbol of the sacred path that I was to take on my way into a miracle healing. It might be helpful to examine more closely the hints for my healing journey that were being offered in this dream.

1. *The dawning:*

I awoke one morning sick and stayed home in bed. The rest of the family was gone, so I believed that I was the only one in the house at the time. To my surprise, however, it gradually dawned on me that I was hearing voices down in my basement. Curious as to who could possibly be in my basement, I got out of bed and went down to investigate. To my

> *amazement, I discovered an architect's office in my basement. How, I wondered, could I be oblivious to the fact that an architect had an office in my very own basement?*

The dream occurred at dawn, the first of a new day. Soon thereafter, I became aware of activity in my depths—it just "dawned" on me that people were in my basement.

Dawning light is nourishment for the soul, enlightenment its purpose. Like a sunflower that tracks the sun across the sky in order to sip from its energetic light all day long, the human soul hungers and thirsts after the enlightened vision, the inspired insight, or the miraculous dawn of a new day in life's journey. That is why a "dark night of the soul" can be both an agonizing starvation of light as well as the soul's preparation for the deliciously delectable taste of the morning's new and miraculous enlightenment. We survive the dark night with the hope and expectation of the dawn. Then comes the "Ah-ha!" when a soul's new enlightenment causes us to celebrate how an important insight "just dawned" on us.

The ancient Egyptians knew intuitively how important light was to our spiritual lives. They personified the brightest light in the sky, the sun, into the all-powerful sun god Ra, a name that literally means "to rise in brilliance." So, as the sun's light rises in brilliance over the horizon every morning, we can be reminded of how there is always the possibility of a new brilliance rising within the human Soul, a new brilliance that can obliterate the darkness, even the deepest and most painful darkness of the personal soul.

So it can be that a life of pain, suffering, and debilitation, a life that includes both being an invalid and being invalidated, can find its way into a new day of healing and wholeness, through its very natural propensity for the light. Dawn can bring a new vision of possibilities and a revisioning of one's deepest identity. Dawn can bring that single beam of enlightenment that can transform a life.

Enlightenment, however, can be at very different levels, at many different times in our lives, and with very different meanings. The light that dawned on me in 1957 redirected my life from professional athlete to professional minister. But I was unaware for fifteen years as to how limited my notion was of ministry in general and of human potential in particular. God's enlightenment came in the dark night of my soul to dawn on me once again and to enlighten some more of my shadowy depths.

Oh, I had been religious, to be sure. I had been religious about my ministry. I had been religious about my search for pain management and for trying to find a way out of my despair about sinking deeper and deeper into suffering, disability, and depression regarding the loss of my primary soul-self. I had been religious, and I had prayed about it. Actually, I had prayed hard and long, intensively and extensively, about it. There were, in fact, times when my prayers were extremely loud and extraordinarily profane. I was angry and frustrated, feeling helpless and hopeless, all of which simply made me more angry and more frustrated. But nothing seemed to help. The religious stuff didn't do it. What had not dawned on me, until God worked the wondrous, symbolic wake-up call via the Architect in my basement, was how my constricted and restricted notions of human potential were blocking me from the healing I so desperately needed and wanted. A new and wider vision needed to dawn on me. A new and wider soul-self needed to be born.

2. The Architect Expands My Vision of Human Potential:

I got into a conversation with the architect who, by the way, seemed to know me very well and not be at all surprised to have me discover his office. He explained to me, in the tone of a gentle, compassionate teacher, that he not only was a designer of homes in general but that he had designed my home in particular. The punch line came when he informed me that he had designed many rooms in my house of which I was, to this point, totally unaware.

In the dream, I felt incredibly reassured that I was so "at home with the Architect"—pun intended. I initially went down into my basement with a curiosity and an edge, as one might expect when you think you hear uninvited strangers invading the basement of your home. But the profound sense that the Architect knew me well and was so calm and nonthreatening immediately put me at ease. It was as if he was an inner guide who had been waiting patiently for me to discover his presence, the theological implications of which are obvious.

What felt extremely important, and what has grown in significance over the succeeding thirty years, is that it was not just any home, it was *my* home. My home was unique and personal, much more wonderful and larger than I had known. It wasn't only about houses in general; it was specifically about *my* house. A theme that we will return to over and over again throughout this book is that you and I are not like track homes; we are not simply cookie-cutter versions of Soul. Rather, each of us, although sharing some similarities with others of our species, gender, and family, is unique in some very important respects. We will never know our full potential for health promotion, disease prevention, and participating in healing processes until we explore that uniqueness completely and thoroughly. In the same manner, as a culture in general and as health professionals and caregivers in particular, we will never be able fully and effectively to enable and facilitate those processes with others until we honor, affirm, and address their unique individuality. The "door" into that unique personal territory is the soul-journey work that will permeate the rest of this book.

Later on, when we return to this theme, we will try to discern the appropriate balance between the medical scientific paradigm that emphasizes group statistical analysis and the spiritual paradigm that stresses individuality and uniqueness of a person's journey of soul. Until we find that appropriate balance, we will continue to trivialize and marginalize miracle healings, and we will tolerate far too much pathology, continue to be mystified by the recurrence of disease, and underestimate and underutilize the individual's extraordinary capacity for miracle healings.

3. The Prediction:

The rest of the dream consisted of the architect's giving me a tour of my house, showing me room after room that I had not known existed in my house. When the dream concluded, I was so changed by what the architect had shown me, in this much larger and much more wonderful home, that I decided not to go back to my former job, but began giving tours of the house.

The dream indicated that the Architect would introduce me to that larger context of expanded human potential that existed within me and that increased awareness would change my life. The dream predicted a process that would transform the texture of my pain-wracked and broken body, and write a different text to the upcoming chapter of my life's story. The discovery of a wide range of potentialities that existed within me led not only to a dramatic and miraculous healing but, as the dream predicted, resulted in a totally different direction and content to my life and my ministry. And that, to adapt Paul Harvey's famous phrase, is what you will come to know as "the rest of the story."

In Preparation for a Miracle

One of the more famous of the stories about the Buddha, and certainly one of my favorites, tells about how, following the Buddha's enlightenment, a passerby was taken by his extraordinarily peaceful presence and asked, "Are you a magician or a wizard?"

"No," said the Buddha.

"Are you an angel?"

Again, the Buddha said, "No."

"Are you a god?"

"No."

"Well, then," said the man, "if you are none of these, what are you?"

The Buddha replied, "I am awake."

Awakening is not only an appropriate metaphor for my dream but is a helpful way to think about enlightenment in general. We probably would not be able to handle the brilliant glare if all the enlightenment that we were to gain in a lifetime happened all at once. Thus, enlightenment comes gradually, as if by a cosmic rheostat. For me, and quite possibly for others as well, there was a time of preparation before the miracle, a time of gradual awakening before "it dawns on us."

Interestingly enough, as if to demonstrate how it would take me a while to awaken to the full import of that dream, I wrote it down the next morning and then promptly forgot about it. I did not discover the written account of the dream until after the miraculous healing that was soon to occur. This forgetfulness, or perhaps unconsciousness, demonstrates not only how slow I may be to awaken, but how profoundly the unconscious can work on us even while we are unaware.

In spite of my not consciously remembering the Architect Dream for the first few months, I felt a profound hope that a healing could be experienced and a strong motivation to explore "outside the box," or what I later realized was the process of discovering the additional "rooms in my house."

1. Outside the box:

The conventional medical "box"—the understanding of health, illness, and the processes of healing that were in vogue at the time—did not have any satisfactory answers for me. So I would just have to explore the territory outside that box. From the morning after that dream, I found myself driven with hope and motivation. I knew that there were no guarantees that I would find a healing, but it would not be for lack of trying. The conventional medical box would not be my coffin. I was on an adventure, a journey, a path.

As my path crossed the boundaries of medical orthodoxy, there was no shortage of warnings from the gatekeepers—dangerous ideas were out there in that unexplored territory, they said—modalities outside the box lack scientific verification, they warned—that's the territory where the quacks hang out, they cautioned. But for someone living in hell who had been given the best orthodox medicine could provide—a future of severe chronic pain, strong narcotics, and confinement to a wheelchair—such warnings carried little credibility.

This was a time, particularly in Middle America, where there were few if any maps, teachers, or field guides for a venture outside the conventional medical box into foreign and forbidden territory. Keep in mind, that was in the days before we even used terms such as "alternative" or "complimentary" medicine. We did not even call the medical paradigm "conventional" medicine, for few of us ever thought about anything "unconventional" when it came to health and illness. The medical paradigm was god, the physicians were the priests, and the promise of salvation, or official damnation, was for those who were obedient and subservient to the established dogma. For a long time, I was just that—a good patient who followed the doctor's orders and did not question the medical "theology."

A paradigm defines what we think is possible and what is deemed impossible. But given what medical authorities were saying was the only possibility for my future, I could either accept that fate or I could begin to explore what I was being told was impossible.

To harken back to the symbolism of my Architect dream, my own vision, as well as the official medical vision of the possible was what we all *thought* was the size of my house, prior to the tour by the Architect. It also means that the former house is still part of the new larger image.

Consequently, my ventures into new territory did not mean that I discounted all that conventional medical science had to offer. Far from it. I think much of it was, and is, very helpful. My point was simply that I would not let that, or any other orthodoxy, determine the parameters of my search or the boundaries of my quest. I continued to consider all that medical science could offer but just did not stop there. I had to explore the other rooms that I previously did not know were there.

Writing this now, some thirty years later, I should make clear that what was outside the box in the 1970s is, for many of us, now inside the box. That is the marvelous thing about growth, maturation, and the evolution of our paradigm of health and illness. It is what we will be exploring increasingly throughout this book.

But to put my healing into historical perspective, put yourself back into the 1970s with me. To make a long and complex process short, I began to read everything I could get my hands on that dealt with extended human potential and to personally experiment with many of the new emerging mind-body-spirit modalities. I explored a wide variety of ideas and modalities in the then-new, emerging human-potential movement. Particularly, I studied closely and experimented widely with stress research, biofeedback, and clinical and experimental hypnosis, as well as various meditative disciplines. On one trip to Denver, Colorado, I worked extensively with biofeedback expert Dr. Tom Budzynski at the University of Colorado Medical Center, and while there, took meditation training from a woman named Diana—the woman who would two years later become my wife, but I'll return to that part of the story a bit later.

The Miracle in Park City

One of the most wonderful physicians I had come to know at The Ohio State University medical school was Dr. Ernie Johnson, whom I mentioned earlier. He was involved in my original diagnostic work; but, unlike most of his colleagues, he did not simply dismiss my future as strictly and hopelessly ordained to be in pain, on drugs, and in a wheelchair.

I received a telephone call one day from Ernie. He had been thinking about my situation and wondered if I would be willing to try medical hypnosis for pain control. "Of course," I replied, "I'm trying anything and everything that might hold the possibility for pain management."

"I have this good friend," continued Dr. Johnson, "who is one of the country's leading experts in medical hypnosis for pain control, Dr. Robert Baer. Bob is a professor in the medical school at the University of Utah. He has offered to let you, as his guest, participate in an upcoming medical conference on hypnosis that will be held at the ski resort in Park City, Utah."

It was a cold and snowy February day in 1973 when I arrived in Salt Lake City and was picked up by Dr. Baer at the airport. We stopped by his home before we headed up to Park City, and he started loading ski equipment into the back of his van.

"What length of ski do you want?" Dr. Baer asked.

"What do you mean? I don't even know how to ski," I said.

"That's all right," Dr. Baer continued without missing a beat. "I'll teach you."

"But," I stammered, "don't you know why I am here? Don't you know that I am in a great deal of pain? I need your help with pain management, not to teach me how to ski."

With a slight grin, Dr. Baer simply replied, "Well, I figure that if we break your leg skiing, you'll forget about your back."

I knew right off that I liked this guy's sense of humor, but I wasn't sure that he understood how desperate I was, how much pain I was in, or that I could only stand for about five minutes at a time. I love to have a little humor in most any situation, but at the moment I flat-out needed pain management, not jokes.

It turned out that Bob Baer was not only an expert in teaching self-hypnosis for pain management, but he was a generous, gentle, and compassionate man. His quiet and unassuming manner hid the fact that he was highly respected for his expertise. Most extraordinary was that, in spite of running a medical conference, he always seemed to have both the time and concern to give me his attention as I needed it. He would translate for me some of the medical jargon being used in the conference and told me to practice my self-hypnotic induction every hour on the hour, no matter what was going on or who was speaking, stressing how much it was a matter of practice, practice, practice.

Several days into the conference, during an afternoon break in the schedule and while most of the other conferees were on the ski-slopes, I was in my room alone practicing the process of going deeply within and using mental imagery to attempt to control the severe pain. I had become convinced, through my investigations of both Eastern and Western forms of meditation, guided-imagery, biofeedback research, deep-relaxation techniques, the implications of placebo research, fascinating evidence on stigmata (spiritual wounding) and faith healing, as well as my current involvement in the seminar on medical hypnosis, that there was great untapped power in the mind-body "dialogue" facilitated by mental imagery. I was gradually developing my own somewhat eclectic and unique synthesis of all those disciplines and all the implications from those various areas of scientific research.

When I began meditating that afternoon, however, I had no preliminary hints or intuitive premonitions that my life was about to change dramatically. I began, as usual, trying to relax very deeply, using breathing techniques—imagining that, with every exhalation, I was getting rid of all excess stress throughout my body and mind. I spent probably six-to-eight minutes in a patient and consistent process of relaxing and going deeply into an altered state of consciousness. Then I shifted to the primary content of the meditation.

I know intellectually that my lungs are not connected to my lower back, but that is irrelevant. The left-brain, if you will, needs to step aside in a meditation such as this and let the right-brain exercise its power. Experientially, when I would take a deep breath and expand my rib cage, I would feel extra twinges of pain in my back. Consequently, it provided a good "feeling" imagery with which to work.

I gradually shifted my concentration from breathing away stress to imagining that, during my inhalation (when I could actually feel the pain), I would be gathering the pain into my lungs, so that when I exhaled, I would be releasing the pain from my body, breathing it away, as it were.

I did not keep track of time per se, but I was probably fifteen minutes into this meditation when it happened. Unexpectedly, like the exquisite feeling of diving into a cool pool after having your body burning for years, I was suddenly free of about 80 percent of my usually severe level of pain.

The relief was so sudden, so dramatic, and so profound that I was startled out of the deep concentrating meditation and into a litany of reality checks. Was I hallucinating? Did I all of a sudden lose touch with reality? Did my body, for some strange reason, go numb? Had I lost the capacity to feel after years of constant and severe pain? Was I dreaming? Was this just a temporary and passing moment of relief, only to have the pain return? I sat quietly as my mind raced trying to figure it out, surveying my body for confirmation.

But, indeed, the relief was real. *Really* real. Not that I was completely pain-free, but I had been unmistakably and miraculously relieved of the severe levels of pain. I still had some pain, but the difference before and after that moment was unbelievable. Instantaneously, I had been catapulted into a different world of physical experience. Without any warning, I suddenly found myself in completely new territory.

As the reality sunk in, I began to realize that I would never return to that previous hell. I literally and symbolically threw away the powerful prescribed narcotics that I had been taking.

An overwhelming sense of relief and a deep and abiding peace replaced the momentary skepticism that doubted the reality of the experience. I was transformed from fearing that I might be hallucinating into a celebration of a profoundly miraculous fact. The moment was more real than any previous moment in my life!

Tears of joy streamed down my face. In fact, the joy was so profound that, even as I remember it and write this description almost thirty years later, fresh tears of joy cloud my vision of the computer screen. Like the radiation left over from the creation of the universe that can be detected fifteen billion years later, the energy of that miracle is still present at a visceral level after almost half a lifetime.

"Now," I told the delighted and celebrative Dr. Baer, "I'm ready to learn how to ski."

After the physical and emotional relief came the intellectual curiosity. How could this pain relief happen when all the experts said it was impossible? Following the intellectual passion came a spiritual compassion: if I could understand how this miracle came to be, could I be of help to the many other people who are suffering severe chronic pain? Perhaps there would even be insights relevant to any process of health promotion, disease prevention, and healing. The intellectual and spiritual quest, the passion and compassion, the synchronistic synergy of body, mind, and spirit, the daily existential struggle with continuing the healing, and the theoretical, medical, philosophical, and theological reflections—those have been continuing themes for the succeeding thirty years of my life story. And that is what the rest of this book is about.

I want, however, to share two very personal parts of the story that followed the miracle in Park City, before moving on to the more general matters of health and illness.

The first has to do with Diana, whom, as I mentioned in the dedication, has become the most powerful healing force in my life. After Park City, and the fact that I was now single, I began to get more energized about finding the woman with whom I would spend the rest of my life. I began dating some in Columbus but also reconnected with Diana, who had been my meditation teacher while on the biofeedback research trip into Denver.

Over the following two years, with huge telephone bills and

frequent trips into Denver, Diana's and my love for each other grew profoundly deep and meaningful, and we were married in 1975.

In Diana I found a relationship in which we could know and affirm each other completely and unconditionally. In Diana I found one who knew and loved me more than I thought possible and who could receive all the love I wanted to give her. More than that, I found a partner who was able to teach me more about living, giving, and receiving healing love than even I, in all my desperation, knew I needed. No single process has been more crucial to my healing than the presence of Diana in my life, and every day I appreciate her more. Besides, she was a good meditation teacher, and I was a slow learner—so I desperately needed her to accept my offer of marriage!

The other personal story involved my friend Dr. Ken Johnson at the Mayo Clinic in Rochester, Minnesota. He was one of a number of friends to whom I wrote to share my good news. I was particularly delighted to tell Ken about my breakthrough, for it gave me hope that I might be able to return to handball someday.

Given our long and close friendship, I naturally expected Ken to be thrilled with the miracle I had just experienced. I expected that he would not only celebrate my breakthrough on the severe chronic pain, but that he might be curious enough about the medical implications of the meditative synthesis that I had developed that he would be interested in exploring those implications with me. Perhaps a new dimension of our old friendship was about to be launched.

Oh, how naive I was and how completely shocked when I received Ken's letter. His response was quick, simple, direct, and blunt—he was sorry that I had "gone off the deep end" into all that mind-body mumbo-jumbo. How, he wondered, could the athlete whom he had felt such a kinship with, the man with the intellectual abilities that he had so highly respected (notice the past tense) be so taken in by such esoteric, woo-woo, New Age fantasy. "There is simply no medical legitimation in what you describe, Bob, or in what you claim to have experienced."

No celebration of my pain relief! No spiritual compassion for what had been, for me, a dramatic shift from hell into heaven. No intellectual curiosity about a sudden, miraculous, healing. No desire to explore the wonders of my experience, nor wonder about the medical implications. Just the refusal to accept even the truthfulness of my experience by a tragic prisoner of the narrowest of paradigms. Just disgust and disdain for my going "off the deep end."

"I'm not interested in that stuff," he concluded.

It was a sad fracturing of a valued relationship with a good friend. I thought about arguing with him. I thought about telling him how disappointed I was in his reaction. But I had learned by this time that you rarely argue someone into a new paradigm. As I once heard Joseph Chilton Pierce say in a lecture, "One's cosmic egg has to crack from the inside out."

I thought it would do little or no good to try to convince Ken of my point of view, or even of my experience, and decided to honor his right to end the friendship. After all, I had a lot more healing to do, and it wouldn't help to be combative or competitive across paradigmatic boundaries. I needed to move ahead, to build on the miracle that had begun a new life for me—not expending time and energy trying to convince others to come along with me if they did not want to.

Still, I did wonder. Why was this physician friend of mine so unable to celebrate my miracle? How could he be so singularly committed to a medical orthodoxy, so certain that it and it alone knew the truth about healing that he could not accept an exception, particularly when it was with a friend whose life had been transformed from severe pain, drugs, suffering, and a totally negative prognosis into a life of new and exciting possibilities?

There were obviously deep and profoundly influential roots to this kind of medical reaction. I needed to go digging into those roots in order to understand why miracles were in medical exile—so exiled, in fact, that it could rend asunder a previously close friendship.

PART II

The Medical Story: Past and Present

CHAPTER FOUR

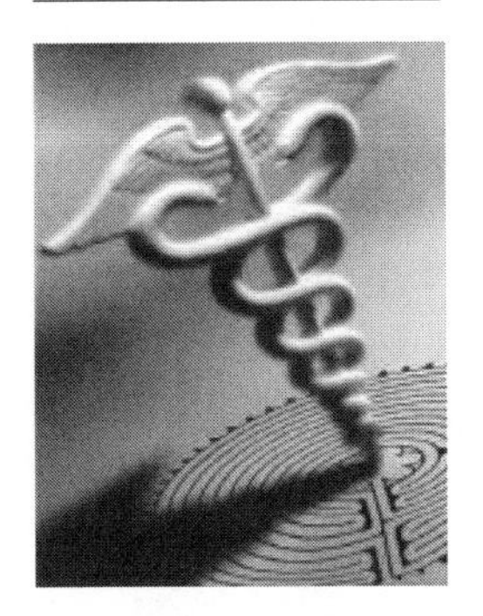

MIRACLES *in* MEDICAL EXILE

Medicine grows out of a culture; it is never isolated and self-contained.

LARRY DOSSEY, M.D.

Why did my friend Dr. Ken Johnson reject the entire notion of miracle healing? Why was he, in fact, not alone within the medical profession? How did it come to be that the medical paradigm banished miracles from the Land of Medical Acceptability and exiled them out onto the Frontiers of the Fringe, the Territories of the Occult, the Mountains of Mumbo-Jumbo, and the Precipice of Going Off the Deep End? In short, why have miracles been in medical exile?

To answer that question we need, once again, to consider context. The text of the modern medical story in general and the texture of its feelings about the role of spirituality in healing in particular were created by a very particular historical context—namely, the

Middle Ages and the Enlightenment—the cultural, intellectual, ecclesiastical, theological, and scientific content of the past six hundred years.

We begin with what may come as a surprise—namely, medieval Christianity's culpability in the eventual medical banishment of miracles.

Christianity's Culpability

Sounds strange, doesn't it? To suggest that Christianity played a role in the banishment of miracles sounds counter intuitive. After all, hasn't Christianity always been in the business of *promoting* miracles? Were not miracle healings a very central activity of Jesus' life and ministry? The answers are, of course, yes and yes.

Nevertheless, it was Christianity's traditional theology that, in fact, set the stage for the eventual marginalization and trivialization of spirituality in the emergent modern Western medical understanding of healing. It certainly was not the intention of Christianity to do so; but when we look at why and how a materialistic and secular medical science developed, we can see how traditional theology was responsible.

Christianity was, far and away, the most influential institution in the European Middle Ages just prior to the rise of modern medicine. Virtually all of Europe was under the influence of the Roman Catholic Church, and there was, as historian Richard Tarnas put it succinctly, an "omnipresence of the Church and Christian religiosity in every sphere of human activity."[1]

Although its theology, in many respects, was not all that different from that of other major monotheistic religions—Judaism and Islam—Christianity had the overwhelming theological influence on the womb that gave birth to modern Western medical science. So what was it about the church's theology that resulted in the eventual banishment of miracles into medical exile?

I have discussed at some length, in earlier books, the several-millennia-long, deep soul-level influences that led to the creation of this theology.[2] For our purposes here, we can boil it down to a fairly simple and straightforward theological structure—(1) a reductionistic and fractured world in which all reality was broken up into pieces, (2) the pieces then arranged in a hierarchical manner, with (3) judgment, power, and absolute control reigning down from above.

1. *A Reductionistic and Fractured World:*
Christianity took the cosmos and broke it up into pieces, fracturing the whole while reducing it to parts—heaven and earth, divine and human, spirit and matter, those inside the church and those outside, those who are saved and those who are damned. Once the world was understood as comprised of parts, rather than a whole, and each part was defined as separate and distinct, we came to believe that each part was fundamentally different and mutually exclusive from the other parts. God, therefore, was separate and totally different from humanity. Heaven was distinct from and completely unlike earth, and the same distinction was believed to exist between spirit and matter, this world and the next, the sinful and the saved, those inside the Church and those outside.

2. *A Hierarchical Arrangement:*
Once all of reality was reduced to individual and disparate parts, the parts were arranged vertically with the higher clearly considered to be the better. God was above, over, and better than humans. Heaven was above, over, and better than earth, etc. Keep in mind that such notions have been so paradigmatic, so unconscious, and so influential for so long that it may seem strange to even question them. After all, we tend to think that is simply the way things are. But we created this structure intellectually and theologically and then came to worship our own creation.

Once we had separated all the parts of the cosmos and arranged them hierarchically, we developed the habit of thinking and speaking of God in the most lofty and grandiose terms—omniscient, omnipresent, and omnipotent—while we thought and spoke of human beings as totally depraved and, following St. Augustine's lead, considered humanity as guilty of "Original Sin." It was, to put it bluntly, a theological and hierarchical structure that had the Almighty at Altitude with an Attitude. A Father God was up in his heaven, doling out love, justice, and judgment upon his children down on earth. The Grand Parent in the sky was the all-powerful giver of both good and bad, whereas the children on earth were the powerless, passive, and submissive recipients.

This complete separation between the omnipotent and the impotent, the good and the depraved, this life and the next, led inevitably to the notion that the very purpose of human life was to be "saved"—saved *from* our completely sinful condition and *to* a reconciled status with God, to be saved *from* this world and *into* the next. Our job, our task, if you will, was to "get into" heaven. We could not do that on our own, however, because of our depravity. The Church claimed exclusive salvic power, the one and only conduit through which human beings could be reconciled with God.

In a brilliant accomplishment of theological spin that would humble even the best of today's political "spin-meisters," the Church got us to believe that it was not the institutional Church that created this fracturing of the world or defined these power-down relationships: it was God. It was, we were told, a divinely ordained arrangement.

The Church's theology regarding Jesus as the Christ—that is, its "Christology"—was an understandable result of its reductionistic and hierarchical theological structure. Once God and humanity and heaven and earth were totally and completely separated, an intermediary, a Savior, was necessary. Thus, God "sent His only Son" to bridge the gap and to save the sinners, so that "whosoever believeth in Him shall have everlasting life." The medieval version of this was stated with absolute certainty and absolute exclusivity. God, Christ, and the Church were the *only* ways by which we could be saved. This, as we shall soon see, played an important role in why modern medical science developed in such a reactionary manner—secular and materialistic in contrast to the prevailing religious and spiritual, and self-sufficient in contrast to being dependent upon divine intervention.

So paradigmatic was this theological structure in the Middle Ages that no alternative way of constructing reality ever had a chance. It was powerfully unconscious and virtually unanimous. It was self-evident and unquestioned. (Of course, in reality it wasn't totally unanimous and was sometimes questioned, but those who were so foolish as to think independently were generally killed as heretics.) For the orthodox version was the accurate understanding of how God created the world—period. This was the shape and purpose of human existence—period. This was the divinely ordained authority of the Church—exclamation point!

3. *Total Power and Control From Above:*

Although it is obvious that versions of this traditional Christian theology continue their influence even into our day and our lives, we should not underestimate how different the Western world of Christendom was then compared to now, particularly as it regards absolute external power and control. We who are writing and reading these words in the twenty-first century should keep in mind that we come after the historical impact of the fourteenth through the twentieth centuries and are, therefore, different in some important respects from the people of the fourteenth century, particularly regarding our attitude toward authority.

In the medieval world that preceded the rise of modern scientific medicine, God was seen as omnipotent and completely in control. This absolute power was mediated to earth, singularly and completely, through Christ, the Church, the popes and cardinals, and on down the ladder of authority. The truths of Scripture were comprehensive and authoritative, and the Church was the official interpreter. The Church would tell everyone precisely what the Bible said, what it meant, and how one was to behave. (Keep in mind, this was before the time when the Bible was in the hands of the common person. Even more importantly, these were the days before we would have thought we even had the right to question this arrangement or to think independently about the meaning of biblical passages.)

The individual was at the bottom of the hierarchy of power and control—completely impotent, weak, inferior, and utterly subservient to the Church. Individuality, personal questing, questioning, and independent thinking, if even thought of at all, were certainly dangerous to one's health. You could and would be tortured until you agreed to the Church's dogma and/or killed in order to save your soul. This degree of power and authority claimed by the Church, along with the unquestioned assumption of individual submission, is extremely difficult for those of us living in the twenty-first century to even imagine.

The critical point in understanding Christianity's culpability in the eventual banishment of miracle healing by the medical science was the assumption that everything good that happened to a person (for example, healing) was a direct reward by this all-powerful and all-controlling God, and everything bad that happened (for example, illness) was a direct punishment for one's sin. It was virtually a child-and-Santa-Claus kind of relationship, with God's keeping track of who was naughty or nice and dolling out punishments of illness or gifts of healing.

It was a simple and straightforward cause-and-effect: you got what you deserved. If you sinned, you were given a grave disease; but if you were good, you were rewarded with being healthy, wealthy, and wise. The opposite was also true: if you became ill, it was clear evidence that you had sinned; but if you were healthy, wealthy, and wise, it was obvious that you were righteous. Consequently, whether it was pestilence or miracles, they came directly from God on high. Because God was outside the natural world, both "judgments" were thought to be supernatural events. Miracles, in other words, were God's interventions into the natural processes of life, as a result of prayer and/or of living a righteous and blameless life.

Make no mistake about it, the clear promise was that God could and would intervene into the natural order to perform supernatural acts—either out of wrath in the form of disasters or, in the special occasion of miracles, because of his love and grace. The assumption was that if you accepted Christ as your Savior, if you were religious and rigorous about the Church's rituals, and if you prayed often and fervently enough, God might reach down out of his heaven and provide you with a miracle healing. It was a theology that emphasized the all-powerful and transcendent God, heaven, and the afterlife, while also emphasizing the lack of power in the immanent, the human, and the here-and-now.

It was, however, a Humpty-Dumpty theological structure that would have a great fall in the fourteenth century; and all the Kingdom's popes and cardinals and all the Church's desperate attempts at damage control could not put Humpty-Dumpty back together again.

History would eventually record this transformation of the divine-human relationship as the Enlightenment, the combined and synergistic effect of the Renaissance, the Reformation, the Scientific Revolution, and the Industrial Revolution. The resultant "new" human being, duly enlightened, reformed, and revolted, would banish miracles into exile and would take a thoroughly secular, materialistic, and self-sufficient approach to health and illness. It would be the beginning of modern scientific medicine.

Historian and Pulitzer-Prize winner Barbara Tuchman underscores what a substantial change in the human psyche took place between medieval Christianity and the modern era. Before this dramatic shift, Christianity was, in her words,

> The matrix and law of medieval life, omnipresent, indeed compulsory . . . [and] . . . its insistent principle that the life of the spirit and of the afterworld was superior to the here and now, to material life on earth, is one that the modern world does not share, no matter how devout some present-day Christians may be. The rupture of this principle and its replacement by belief in the worth of the individual and of an active life not necessarily focused on God is, in fact, what created the modern world and ended the Middle Ages.[3]

To understand fully what triggered this incredible transformation and how its influence led to the development of modern medical science, we need to look a bit more carefully at the impact, the massive physical death and faith destruction of what was known as the Plague, or the Black Death, in the fourteenth century.

The Fourteenth Century's Crisis of Faith

Ring around the rosies
A pocketful of posies
Ashes, ashes
We all fall down

Some of us are old enough to remember having played "Ring Around the Rosies," wherein we held the hands of other children while singing the rhyme and moving around in a circle. Child psychologists, folklorists, and nursery-rhyme mythologists now explain this behavior as an unconscious effort to deal with the tragedy of a major devastating event. What is particularly interesting in this case, however, is that it was an unconscious memory of an event some six-hundred years earlier.

The rhyme refers to the skin discolorations and widespread devastation of what at the time was called the Pestilence or the Great

Mortality, but which later was referred to as the Black Death, the Bubonic Plague, or simply the Plague.[4]

It is almost impossible to exaggerate the impact that the Plague had upon the human population in Europe—physically, mentally, and spiritually—in just four short years from 1347 to 1351.

Although there is considerable uncertainty as to precisely where it started and even how many it killed—record-keeping was certainly not an exact science at that time in history—this enormous trauma may have begun somewhere in Asia, perhaps China. Tuchman calls it "the most lethal disaster of recorded history" and suggests that it "killed an estimated one third of the population living between India and Iceland."[5]

Professor Norman Cantor of New York University, considered by many to be the premier historian of the Middle Ages, suggests that Tuchman was not exaggerating. He himself calls the Plague "the greatest biomedical disaster in European and possibly in world history" and says that it left many with the feeling that humanity itself was being exterminated.[6]

Anyone who contracted the Plague had an 80 percent probability of being dead within two weeks; many died within three or four days of being infected, and some overnight. The devastation was overwhelming; in many places, there were not enough people left alive so as to bury the dead. Bodies were strewn across the countryside. In the cities, they were stacked up in the streets. Paris is reported to have had, on average, 800 people die every day, eventually wiping out half its population, or 50,000 people. Florence lost 60 to 80 percent of its population, and Venice two-thirds. In one city, out of twenty-four physicians, twenty died, and Cantor estimates that throughout Europe some 40 percent of all clergy perished.

The psychological and spiritual impact was extreme, exacerbated by the fact that, at this time in history, virtually nothing was known about infectious diseases and phenomenon of contagion. We knew of no prevention and had no remedy. Consequently, there was widespread hopelessness, pessimism, despair, and submissiveness. Many people believed it was the end of the world.

Most important, however, was the resultant quake in the soul-scape of the faithful. Since it was believed that everything was a direct act from God, then *this* devastation must have God's intentionality behind it, God's fingerprints all over it. What incredible sin, humanity wondered, had it committed? Was our sin so severe that God was trying to exterminate the entire human race?

People prayed fervently and often, yet kept dying. What contributed to the despair was that the priests were also dying. Again, without the knowledge of contagion, we couldn't figure out why God's favorites, the monks in their monasteries, were not spared; in fact, they were dying faster than anyone else. If one monk got infected, virtually all within the monastery died within days. It was a massive destruction of hope, severely destroying our faith in God's saving grace. Barbara Tuchman explains:

> If a disaster of such magnitude, the most lethal ever known, was a mere wanton act of God or perhaps not God's work at all, then the absolutes of a fixed order were loosed from their moorings. Minds that opened to admit these questions could never again be shut. Once people envisioned the possibility of change in a fixed order, the end of an age of submission came insight; the turn to individual conscience lay ahead. To that extent the Black Death may have been the unrecognized beginning of modern man.[7]

The resulting faith-quake created a tsunami that rearranged the entire landscape of the human mind and spirit—particularly the landscape of power regarding salvation from disease. If God had become impotent to save us, we would just have to save ourselves. If the power of God was insufficient, human mental powers would have to become sufficient. While losing faith in God, the vacuum was filled to overflowing with faith in ourselves.

In the succeeding four centuries, with the collective impact of the Renaissance, the Reformation, the Scientific and Industrial

Revolutions, and the Enlightenment, human self-confidence grew to gargantuan proportions. As historian Tarnas writes:

> The direction and quality of [the Modern Age] character reflected a gradual but finally radical shift of psychological allegiance from God to man, from dependence to independence, from other-worldliness to this world, from the transcendent to the empirical. . . .
>
> Modern man's capacity to understand the natural order and to bend that order to his own benefit could not but diminish his former sense of contingency upon God. . . . This new sense of human dignity and power inevitably moved man toward his secular self. . . .
>
> Man was responsible for his own earthly destiny. . . . And as modern man continued to mature, his striving for intellectual independence grew more absolute.[8]

As medical science developed, we became increasingly confident that we could figure out both the cause and the cure for diseases of the body. God and heaven-sent miracles were no longer a necessary part of the equation—in fact, given our experience in the fourteenth century, we knew that we could not count on divine intervention. The physical body became the territory of health and illness and the province of the physician. The human mind through scientific medicine would solve all physical problems, while the metaphysical and the miraculous were exiled into the land of oblivion.

Consequently, if Christianity's transcendent spiritual faith was the initial thesis regarding the power to heal, the antithesis was the secular and materialistic faith in modern medical science's ability to figure out the causes and cures of illness in the here and now. In other words, the faith-quake and its aftershocks shifted the landscape of power and authority regarding health and illness from the Divine to the human, from heaven to earth, from priest to physician, and from imploring God for supernatural favors to scientifically exploring the human body for natural causes and medical cures.

The overall result was that the spiritual role in health and illness was marginalized and trivialized. Miracle healings were banished into exile. Consequently, the talk that modern medical science walked was as follows:

1. We can and need to be certain:

It is understandable that our "blind faith" was shaken, when people were dying all around us in massive numbers and we had no sense as to why or what could be done about it. None of our traditional religious answers was working. Coming out of that trauma, we were left with a strong need for certainty. We desperately wanted to know *why* people got sick, *how* we could make them well, *when* they would be well again, and *who* would do it. We no longer tolerated the ambiguity and uncertainty we had just experienced: we demanded absolute clarity and certainty in matters of health and illness.

It was a receptive time in history, therefore, when René Descartes (1596–1650), who was to become one of the most influential philosophical fathers of modern science, announced that, through disciplined critical rationality and mathematics, he had found a means by which we could attain absolute certainty and total control.

For rationality and mathematics to provide us with absolute certainty, however, we obviously needed to narrow the field of inquiry to that which lent itself to rationality and mathematics—namely, an objective, measurable, quantifiable, material world that is, in essence, like a machine.

2. Matter is what matters:

Following the Church's lead in splitting spirit and matter, wherein the Church's interest was primarily in the spiritual and metaphysical realm, science took the other side of the dualism and emphasized matter and the physical. The job of science, as it was then conceived, was to gain certainty and control by measuring and quantifying physical matter.

Descartes conceptually split the human being into two distinct and fundamentally different parts, mind and body; the Greek roots that came to be used more in medicine were *psyche* (mind and soul) and *soma* (body). Descartes was most interested in restricting medical thinking to the territory that could gain mathematical certainty, predictability, and repeatability for scientific research. The effect, therefore, was that the psyche was also reduced to parts—the soul was irrelevant to medical science, and the mind would be used to analyze the separate and distinct body. Descartes basically gave the soul back to the Church for its metaphysical activity and focused his mind upon the physical, the soma, the body, and the material universe.

This contributed to the reductionism that came to permeate academia, the sciences in general and medical science in particular. It became so specialized and so fragmented that it makes seeing interconnections very difficult. Each discipline has its own jargon, its own way of addressing issues, and its own way of coming to conclusions. Consequently, we have come to know a lot about small parts but very little about the dynamics of the whole. We are impressed and excited about discoveries of the material universe but know little or nothing about the nonmaterial universe.

Consider, for instance, how much money we have invested in the human genome project, the science of mapping our body's genetic code. What we are learning is certainly valuable and exciting, but I would raise the question of what we have overlooked, what we don't know, because of not investing funds into researching the soul's code. Are we so sure that spirituality does not or cannot play a role in our state of health and illness? Or is it simply a matter of not having devoted the resources to finding that out?

Consider how delighted we are if a physical gene is identified as contributing to obesity, or to alcoholism, or to breast cancer, etc. But how do we know if an individual's soul journey is not also a contributing factor?

The materialistic paradigm of medical science has invested in and focused its spotlight on physical causes and interventions. We are reminded, however, of the old fable about a man looking for his lost key only under the street light, not because he is sure that he lost it there but because that is where the light is. It would be one thing if we had invested equally in the physical and the metaphysical and decided that only the physical impacts health and illness. It is quite another thing, however, to put all our investment into a strictly materialistic search and then proclaim, "Why, of course, cancer is strictly a biological and genetic matter. We have the evidence to back us up on that. Where is the evidence for those of you who suggest spirituality might play a role?"

To step back away from this particular discussion and state a larger principal, it is important to keep in mind that nowhere in this book will I be suggesting that we simply replace one tunnel vision (materialism) with another (spirituality). An underlying principal here is that an important ingredient in discovering that healing has spiritual and sacred components is in discovering that it is holistic—our health and illness have physical, psychological, emotional, environmental, and spiritual elements.

Reducing our search to the physical may be simple, clean, and easy. It may be what specialists are most comfortable with. It is not, however, the route to maximum healing, high-level wellness, or understanding how miracle healings can become commonplace. My personal experience, and the ideas explored in this book, suggest that neither tunnel will lead us into the promised land. Only a synthesis of the best that both science and spirituality can contribute will allow miracle healings to become commonplace.

In order for medical science to progress down the materialistic tunnel, matter had to be desacralized. Prior to this time, and particularly within traditional cultures, nature, including the human body, was thought to be imbued with spirits. But the three major architects of the Scientific Revolution—Francis Bacon, René Descartes, and Isaac Newton—accomplished a transformation of nature from living organism to dead, inert, machine parts.

Francis Bacon (1561–1626) began the transition with a concept that revealed the patriarchal, sexist, and violent underpinnings of his time in history. He thought of nature as a rebellious female, a "common harlot," that could be unruly, untamed, unpredictable, and uncertain—all anathema to the purposes of science—and considered it the task of male scientists to use torture, "to put her on the rack," so as to learn her secrets.

Whether it was because René Descartes (1596–1650) and Isaac Newton (1642–1727) were repulsed by this imagery, or for other reasons, they completed the desacralization of nature by taking all the life out of it and turning nature into a lifeless machine. We were then able to escape the guilt of torturing and violating living and spiritually imbued matter and considered ourselves as mechanics simply tinkering with the machinery of nature.

3. Nature and the human body are like machines: Historian of science Carolyn Merchant describes the consequences of this development within science:

> The removal of animistic, organic assumptions about the cosmos constituted the death of nature, the most far-reaching effect of the Scientific Revolution. Because nature was now viewed as a system of dead, inert particles moved by external, rather than inherent forces, the mechanical framework itself could legitimate the manipulation of nature.[9]

When the mechanistic metaphor was applied to the human body, Descartes likened us to a clock—a healthy person was like a well-made and functioning clock, an ill person was a clock that needed repair. We followed suit by generally thinking about the human body in mechanistic terms: the digestive track as a plumbing system, the heart as a pump, the lungs as bellows; and as we moved into the late twentieth century, we began to think of the brain as computer.

Consider, however, how mechanistic metaphors eliminate any notion of individual differences—after all, the same "species" of machines are manufactured precisely the same. Notice how there is little room for spirituality or miracle healing if the body is "nothing but" a machine. Once the body is considered to be a collection of machine parts, disease is seen as a breakdown of the machine, with the physician's being the expert mechanic, able to repair, extract, or replace the parts of the machine. Spirituality has no role.

Few would argue against the notion that materialistic and mechanistic medicine has made remarkable progress in our understanding of health and disease. But permit me to play the angel's advocate for a moment. When the Church was in charge, humans were considered to have been created in the image of God. But when science began its rise, we were considered to have been constructed in the image of a machine. (Not to be lost in this quick overview of the historical development of materialistic science is the ironic fact that most of the people who contributed to the desacralization of matter and the human body were, themselves, very devoutly religious people. They tended to believe, however, in the absent, transcendent, Father God who was, in effect, the creator of the "machines" in the universe and on earth. In Descartes' mind, God was the Grand Watchmaker.)

4. The experts are in charge:

Authoritarianism characterized the development of the medical profession in a remarkably similar way to that of the traditional religion. At one time, the imperialistic Church claimed to be the only authority for salvation. In similar fashion, an imperialistic allopathic medical establishment claimed to be the only legitimate means of salvation from illness and disease.

Following in the Church's footsteps, the modern medical establishment adopted a paternalistic pattern of authority. As the sole guardian of the "truth" about health and illness, it alone would decide what must be done to save us from illness and how and for whom certain remedies would be dispensed. It alone had the elite knowledge regarding good and bad approaches to illness, and it purported the dogma that it would be down-right dangerous for the common person to make decisions on these very complex matters. The patient was considered ignorant of what was happening to her or his body and was expected to be passive, subservient, and obedient to the doctor's orders. (Isn't it revealing that we have come to speak of "doctor's orders" rather than the advice and counsel of someone who has valuable and specialized knowledge?) Consequently, laws were passed against anyone who "practiced medicine without a license."

Consider, however, where and how an individual's unique spiritual journey would fit into this arrangement. Since the medical establishment has total authority and control and since it does not consider spirituality to have any role in physical health or pathology, facilitating an individual's spiritual journey has not been part of the medical school curriculum. (Keep in mind that, although this began to change in the 1990s, as we will soon discuss, here we are considering the historical development to understand why, for most of the history of medical science, spirituality was considered irrelevant to health and illness, and miracle healings were in exile.)

Throughout the rest of this book, I will be suggesting and illustrating how the future of healing will be a cooperative and synergistic interplay between three powerfully important "players:" (1) physicians who are highly trained in medical science but who also humbly understand that health and illness involve a larger "playing field" than their training can cover, including spirituality; (2) clergy who will become highly trained in the knowledge of how spirituality participates in health and illness, as well as in the skills to facilitate individual soul-journey; and (3) the one who probably matters the most, the individual in question, who will become increasingly empowered regarding his or her enormous abilities to influence states of health or illness and to cultivate the processes of healing.

As this is being written, however, physicians are all too narrow and uninformed regarding spirituality, clergy have little or no training in the applicable knowledge and skills, and the individual patient is largely uninformed and disempowered. While I consider this current state to be disturbing, given the size of the challenge and opportunity before us, the rest of this book will show why I am also very optimistic about what the future holds regarding this cooperation and liberation of miraculous potentialities.

Let us return for the moment, however, to our understanding of why, for so long, miracle healings have been in exile. Only by knowing where we have been can we fully appreciate and understand where we are going.

5. Health as the absence of illness:

One particularly critical consequence of authoritarianism is the decision as to who gets to do the defining. The medical establishment, therefore, claimed the total and unilateral power to define what health is and what constitutes pathology. With a profession that gave all its attention to diagnosing and treating pathology, it is not surprising that health was defined as simply the absence of disease. When machines are the primary metaphor for thinking about health and illness and the professional is primarily trained in fixing what is wrong, it is not surprising that, if the machine is fixed so as to run as before, it is considered healthy. Thus, what we curiously call our primary "health professionals" are people trained not in health and well-being so much as in diagnosing and treating pathology.

A related consequence of this paradigm is the focus on symptom eradication rather than the spiritual, psychological, or emotional meaning or message that the symptom may be offering us. If something is wrong with the machine, fix it. If a part of the machine has worn out, replace it. If an impediment to the operation of the machine has occurred, extract it. To suggest that a symptom may be a spiritual message has been tantamount to medical heresy.

In contrast, what we are moving towards is the recognition that we do little to enable a person's sacred path into wholeness, healing, and high-level wellness simply by eliminating the symptoms of disease. We have to ask why the symptom is there. Why is this particular message coming now? Is my body trying to tell me something? Knowing that this particular point has often been oversimplified—and we will try to deal with that problem more later—the messages may come from a variety of sources. The "why" may be a genetic predisposition, but even then we need to look more deeply as to why that predisposition was triggered at this particular time. The "why" may be environmental assaults. The "why" may also be emotional predispositions, habits of coping with stress, or a message that is trying to get through to your consciousness from your soul regarding the next step in your journey towards health and wholeness. The point is that the territory at which we have looked for the "why" has simply been too narrow and too superficial.

As we learn more in the future, as medical science and spirituality grow into a synergistic partnership, physical symptoms will be seen as giving us important spiritual messages. Perhaps some day we will have the eyes to see and the ears to hear those messages.

Modern medical science, for identifiable and understandable historical reasons, developed in a way that denied spiritual involvement in health and illness, a very narrow paradigm of legitimacy. Miracle healings, with Christianity as a co-conspirator, were exiled into oblivion. It has been a Procrustean story.

In Greek mythology, Procrustes, who was called "The Stretcher," was a robber and a villain who had an iron bed into which he would "fit" his victims. If they were too short, Procrustes would stretch their legs until they fit. If they were too long, he would cut off their legs until they fit.

Any paradigm is kind of like that—we stretch or cut any ideas until they "fit," and that sometimes involves a great deal of violence. Ideas about health and illness that won't "fit" are summarily declared as irrelevant, too far out, dangerous, untested, and unscientific.

The question is not if the scientific methods of research are valuable—of course they are. We have gained and will continue to gain much from this methodology. The question, rather, is whether or not scientific methodologies can and should be the *only* means of legitimation. Can elements of human life, elements that do not lend themselves to scientific quantification and replication, be important to health and illness? The answer is: absolutely. We will explore later how an individual's unique and personal soul journey cannot be reduced to statistical analysis or conform to cookie-cutter evaluation, yet it is, in my opinion, a crucial player in determining one's state of health or illness and a powerful influence in the processes of healing.

Certainty, predictability, and repeatability have little tolerance for the mysterious, the changing, the uncertain, the mystical, the spiritual, and the uniqueness of the individual. When we eliminate these qualities and experiences from consideration, don't we severely restrict who we are? If we, by paradigmatic necessity, ignore all those aspects of our lives that do not lend themselves to absolute certainty, do we really think—I mean *really* think—we can predict how anything and everything in our lives will participate in our state of health or illness? If we eliminate the mystical and the mysterious, haven't we robbed life of much of its flavorful texture? If we eliminate dreams and spiritual experiences, we ignore anything sacred as essential to our health and illness.

One could say, with considerable legitimacy, that materialistic and mechanistic medicine went a long way in accomplishing the initial scientific goal coming out of the Enlightenment—namely, that we gain confidence in our abilities to understand and control disease. Now, however, the question is whether we have been too arrogant and too narrow in our understanding.

Both the extent of that arrogant confidence and the extent of its built-in naivete were powerfully symbolized by President Richard Nixon's declaration, in 1970, of a "War on Cancer" and how congressional funding and the public's attitudes enlisted in that "war." Remember how Nixon promised that, if we were committed to throw enough money at solving the cancer problem, we had the science by which we could cure cancer in six years. We would celebrate our nation's birthday in 1976, we were told, with a triumph over the scourge of cancer. The war would be won. Victory would be proclaimed! Remember?

Oh, by the way, in spite of our enlisting massively in that war—in terms of the numbers of scientists devoted and untold billions of dollars spent—when we reached the year of our birthday celebration, 1976, we not only had *not* won the war, but we had to bury 330,000 Americans who had died that year from cancer. We fought on, however, rarely if ever questioning the assumptions upon which the paradigm was based. A quarter of a century later, half a million Americans die every year from cancer.

Materialistic mechanical medicine did, indeed, accomplish some great things, but we are also beginning to recognize its limitations. Yes, we have made great strides with some cancers; but, no, we do not as yet have the science that completely eliminates cancer from the human condition—or even comes close. Yes, we have the science to eliminate polio from the world; but, no, we do not as yet have the science to help those of us with the later effects of polio, the so-called post-polio syndrome. Yes, we have the science that could perform the remarkable surgery on my severely broken back; but, no, we do not as yet have the full understanding as to how mental and spiritual factors contribute to one's experience of pain, particularly chronic pain.

There are many challenges that remain in health promotion, disease prevention, and the processes of healing, and a science that is singularly devoted to diagnosing only the physical causation of illness and its cure is not a science that is big enough to meet those challenges. To enlarge those medical possibilities we need to include the spiritual. We need to bring it back from exile.

Our country's largest philanthropy devoted exclusively to health and healthcare, The Robert Wood Johnson Foundation, asked the prestigious Institute for the Future in Menlo Park, California, to assess the state of healthcare in America at the end of the twentieth century and to forecast where it would be going over the next ten years. The report, in part, reads as follows:

> In the past quarter century, the record of biomedical discovery and progress has been spectacular, and yet on critical analysis our ability to diagnose and treat disease has had no more than a modest impact on the public's health. Despite improved diagnostic and therapeutic capabilities and an unprecedented expenditure of resources, we are not the most healthy of peoples among the developed nations. Perhaps an obsession with disease has unintentionally relegated health to a position of secondary importance. The health care delivery system is still organized, staffed, and financed on the assumption that its central task is to use biomedical interventions to provide care for people facing acute episodes of illness.
>
> From many quarters comes evidence that our view of health should be expanded to encompass mental, social, and spiritual well-being.[10]

One of the reasons I am so optimistic about the future expansion of our paradigm regarding health, illness, and healing is that medicine has the built-in saving grace of a scientific soul. The soul of science, by its very nature, quests and questions after the newer and the better. It is willing to challenge old dogma and look for better ways to both understand and deal with the world. Thus, medical science has a soul that draws it into a new and different future. That will be the subject of our next chapter: the hope that emerges from a soul with the habit of challenging the old, growing into the new, embracing novelty and evolutionary change.

Before turning to that evolutionary paradigm and the hope that it engenders, I want to bring back to center-stage my previously treasured and then regretfully fractured friendship with Dr. Ken Johnson of The Mayo Clinic in Rochester, Minnesota. For it, too, symbolized the possibilities of change for the better.

As I walked out of the Boulder Post Office on Saturday morning, December 4, 1993, I was casually flipping through the letters, the magazines, and the junk, just to get a general impression of what the mail contained. I stopped dead in my tracks, however, right in the middle of the sidewalk just a few feet from my car, when my fingers flipped past a piece of junk mail only to find my eyes riveted upon the next letter in line. It was an envelope with the logo of The Mayo Clinic at Scottsdale, Arizona, with a hand-written "Ken Johnson" up in the left-hand corner above the logo.

This was my friend from twenty years ago, who back then was on the staff of The Mayo Clinic in Rochester, Minnesota. This was the guy who guided my diagnostic work and who predicted that I would spend the rest of my life in pain, on drugs, and in a wheelchair. This was the guy who treated with complete disdain and ridicule my miraculous healing in 1973, who could not even celebrate my freedom from pain and drugs, my reprieve from the wheelchair, and my return to the handball court. This was the guy who broke off our friendship because I had "gone off the deep end" and who felt that I was involved in ridiculous New Age "mumbo-jumbo." Why, I wondered, am I now receiving a letter from Ken Johnson?

Still standing in the middle of the Boulder sidewalk, I hastily tore open the envelop and read the letter.

Ken began with an apology for his attitude back in 1973 and his regret at letting a valued friendship die. He explained how his understanding of health and illness had grown through the years and that he wanted to get back in touch, but just never got around to it. Life just kept moving on, he said, until the many years had passed.

Recently, Ken went on to say, in a discussion with a friend at a cocktail party, his friend began telling him about a book he had just finished reading. The book, he said, was *Sacred Eyes*, and the author, a Dr. Keck, was putting his own healing and modern medicine into the context of humanity's evolutionary changes in deep-values. Ken said that, at first surprised, he queried his friend: "Is that author a guy named Bob Keck?" His friend said, "Well, it's an L. Robert Keck, so I guess he might go by Bob."

Ken went on to write that he asked to borrow the book from his friend, read *Sacred Eyes*, and felt a deep delight and desire to reconnect with me. Would I, Ken asked, forgive him for what happened twenty years ago and allow our friendship to begin again? He said that he was now ready to really dig into my ideas and explore the medical implications.

I was thrilled. I was moved emotionally, although physically I continued to stand in the middle of the sidewalk outside the Boulder Post Office in stunned silence. Tears of joy welled up in my eyes. What a marvelous story of a man's being able to grow and change. My primary feeling was that an old valued friend had just been resurrected from the dead. How great it would be to get back together with Ken for what had always been some wonderfully competitive handball: we were extremely evenly matched, back before I started getting lame and pain-wracked, and always had incredible fun and close games. How wonderful to enjoy some golf again together as well and to resume what had always been stimulating conversations. I felt joy and anticipation.

I did not want, however, simply to write Ken a letter. I wanted to tell him over the telephone how delighted I was to be back in touch. I did not have his home telephone number, but his letterhead gave me his office number. So, first thing on Monday morning, I called his office in excited anticipation.

When I asked for Dr. Ken Johnson, a sobbing secretary, barely able to talk, informed me that, "Dr. Johnson was killed yesterday when his small plane crashed into the side of a canyon wall, just about an hour north of here."

Needless to say, I felt a powerful sense of sorrow and grief. It was as if my newfound hope and anticipation of the renewed friendship barely got planted into my heart, when fate reached in and ripped it out.

CHAPTER FIVE

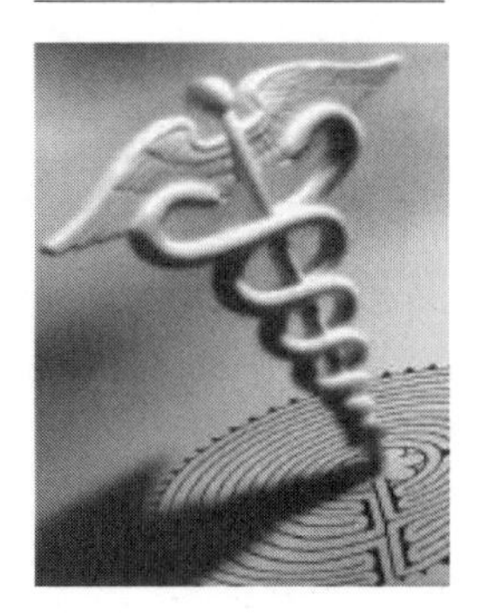

The EMERGING SYNERGY: MEDICINE *and* SPIRITUALITY

[S]cience and religion are not at opposite poles of objectivity and subjectivity. Instead, they form a continuum in which the insights, methods, and discoveries of each can be shared fruitfully with the other. . . . This interaction aims at serving the broader concerns of the global human and ecological communities.

ROBERT RUSSELL, M.DIV., PH.D.

Tremendous advances are occurring in this rapidly evolving field, and there are already over 150 groups doing work in science and theology. . . [and] . . . we believe that only by becoming increasingly open-minded, humble, and eager-to-learn can spiritual information begin to grow rapidly.

HAROLD KOENIG, M.D.

Religion without science is blind; science without religion is lame.

ALBERT EINSTEIN

The first of the above three statements comes from Robert Russell, who has a Ph.D in physics and a master's degree in theology—a highly respected scientist and an ordained minister in the United Church of Christ—and who founded the influential Center for Theology and the Natural Sciences in Berkeley, California.

The second is from Harold G. Koenig, a psychiatrist and associate professor of Medicine at Duke University Medical Center and editor-in-chief of the important monthly newsletter *Research News and Opportunities in Science and Theology*, the purpose of which is to stimulate "the discovery of new spiritual information in order to advance both science and theology for the betterment of humankind."

The third is, of course, from the man whose very name we tend to associate with scientific brilliance, Albert Einstein.

After the initial theological thesis of all-healing power's coming from an external and transcendent God on high and then Western medicine's living through the antithesis of a completely secular scientific paradigm that had banished miracles into exile, we now witness a growing synthesis wherein the newest and best of scientific medicine is engaged in creative dialogue with the newest and best of religion and spirituality. We are fortunate to be living within such a time in history.

As I mentioned before, medicine benefits from being so closely related to the scientific soul that it is graced with an evolutionary spirit: a habit of not resting on its laurels, a propensity for paradigm busting, the courage of challenging old answers and looking for newer and better ones. Consequently, in spite of some small-minded arrogance on the part of some of its adherents who worship certainty, stasis, rigidity, and the status quo—and what field doesn't have its share?—medicine has a soul that is on the go and on the grow.

Medicine on the Grow

Dr. Larry Dossey has been one of our best chroniclers of the changes taking place as this new synthesis emerges. He has also, through his many books, lectures, and public appearances, contributed greatly to the very evolution of medicine and spirituality that we are exploring in this book.

Throughout the last half of the twentieth century, as Dossey points out,

> evidence began to mount suggesting that the mind . . . could affect the body. . . . For example, scientists demonstrated that if rats and mice were confined in close quarters or were stressed by exposure to electrical shocks, they developed gastrointestinal ulcerations, hypertension, and heart disease and often died. Humans, it was discovered, reacted similarly when under stress. Eventually it became clear that our emotions, attitudes, and thoughts profoundly affect our bodies, sometimes to the degree of life or death.[1]

Stress research became mainstream and very convincing. Research also increasingly suggested nutritional involvement in disease prevention, along with physical fitness, massage therapy, and a variety of so-called "energy-medicine" interventions. It also documented the deleterious effects of hostility, anger, and depression, and the positive effects of love, compassion, and forgiveness. And now, of particular interest to us in this discussion and certainly parallel to the new dialogue between science and theology, medical research is beginning to take a strong interest in and show substantial efficacy of the role of spirituality in healing.

One of the pioneers in the field is Dr. Herbert Benson, who now heads the Mind/Body Medical Institute at Harvard Medical School. When Dr. Benson was a medical school student in the late 1950s, he was already expressing concern over the "spiritual crisis in medicine." He correctly observed that, if all the attention were given to a materialistic, mechanistic, technology-driven medicine, the patient's own potential for self-healing would be overlooked. Benson now sees his quarter-century's struggle of having some of his ideas languish in the medical wilderness finally coming to fruition and is happy to report that "over the last ten years, we have witnessed a substantial growth in the role and application of spirituality and healing in medicine."[2]

Research News reports that, "since 1990, almost 1,500 research studies, research reviews, articles, and clinical trials have been published on the connection of spirituality or religion to medicine and health—a figure equal to the total of all such pieces published prior to 1990."[3]

Dr. Harold Koenig of Duke University, mentioned earlier, is also a co-author of the gargantuan project that resulted in the publishing of the *Handbook of Religion and Health*, probably the most comprehensive, careful, and systematic analysis of the research in this field to date. Dr. Koenig states:

> The number of research studies documenting the healing effects of spirituality and religion is significant. We are astounded and thrilled with the explosion of research in the past ten years. . . . The collective findings and positive results indicate that we've just broken the surface. Imagine what the next ten years will bring.[4]

A 1999 report by The Association of American Medical Colleges, in which they set forth the learning objectives for medical students, states that one criterion for graduation by future physicians would be "the ability to elicit a spiritual history as well as an understanding that the spiritual dimension of people's lives is an avenue for compassionate care giving."[5] That may be a long way from where I think physicians should eventually be regarding their understanding of spirituality in health promotion, disease prevention, and in the processes of healing; but it's a start.

If there is a superstar among the medical pioneers in this emerging field, a professional who recognizes the value of research and curriculum development but who also knows clearly what the priority is—loving and compassionate patient care—it is internist Christina Puchalski, M.D., of George Washington University's Medical Faculty Associates.

From early in her medical training, Dr. Puchalski was concerned that the high-tech method of modern medicine, valuable though it is, too often takes precedence over the high art of compassionately touching the soul of those who are suffering. As we discussed in the previous chapter, medical science has a long history of thinking in machine metaphors; thus, it understandably puts the focus upon technology. However, all sciences, and particularly medical science, need the extraordinary people who match their peers in technical knowledge and skill but go beyond their peers to see the larger picture and how to arrange the priorities. Dr. Puchalski is one of those extraordinary physicians who embodies both the technical knowledge and skill but who knows that, particularly when it comes to helping patients with chronic diseases and end-of-life challenges, nothing is more important than compassionate care.

One of the things that define Puchalski, Benson, Koenig, and Dossey, among other pioneers, is that they understand spirituality not simply as a nice and comforting adjunct to what otherwise might be considered the really important medical high-tech interventions but realize that spirituality can participate in both the causation and healing of physical symptoms.

A *Washington Post* article on Dr. Puchalski recounted the experience of Francine Lima-Cooke, ". . . a 40-year-old Virginia language teacher who suffers from chronic ulcers and insomnia":

> A neurologist had prescribed medication for her insomnia, but Puchalski has been trying to help her understand her anxieties, which the internist believes may be at the root of both illnesses.
>
> "Other doctors just prescribe medication," said Lima-Cooke,

"but Dr. Puchalski looks at the whole you. I feel very close to her. She helped me to understand what was troubling me. I realized that I was very worried about losing my husband, who has prostate cancer, and about being left alone. Often I was so worried I couldn't sleep, even with the medication I was taking."

Puchalski taught Lima-Cooke to meditate to calm her anxieties; she now practices meditation for 15 or 20 minutes in the mornings and at night when she is trying to sleep. She said that she is learning "to take one day at a time and just enjoy life."[6]

Throughout the mid-to-late 1990s, Dr. Puchalski was director of education at the National Institute of Healthcare Research, where she became a crusader for medical-school course development that would emphasize spirituality and compassionate care-giving with medical students. Her efforts may have been the primary reason for the dramatic and remarkable change regarding the curriculum of medical schools—of the 125 medical schools in the United States, only four offered courses in spirituality and healing in 1992, whereas, by the year 2000, seventy-nine did. And that number is growing yearly.

In May of 2001, with the assistance of a $2.4 million grant from the John Templeton Foundation, Dr. Puchalski founded the George Washington University Institute for Spirituality and Health (GWISH), dedicated to spreading the idea that "spirituality is a key dimension for achieving optimal health and for coping with illness." "It is compelling to us both as researchers and physicians," says Dr. Puchalski, "to see physicians emerging from the classroom with a greater understanding of how spirituality and healing can impact medicine."[7]

Dr. Larry Dossey explains: "Many studies reveal that healing can be achieved at a distance by directing loving and compassionate thoughts, intentions, and prayers to others, who may even be unaware these efforts are being extended to them."[8]

When some physicians argue that prayer or spirituality are not appropriate subjects for a doctor to raise with a patient, that it is crossing the line into privacy, Dossey replies, "Any intervention or behavior that adds seven to fourteen years of life to a human being is by definition the concern of physicians and other health care professionals. To argue otherwise strikes me simply as an obfuscation."[9]

James S. Gordon, M.D., is certainly not one who is confused about this issue. Dr. Gordon is clinical professor of Psychiatry and Community and Family Medicine at the Georgetown University School of Medicine and director of The Center for Mind-Body Medicine in Washington, D. C. In his book *Manifesto For A New Medicine,* he suggests that there are five basic principles in the new medicine.[10]

1. Understanding that we are all whole persons—biological, psychological, and spiritual—all of which participates in creating our state of health or illness.
2. Being concerned with enhancing wellness as much as treating illness.
3. Mobilizing our own power to heal and learning to make full use of our extraordinary innate capacities.
4. Drawing upon the perspectives and practices of the world's great healing traditions, including Chinese medicine, Indian Ayurveda, Native-American and African healing, while also giving credence to the therapeutic practices in the West that have previously been scorned by modern allopathic medicine.
5. Exploring the largely untapped power of supportive relationships and communities.

Dr. Gordon writes, "The new medicine, like the oldest healing that humans have known, recognizes that illness is a teacher on each of our spiritual journeys, as well as a physical misfortune and psychological challenge. It insists, as did the tribal shamans who were our first healers, that the work, the 'profession' of those who 'provide' healthcare, is itself a spiritual path."[11]

Pioneers such as these courageous medical visionaries are changing the content of medical practice and challenging the boundaries of the materialistic and mechanistic medical paradigm. They are keeping medicine, as all scientific disciplines ultimately must be, on the grow.

Least we become too optimistic about the *pace* of change, we would do well to listen to the sobering evaluation by the Institute for the Future. While its report emphasizes that "physician-led advocacy is a necessary prerequisite for meaningful change," it also recognizes that such advocacy may be slower than we would like:

> Physicians will be reluctant change makers because the generations of physicians in the current workforce learned, believe in, and practice according to the biomedical, bipolar view of disease and health. Interviews with practicing physicians provide ample evidence that medicine's disdain for soft science—and in their view the psycho-social sciences are soft—is alive and well.[12]

I have no basic disagreement with their evaluation. But the point here is not so much regarding the *pace* of change, which I often find discouraging, but the *reality* of change, which is cause for hope. Movement of medical science in the direction we are discussing is, I believe, inevitable. Science is verifying the role of spirituality in healing. But what some of the laggard physicians may not understand is that the very soul of humanity is moving in a direction that will increasingly demand it. (See my book *Sacred Quest* for the larger and more extensive argument on this point.) When the human Soul is transformed and moves into new and different territory, institutions and professionals will either move with it or be left behind. Outdated ideas will die, not because of some violent revolutionary overthrow but because the people will simply withdraw their legitimacy. People will go where their collective Soul leads them, in this case toward a more comprehensive, holistic, integrated, and self-empowered approach to health and illness.

Being one who has lived in, experienced, observed, and pondered the medical paradigm over the past forty years, I can say that both perspectives are true—the *pace* of change is sometimes agonizingly slow and depressing, but the *fact* of change is indisputable and hopeful. There is absolutely no doubt in my mind that all the aforementioned medical pioneers will be joined, daily, by more and more colleagues. Enough physicians are innate scientists who are on the grow and enough are also sensitive and thoughtful about what really goes on within the people they are serving that they are acknowledging how important the spiritual role is in health and illness. The direction of the future, in this regard, is clear.

One of the major cultural and theoretical points of this book is this: *for us to discover and utilize our maximum capacity for health promotion, disease prevention, and miraculous healing, we need a powerful synergy between an evolving medicine and an evolving spirituality.* If one side falls down on the task of growing into an evolutionary paradigm, we simply won't get to the mountaintop of maximum health and wholeness. In point of fact, despite my personal experience and frequent criticism of the medical establishment, I have more concern for the religious and spiritual side of that synergy than I do for the scientific.

As I have noted, as long as medicine is a scientific discipline, it will continue to grow, change, evolve, and mature. Anyone within a scientific discipline, with any sense at all, must have a huge dose of humility regarding the existing knowledge at any given time in history. Human life is far too mysterious and complex for us to ever think that we have it all figured out, or the flip side of that coin, to think that we can be absolutely sure that an inexplicable and miraculous healing cannot happen to any given person at any given time. Medical paradigms can and have shifted over the years. In contrast, a similar evolutionary spirit is not so evident in the spiritual and religious realms. This represents a critical absence. Those in the forefront of suggesting that religion and spirituality contribute to health and healing, generally speaking, are physicians and psychologists, not trained scholars, theologians, or practitioners in the religious and spiritual disciplines.

It could be argued, with considerable veracity I might add, that religious scholars and spiritual practitioners, again generally speaking, are not trained for this integration of spirituality and healing. But to suggest that we don't need expertise on the religious and theological side of the synergy between science and spirit, medicine and spirituality, is wrong. Trained medical scientists *and* trained religious scholars and spiritual practitioners are needed to create a synergy wherein the whole of our knowledge and practice in health and illness will be more than the sum of the individual parts.

Without this dynamic synergy, ill and suffering people, and those about to become ill, will pay a hefty price. If we don't manifest the most powerful partnership we are capable of between a growing medicine and an open and growing spirituality, it will result in the diminution of human lives. Too many people will suffer unnecessarily. Too many people will have their lives truncated and distorted by drugs. Too many people will experience what might have been preventable disease, the recurrence of disease, and premature death. Too many people will miss experiencing the grandeur of having the miraculous and high-level wellness in their lives.

A primary impediment currently is that . . .

The Very Right Reverend Rigor Mortis Can't Dance

Why would we ever choose rigidity or predictability when we have been invited to be part of the generative processes of the cosmos?

MARGARET J. WHEATLEY, PH.D.

This quote, coming from a business consultant and former professor of management at Brigham Young University, is particularly interesting in its theological, religious, and spiritual implications.

My hypothetical "The Very Right Reverend Rigor Mortis" is a pastor and personification of a religion that stands still. His head is permanently stuck looking back over his Right and rigid shoulder, and he is preoccupied with venerating, protecting, preserving, and defending the past. Isn't it ironic that the Very Right Reverend Rigor Mortis has a "wry neck," which is officially described as "abnormally bent or turned to one side . . . distorted, perverted or misdirected, as in meaning." I describe him with a wry smile—which in this instance means "ironic"—because, in spite of this habit of looking backwards, religion should facilitate a spiritual journey forward into health, wholeness, and holiness. A healthy religious and spiritual influence enables a courageous journey of exploration and discovery, not a timid, cautious stasis that eventually turns into immobile stone.

Medically speaking, *rigor mortis* is the stiffening and rigidity that takes place after death. However, for the Very Right Reverend Rigor Mortis, it's the other way around—he's on the verge of death precisely because he is stiff and rigid. He can't face new and exciting religious and spiritual opportunities because he's looking backwards and busy studying, memorizing, and repeating the past. Most importantly, he cannot bring a full and empowering ministry to the special and unique opportunities that spiritual counselors and communities have for assisting people in promoting health and well-being, preventing dis-ease and disease, and experiencing miraculous healing. Not only is this sad, but it is tragic, a failure of a potentially important and compassionate ministry.

Returning to my own struggle with physical rigor mortis taking over my body as my prior soul-self died, I had been on a downward spiral into becoming stiff, rigid, and incapacitated; and, inevitably, rigor mortis and a wry neck had begun to set in spiritually. I was so physically disabled that I could barely carry on a ministry to other people, particularly when I was looking back over my shoulder to the former athletic soul-self and being depressed about the loss of that past. When rigor mortis and a wry neck begin to take over one's life and spirit, there are two alternatives: either give in to the paralysis, sink into the depression of a lost soul-self, and give up, or use the energy of desperation to face the future, discover new possibilities, and move into a new soul-self.

If necessity is the mother of invention, desperation has to be the father of radical movement and change. In my case, I was desperate enough to begin to question the conventional medical paradigm and begin a search into serendipity. But just as the old medical thinking failed to liberate me, the old religious thinking was also inadequate and restrictive.

Although defining these terms at the beginning of this book, in "An Invitation," it might be helpful to revisit the concepts and elaborate just a bit. However, I would want to preface the following with a disclaimer of sorts. Although I believe strongly that one's theology can be either liberating or constricting, and I am offering what I believe to be the most liberating, I have no need to convince anyone of any precise way to believe. I am more interested in compassion and results than in how any of us articulate our belief system. Each of us needs to find our own way of thinking about God and our relationship with the Divine. As with everything else in this book, however, I will share what I have found to be important and meaningful, but leave it up to you, the reader, to decide what, if anything, applies to your sacred and healing journey.

EXPLORING A LARGER THEOLOGY OF MIRACLES

I was very fortunate to have had Christianity presented to me, from my earliest exposure to today, in ways that facilitated growth, exploration, and new discovery. There was never an emphasis upon holding rigidly to a set of beliefs, no fear of intellectual freedom or spiritual exploration. My mother, undoubtedly the more influential parent regarding my spiritual and intellectual environment, encouraged independent thinking and heretical positions, *if* they were integral to my soul's journey. Consequently, my journey did not need to include denying or rebelling against anything of my past. It was always simply a matter of seeking, questing, questioning, searching, and re-searching to find better solutions to the problems that life presented.

Pain, particularly chronic pain, is a message that something has to change. Consequently, in my desperate attempt to find an alternative to severe pain, drugs, and physical deterioration, I began to wonder if my theology needed to change. I wondered if my thinking about God and my relationship with the divine dimension of life was in any way constricting the possibilities for healing.

As I mentioned earlier, my life-changing experience in the Cornell Chapel at age twenty-two never felt as if it fit with the traditional Western religion's externalized notion of God. In addition, over the years I have become increasingly convinced that belief in a completely external God constricts our possibilities for miraculous healing. It certainly restricts the discovery of our enormously untapped inner potential. And it creates a distinction and separation of the natural from the supernatural.

That theological structure became, for me, no longer tenable. It seemed simplistic and moralistic, a theology of healing that has more intellectual and spiritual dead ends than the worst maze one could possibly devise. More importantly, this kind of theology constricts and restricts the opportunities for healing itself and for understanding the natural, accessible, and miraculous nature of healing as a sacred path.

As suggested earlier, it is time for us to leave behind a satellite image wherein we send a request up to God and God sends, or does not send, a healing back down to the person who is praying. It is time for a more holistic and integrated theology wherein we recognize that divine energy permeates all of reality. Rather than God's being "a person," separate from the physical world and our bodies, God is up-close and personal by being the sacred "within-ness" of everything and everybody.

That powerful healing presence of the love and grace of God is, in other words, always present. It does not need to be granted, earned, dispensed, brokered, awarded, or given. It is fore-given. It is built-in "standard equipment," or as Matthew Fox terms it, it is an "original blessing." It comes with life and creation itself. It is there before we ask, before we awaken to its presence, before we become aware of its essence. Before we know it, accept it, absorb its reality, or appropriate its power, it is here and now, accessible and available. We need but to awaken to this reality.

All of reality has the miraculous embedded deep within. All life has the miraculous and the mysterious, mysterious because we can rarely, if ever, experience it in all its fullness or comprehend it completely. That, in fact, is how I have come to think of the concept of transcendence. God is transcendent, not by being completely separate from and "above" the human being, but by being within yet *beyond* any one of us, and definitely beyond our current and limited notions of reality.

Healing becomes a sacred path when we realize that the miraculous is in transcending what we have previously known about the cosmos in general and health and illness in particular. The potentialities for healing transcend what we have previously thought and done, transcend anything we have understood about health and illness—indeed, transcend anything we can *ever* understand. Healing can be a sacred awakening to that divine presence, essence, and mystery.

A "miracle" occurs when we experience a dramatic breakthrough or awakening—sometimes sudden, sometimes over time—so different from our previous experience that we want to speak of it as something coming from the outside, something qualitatively different from what we have known before. Our previous soul-self was, perhaps, unable to imagine or experience that power as having been within, so we conceptualize it as coming from the outside. But that says more about our limited notions of "self" than it does about the actual location of the miraculous power. We have sought a way of thinking about that which feels, at the moment, as clearly beyond the normal and natural world of our daily experience. So we have spoken of the "supernatural" and "a special intervention by an external God."

"Miracle" is a legitimate word to use in our attempt to understand the mysterious healings that can and do occur. It is, however, not something conferred upon one from the outside, but something that breaks through from within, an awakening to the potential that was and is always there. Developing our awareness of that is part of the miracle.

There is a grand expression of this insight, that was ostensibly original with Michelangelo but has been told and retold by many sculptors since who sensed the same truth. As the story goes, Michelangelo was asked how he created beautiful images, such as the Pieta or his statue of David, out of an undefined, cold, hard slab of marble. He is reported to have replied, "They were already in the marble. God put them there. I simply carved away the excess marble that kept you from seeing them."

In similar fashion, God has created each of us with divine, miraculous potential. Miracles are already within us. Our job is to do the best we can to allow them to manifest in our lives, to awaken to their presence, to strip away the layers of personae that hide Divinity, to grow beyond the previous truncated soul-self, and to allow those miracles to come forth so that they can transform our lives. Of course, as my own experience would attest, we can experience miracles wherein no particular effort on our part seems to be the catalyst—the miracle just happens, seemingly by the grace of God. Just because we are unaware of it, however, does not eliminate the possibility that we may have been preparing for it for some time. Some of the grace is found in the fact that, whether conscious or unconscious, our soul may have been leading us into the miracle that occurred seemingly so suddenly and dramatically that it feels as if it came from the outside.

This is not, in fact, a new idea. Jesus, in stark contrast to the externalization of God and salvation espoused by many of his followers for the past two thousand years, said, "If you bring forth what is within you, what you bring forth will save you. If you do not bring forth what is within you, what you do not bring forth will destroy you" (Gospel of Thomas 70:1–2).

Jesus appeared to be saying, and in the interest of healing, wholeness, and holiness we would do well to listen, that salvation is already within us and we will find our lives to be truly miraculous if we but allow the miracle to come forth. It is an insight—literally, seeing what is within—that, as Jungian psychotherapist Kathleen Brehony points out, has been expressed by many through the years:

> Abraham Maslow, for example, called this journey of growth and self-awareness *self-actualization*. Others have referred to it as *self-realization*. On the cave wall at the Temple to Apollo at Delphi from whence the oracle spoke, ancient Greeks carved these plain words, "Know thyself." The Tao te Ching teaches that "knowing others is intelligence; knowing yourself is true wisdom."[13]

It is important in this context to mention briefly—we'll expand on this theme in the next chapter—that this going within does not mean a narrowing, constricting, or restricting individualistic self-centeredness. Since the essence of *Being Itself* is that it permeates *everything* and *everyone*, to explore one's depths with a truly mature vision is to see how we share this holistic and miraculous reality with everything and everyone. There is a fundamental democracy and intimate relationality in the world of miracles.

The sacred path, the sacred seeking, or the sacred quest is one of searching one's own depths and the world at large with sacred eyes and perceiving that the Divine permeates and penetrates everything. And if Jesus was *way* ahead of his time in suggesting that we are saved by bringing forth what is within us, the eighteenth-century Swedish spiritual genius Emanuel Swedenborg was at least slightly ahead of his time. A maverick in his religious environment and a spiritual intellect unparalleled by his contemporaries, Swedenborg held the panentheistic theology to which we are just now awakening: "Heaven is not on high but within. . . . [it] is in fact within people wherever they may be. . . . an individual can be in heaven without being led out of his body."[14]

As Saint Augustine observed long ago, miracles are not in contradiction to nature, only in contradiction to what we *know* about nature. Miracles are moments of transformation, transforming our ordinary perception of life, transforming our ordinary experience of being, transforming our ordinary processes of becoming, sometimes transforming illness into wellness, pain and suffering into meaning and well-being, and sometimes even allowing the proverbial blind to see and the lame to walk. Miracles are mysterious, magnificent, marvelous, and more accessible than our outdated theologies have led us to believe.

Because it is the Divine we are talking about, we will never arrive at complete understanding nor complete actualization. That is precisely why we speak of a *journey* of growth, a *process* of awakening, and healing as a sacred *path*. That is why the Chinese refer to the ultimate spiritual process as the *Tao*, or the *Way*. It is why the Sioux refer to it as the *Good Red Road* and why the Navajo call it the *Pollen Path*. Any life that is a sacred journey, and particularly any life that needs healing, may find that the metaphor of awakening to the Divinity within turns out to be the path of enlightenment as well as the path into healing and wholeness. There is an innate wisdom in the ancient etymology that links together the words *health*, *wholeness*, and *holy*.

Speaking of etymology, *prayer* in the "true sense of the word" according to the Latin root meant "obtained by begging," which certainly was consistent with the theology of an external "Father God up in heaven," but is precisely the wrong concept of prayer, in my opinion, for liberating maximum human potential and for facilitating the emerging synergy with scientific medicine.

EXPANDING THE CONCEPT AND PRACTICE OF PRAYER

As mentioned earlier in my personal story of healing, I had begun to explore more expanded ways of using the mind. Many areas of research that I investigated suggested a wide range of capacities in the human mind that we had not generally utilized—including biofeedback, Eastern meditative practices, guided imagery, clinical and experimental hypnosis, placebo research, faith healing, and faith wounding (stigmata). My breakthrough in Park City, as you recall, came when I was experimenting with a synthesis of all that I had been learning about these various ways to access the potential that God had created within our minds.

It was only natural that I explored how these expanded notions of mind informed, along with the theology discussed above, my concept and practice of prayer. The habit of considering prayer only as a left-brained, verbal, rational exercise seemed, well, half-brained to say the least. Those of us who grew up in the conventional Judeo-Christian tradition generally prayed with words; or if we were engaging in a silent prayer, we simply thought the prayer out in words. I began to see this as a terribly limited concept of prayer.

The Lilly Endowment provided a generous grant with which I was able to conduct the search and research, the investigation and experimentation, by which to develop an innovation in a Christian approach to prayer that I eventually called, simply, "Meditative Prayer"—namely, a Christian concept of prayer utilizing the meditative state of consciousness. With the grant, I was also able to engage a very prestigious group of biblical scholars and theologians, chaired by John Cobb Jr. of the Claremont School of Theology, to provide an in-depth critique of the innovation while it was in development.

I took a thorough and careful look at many different disciplines, practices, and areas of research that appear to recognize, tap into, and facilitate a broader range of divine-human abilities and communication, as well as those that recognize and manifest a holistic body-mind-spirit synthesis.

My goal was to find out what force was at work underneath the particular vocabulary and belief structure of each and every system. The search encompassed traditional concepts of Christian prayer,

Eastern forms of meditation, biofeedback, clinical and experimental hypnosis, psychic research, dream research, Jungian and transpersonal psychologies, quantum physics, bioenergetics, split-brain theory, psychosynthesis, and many more.

This was a time in my life when I was actively involved in the Christian pastoral ministry, so the people at the congregation I was serving, First Community Church in Columbus, Ohio, played a significant role in helping me fashion, develop, and refine Meditative Prayer. We also field-tested it with some five-thousand people in churches from Massachusetts to Hawaii and from Canada to Texas.

There is, however, absolutely nothing exclusively Christian about this capacity to communicate with God in a prayerful manner. The very same power and principles of access are available to anyone, regardless of religious or denominational affiliation. In other words, Meditative Prayer is a means of divine-human communication that can be infused with the theology and images of whatever is most integral to the person who is praying.

Meditative Prayer was and continues to be a powerful and meaningful means of prayer for me. In my practice, I generally utilize imagery in one or more of five different ways, always preceded by a process of relaxation facilitated by deep breathing.

1. Communion:

The first "way" for me is com-union and being at-one with the divine energy within, while letting go of my daily agenda, intellectual activity, emotional stresses, and preoccupations. I try to drift deeply into that mystical union with the Divine. I find enormous value in recognizing and communing with the love energy that transcends any small ego notion of self or any truncated understanding of reality.

2. An attitude of gratitude and appropriation of appreciation:

A second "way" is to focus upon how, in spite of the toils and troubles, the pain and the problems that grab our attention for so much of our time, we are richly blessed to be participating in this magnificent universe and the opportunity to love and be loved. This kind of Meditative Prayer is good for the necessary act of soul-balancing.

3. Receptivity:

This "way" of praying is in stark contrast to the traditional verbal prayer when we are always thinking and talking. When we are busy thinking about what we want to pray about and how we are going to phrase it, we have little time or state of mind with which to listen. With the left-brain, we are generally *telling* God what we want. In deep Meditative Prayer, however, the state of mind more easily facilitates *listening* to what the divine energy of the universe wants to "say" to us.

For instance, living where I do, along the Front Range of the Colorado Rocky Mountains, I can symbolize and ritualize the dawn of a new day by asking in meditation what new enlightenment God has for me. In this case, I meditate with my eyes open, for I can see the sun rise over the eastern plains; and at that very special moment in the midst of the sunrise, a colorful lavender hue splashes the snow-capped mountains of the Continental Divide. I ask that, as the Divine splashes the Divide with the new morning's light, I be receptive to new light in my soul. And I listen and watch and wait. Sometimes the answer is obvious and clear, sometimes subtle and barely discernible. Sometimes it comes now, sometimes later.

4. Intercession:

The fourth "way" is that of sending love to someone in particular need and asking that he or she be receptive to the powerful and power-filled love of God that is within that person and between us.

5. Personal transformation:

Virtually any area of one's life can be transformed and can grow into greater maturity and wholeness. The inner transformative power that is available in the deep body-mind-spirit is so much more substantial than simply thinking, wishing, wanting, or talking about it.

For me personally, prior to "the miracle in Park City," I desperately needed to transform a severe level of physical pain. The extreme nature of my motivation was unquestionably significant in preparing me for that miraculous breakthrough. Nevertheless, the transforming power is always there—however dormant, unrecognized, or untapped—if we only believe in it and begin to cultivate its emergence.

Hearkening back to my seminal Architect dream, it would not be off the mark to say that God, symbolized by the Architect, over a period of time introduced me to these deeper capacities "designed into" and "original equipment of" my very own nature (symbolized by previously unknown and undiscovered "rooms" in my very own "home"). So, in essence, God gave me the tour that introduced me to the powerful capabilities available in Meditative Prayer.

My pain relief, through Deep Meditative prayer, is probably due to the capacity of mental imagery to change body chemistry, releasing so-called endorphins. "Endorphins" is an umbrella term for more than fifty neuropeptides that our bodies produce—our own internal naturally occurring pain medication. Endorphin research, in fact, provides both an interesting parallel with my own "healing," while at the same time giving us a powerful testimony to the miraculous capacities that have been created within us.

I experienced my "miracle in Park City" in 1973 while experimenting with a deep Meditative Prayer discipline. At that time, nothing was known about our internal endorphins, so the general public called my healing a "miracle" (meaning, for them, that it came from an external God), and medical people either totally discounted my experience or called it a "spontaneous remission"—a euphemism for saying, "We have no idea as to why Keck is now able to be pain-free much of the time and has been able to return to playing handball."

Virtually coincidental with my "discovery" of pain relief, a doctoral candidate in pharmacology at Johns Hopkins University, Candace Pert, was discovering that our own bodies had opiate receptors, which meant by implication, that our own bodies also were able to produce naturally powerful pain-killing opiates.

By 1975, scientists around the world were discovering that the human body produces its own morphine-like substances. Scottish researchers called them *enkephalins,* which is Greek for "from the head." American researchers dubbed them *endorphins,* which means "endogenous morphine." The American term stuck.

What is perhaps most amazing about the discovery of endorphins, and what is particularly relevant to my own healing, is that it appears that some of the endorphins are *more powerful* than the artificial drugs that are typically given us for pain relief.

All the time that I was being injected with or swallowing the strong narcotics, I was *never* free of pain. Yet after learning how to increase my own internal naturally occurring endorphins, I was able to be pain-free for periods of time. It made no sense, until more research discovered something very interesting. Avram Goldstein and his associates discovered that one particular neuropeptide was *"seven hundred times more potent than Leu-enkephalin,"* another of the endorphins. Due to its incredible potency, Goldstein named it *dynorphin,* which means, literally, "powerful endorphin."[15]

> Dynorphin is a real blockbuster of an opiod peptide. In standard tests of opiate potency, dynorphin was 50 times as powerful as camel beta-endorphin, some 190 times as powerful as morphine, and 700 times as potent as Leu-enkephalin.[16]

As the years went by, more was learned about both the variety of endorphins and what kind of activity apparently enhanced their internal production. Several teams of researchers, for instance, in 1980 discovered that physical exercise, running, and endurance training enhanced the production of endorphins. In one study, researchers at the University of Wisconsin in Milwaukee used five subjects, tested their blood before hand, had them run for twenty minutes on a treadmill, and then ran blood samples afterwards. It was reported that "they found evidence of a huge increase in plasma levels of beta-endorphin, up to 440 percent."[17]

Other studies suggest that endorphins may be enhanced by laughter, by touching and hugging, and yes, by sexual activity. Ah, yes, pain management can be fun!

Evidence suggests that the pain relief some people get from acupuncture, as well as the various methods of electrical stimulation (Transcutaneous Electrical Nerve Stimulation—TENS equipment) is due to the release of endorphins. Endorphins appear to play a role in healing heart disease, enhancing the immune system, slowing down the effects of aging, and enhancing one's memory.

It may be that my Meditative Prayer is so effective in managing a severe chronic level of pain, in part, because of the deep breathing that I use to enter the meditative state.

Candace Pert writes:

> We've all heard of the yogis of the East and practitioners of certain mystical disciplines who have been able, through breath training, to alter their perceptions of physical pain. (Other people, known as mothers, demonstrate mastery equal to that of the yogis, when, with proper training such as Lamaze, they use breathing techniques to control pain in childbirth.) . . . .
>
> There is a wealth of data showing that changes in the rate and depth of breathing produce changes in the quantity and kind of peptides that are released from the brain stem.[18]

God has created an enormous range of potential within the human being; and as exciting as our discoveries have been to date, we have just begun to scratch the surface. Prayerful communion with the Divine both without and within has many miracles for us yet to experience. If we don't let our theologies constrict and restrict our quest, block our path, or condemn our journey, life can indeed be a wondrous adventure in and out of miraculous healings.

The rest of this book is comprised of what I believe makes up the emerging partnership and synergy between a new and evolutionary scientific medicine and a new and evolutionary spirituality. The potential is exciting and awaits our awakening.

PART III

The Future Story of Miraculous Healing

CHAPTER SIX

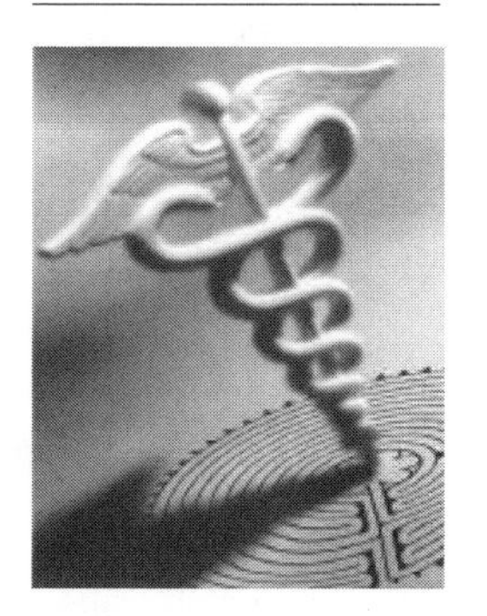

An ECOLOGY *of the* HEART: NATURE *and* ANIMALS

Tell me a story, a story that will be my story as well as the story of everyone and everything about me, the story that brings us together in a valley community, a story that brings together the human community with every living being in the valley, a story that brings us together under the arc of the great blue sky in the day and the starry heavens at night.

THOMAS BERRY

This book is about stories. In part 1, it was my personal story of several descents into a painful hell and back again, my first powerful life-changing mystical experience, and my miraculous miracle healing. In part 2, it was the story of medical and spiritual evolution, how paradigms can either constrict or liberate an individual's potential for healing, and the new emergent partnership and synergy between medicine and spirituality. Now, in part 3, we explore the future—what I believe will become a wonderful, magnanimous, and magnificent story of miraculous healings becoming increasingly available to larger numbers of people and, thus, virtually commonplace.

Stories, of course, use language, and etymology has to do with the origins of words. The very word itself, *etymology*, comes from the Greek *etumon*, which means the "true sense of the word." It is significant, therefore, that the words *health*, *wholeness*, and *holiness* are etymologically connected. The "true sense" of health is fundamentally connected with the "true sense" of wholeness. The same "true sense" includes the holy. Holistic health, therefore, is a redundancy. So too is sacred healing, if and when we come to understand fully both the sacred and the nature of healing. Thus, any separation of sacred and secular, physical and spiritual, heaven and earth, human and divine, humanity and nature—any such notions that assume absolute distinction and separation are not "true" in the original "sense" of the words. So, let's try to make sense of all this.

Is it possible that a deep value of living more holistically can play a significant role in the sacred search for miraculous healings—i.e., healing that is unexpected, unpredictable, seemingly inaccessible, and under-facilitated precisely because of considering too small a context? My life's story would suggest that it is.

Western science has had a long, well-established habit of taking things apart and emphasizing separateness and distinction. Western medicine, repeating that reductionistic story, assumed that our understanding of healing would be enhanced conceptually and our effectiveness in helping people would be increased if we reduced the whole human being into a number of separate specialities.

In this chapter and the next, we will explore what Thomas Berry suggested in his opening statement, "a story that brings us together." It is a story about the kind of healing that results from enlarging our sense of self to include a lot more togetherness—an ecological self, if you will. To begin, revisit with me the issue I raised earlier—about how our primary identity, or soul-self, may participate both in illness and in healing.

At any given moment in our lives, we operate out of a primary self-identity or a deep soul-self. That soul-self provides the lens through which we view the world, ourselves, our experiences and, perhaps most importantly, our future possibilities. Consequently, that soul-self participates in the development of any illness, in our reactions to and interpretations of an illness, and our expectations regarding the future of that illness.

But as pointed out earlier, our soul-self can change. It can grow. It can become healthier, more whole, and more attuned to the sacred. Further, the transformation of a former soul-self, or to put it a slightly different way, the discovery of a new, deeper, or larger soul-self, may be the most important thing we do to liberate the kind of healing that we previously thought impossible.

Miraculous healing and a new soul-self may be profoundly linked. After all, if a miracle is defined as being beyond what we previously thought possible, what we previously thought possible was constrained, at least in part, by our soul-self of the moment. It may sound terribly "new-agey," superficial, or simplistic at first blush; but don't overlook the profound potential power involved if you seriously probe the aphorism—discover a new "you," and open your life to a miracle.

The old "you," perhaps one that was too reduced, too small, too separated, too isolated, may very well be the primary impediment to a more health-full future. Conversely, discovering a new and larger soul-self, author-izing a new and larger autobiography, may be the single most important act in your healing story.

Ecological is an appropriate word for our exploration of the web of relationships. Because love is the fundamental energy for healing fractures, splits, estrangements, and separation, *heart* is the appropriate metaphor for that loving power. Thus, this is a "story that brings us together" via an *ecology of the heart.*

An Ecological Soul-Self

One of the most profoundly insightful books on healing that I have ever read is *The Healing Path: A Soul Approach to Illness,* by Marc Ian Barasch. Barasch, a cancer patient and journalist, writes:

> Each of our stories, no matter how mundane, is a tale of spiritual growth embraced or denied. Beneath the surfaces of everyday awareness, a larger and more inclusive self is ever pressing for realization. Ironically, even inconveniently, it is in moments of deepest crisis that this self may become most insistent, and its story most demanding of realization.[1]

Deep-Value Research suggests that this is a time in the evolutionary history of humanity when a "more inclusive self" is, indeed, "pressing for realization." After ten thousand years of an evolutionary epoch with the purpose of ego development, which inevitably narrows our identities into smaller and smaller compartments, we have arrived at a time when humanity's soul-self must grow up and grow larger if we as a species are to be healthy. It is time for our soul-self to include our relationships with nature, with animals, and with the people we have defined as "other." It is, for humanity at large, a more inclusive self pressing for realization, and it will be "a tale of spiritual growth embraced or denied." We will grow towards a larger health, or we will slide into greater pathology.

For both a collective human level, as well as an individual level, Jungian analyst James Hillman poses the appropriate questions: "*Where is the 'me'?* Where does the 'me' begin? Where does the 'me' stop? Where does the 'other' begin?"[2]

The ecological soul-self is not a skin-encapsulated self. It is, rather, an identity that finds its fullness in its many relationships and, in many ways, is defined by those larger connections.

The Heart of the Matter

The utterances of the heart—unlike those of the discriminating intellect—always relate to the whole. The heartstrings sing like an Aeolian harp only to the gentle breath of a premonitory mood, which does not drown the song but listens. What the heart hears are the great things that span our whole lives.

C. G. JUNG

Not the collective human heart, my personal heart, nor the heart as a metaphor were on my mind when I climbed the stairs up to the home of cardiologist Dr. Dean Ornish on a sunny spring day in 1989. My mission was to help a new graduate school get off the ground, and I had an appointment with Dr. Ornish to discuss his potential involvement with the school. We were developing an impressive and prestigious group of creative thinkers and innovators in the fields related to health as an advisory board for the new school. Ornish was high on our list.

Ornish welcomed me warmly, offered a cup of tea, and led me out onto the deck of his home, a virtual tree-house in the wooded hills of Sausalito, California. Surrounded by a thick stand of trees, his deck provided an environment that seemed to be actively welcoming a valued guest. Branches and leaves reached over the railings as if to shake my hand, and the chirping birds seemed anxious to be in conversation. It was a very relaxed and natural setting within which to commune with the spirit of Dean Ornish.

I had been aware for some time of the seminal and important research that Ornish and his colleagues had been conducting, proving that it was possible to reverse heart disease without the use of surgery or drugs. In addition to an aggressive program of dietary changes, Ornish emphasized the emotional, psychological, and spiritual aspects of getting to the heart of heart disease. Our meeting took place a few months before the book that would make him famous was to be published, but the word was getting out about his important and groundbreaking work.

We covered the primary purpose of my visit, Ornish's potential involvement with the new graduate school—a school which, by the way, eventually "died" of an institutional form of "heart dis- ease"—but the more lasting impact on me personally had to do with his research in and particularly his thinking about the emotional, psychological, and spiritual causes of heart disease.

Dean Ornish is extraordinary among cardiologists in his capacity and interest to look beyond the usual medical process of treating symptoms to consider the deeper level of causation. It was during his early work with famed heart surgeon Dr. Michael DeBakey that Ornish began wondering why, as various studies were indicating, approximately half of the patients who had coronary bypass surgery returned for second and third operations. "Did this indicate," Ornish wondered, "that we were not getting at the primary causes of heart disease?"

Among the most important things that Ornish wrote about, and what he identified as a primary theme of his book, was that *"the farther back in the causal chain of events we can begin treating the problem, the more powerful can be the healing."*[3]

Whereas most cardiologists think only of physiological causes—genetic predisposition, cholesterol count, smoking, weight, and lack of exercise, etc.—Ornish thinks more extensively and more comprehensively as he explores a bigger picture of fundamental causes. "What," Ornish wondered, "leads to the chronic stress that can contribute to eventual heart disease?" And then he began speculating about what he calls a "pretended self."

Ornish suspects that superficial and pretended self-identities are fundamentally stressful, in that they do not fulfill us at a deep level. To put it in a slightly different way, pretended selves cannot provide the level of meaning and purpose in life that are ultimately fulfilling. If our pretended self is an identity found primarily in wielding power and making money or in relationships of exploitation, in competition, or in sexual conquests, in the importance of our professional position or in our possessions, we will live constantly under a deep spiritual stress. If we do not spend our lives in relationships and activities that nourish our souls—those mentioned above may temporarily fool us into thinking that they do but, in fact, they do not—then stress and lack of fundamental nourishment can lead to dis-ease, disease, and meaninglessness. If we are in need of a miraculous healing, or if we want to participate in miraculous living, *that* is the level we must address.

That is precisely what I mean when I talk about the transformation or expansion of our deepest identity, our soul-self. The only argument I have with the term "pretended self" is that most of us are not pretending when we are committed to a superficial and ultimately unfulfilling identity—such as when my primary self-identity was that of an athlete. I was very serious about it; I just did not know how *superficial* it was at the time. That is why I would say the admonition "stop pretending" is not as much to the point as is "wake up to a deeper, more meaningful, more purposeful, and more fulfilling soul-self."

In the realm of the soul, the spiritual and the metaphorical are kissing cousins. In other words, the spiritual and the metaphorical are related as are the earth and the sun—the latter illuminates the former. Metaphors can enlighten and illumine our spiritual journeys.

Ornish refers to the most popular surgery in the United States, coronary bypass surgery, as a metaphor for how many of us, particularly men, have bypassed the heart, the heart being symbolic of loving relationships, tenderness, emotions, forgiveness, and compassion. Sometimes, I would add, the heart has to "attack" us in order to wake us up to those essential qualities. The prevalence of "open-heart surgery," Ornish suggests, is a metaphor for our need to "open our hearts" emotionally and spiritually. It is not coincidental, therefore, that the name selected for Ornish's program, the first program to be scientifically proven as capable of reversing heart disease without drugs or surgery, is "Opening Your Heart." It is also the metaphor I will borrow for our discussion in this chapter.

The heart, we all know, is symbolic of love. If someone simply draws the symbol of a heart, we know that they are not referring to the anatomy of the body, but to the symbol of love. Consider how many love songs are written with the heart as the primary metaphor. Or let the following stream of words wash over your heart and soul.

"Blessed are the pure in heart," said Jesus

"Our hearts are restless til they rest in thee," said the Psalmist.

"Don't be so heartless," we say.

"Purity of heart is to will one thing," said Kierkegaard, and I wonder if he meant, as would I, to put the emphasis upon the word *one*?

"The work of seeing is done," said the poet Rilke. "Now practice heart-work."

"I love you from the bottom of my heart," a lover says.

Novelist and essayist Gail Godwin puts the emphasis where, in an evolutionary sense, it needs to be: "The wisdom of the heart must catch up with our overdeveloped 'thinking heads' if we are to survive."[4]

Certainly, the survival of our species is dependent upon our growing into a wisdom of the heart, and a loving heart has a greater influence on our individual health than most of us realize. In my opinion, of all Dean Ornish's significant contributions, and they are many, his emphasis upon love is the most important, as it was for cancer surgeon Bernie Siegel.

Ornish writes that "increasing scientific evidence from my own research and from the studies of others . . . [leads] . . . me to believe that love and intimacy are among the most powerful factors in health and illness, even though these ideas are largely ignored by the medical profession."[5]

Ornish makes a statement very similar to one Larry Dossey has made frequently throughout his innovative medical books. Ornish writes:

> If a new drug had the same impact, virtually every doctor in the country would be recommending it for their patients. It would be malpractice not to prescribe it—yet, with few exceptions, we doctors do not learn much about the healing power of love, intimacy, and transformation in our medical training.[6]

Let's take the implications of a loving heart to its even larger and more significant implications:

1. What makes love such a powerful healing force is that love is the ontological (the essential) power of whole-making.
2. Conversely, we will never realize all the miracle healings that are possible as long as we continue the habit of focusing on isolated parts.

This brings us back again to the etymological wisdom of linking health, wholeness, and holiness. First of all, every major world religion has associated love with holiness, many stating simply and bluntly, "God is love." Second, love is the power that unites and connects and thus makes everything whole. Third, wholeness is essential to real healing.

The primary problem that keeps us from understanding the role love plays as a fundamental healing force is that we have trivialized our understanding of love. We have associated it with sentiment or emotional associations—"I love chocolate," or "I just love so-and-so's music," or "I'd love to go out to dinner with you."

Love, however, is much more than a sentiment, much more than liking something, and much more than a feeling of emotional attachment. We will never fully understand the role love plays in our world until we grasp its ontological power—in other words, its essential, fundamental, basic, and ultimately important power.

Love is the power that makes this a holistic universe. It is the power that can heal our inner fractures. It can heal our estrangements—human from nature, human from animals, and human from human. There is no more powerful force in the universe that contributes to greater health, wholeness, and holiness than the power of love!

The importance of love-making, health-creating, and the establishment of wholeness in our lives is brought center stage by the very evolutionary energies that are creating our particular time in history. As mentioned in the previous chapter, twenty-three years of researching the deep causal influences within the human journey—Deep-Value Research—has convinced me that we are living in an extraordinary time in history. We are, literally, living right in the midst of a major transformation of the human Soul—in fact, only the second such transformation of Soul in 35,000 years of spiritual evolution. We are in the process of leaving a ten-thousand-year-long emphasis upon ego distinction and separation and are growing into an evolutionary epoch wherein humanity's interdependence with nature and the ubiquity of wholeness are primary deep-values for our time and for the foreseeable future.

It has the impact of a double-whammy. The larger context influences the text and texture of our lives, and the larger evolutionary context is now emphasizing interrelatedness, connections, unity, and the value of our relationships. The implications for health and illness are profound.

Rachel Carson, one of the many courageous prophets of this time, which I call the third epoch of spiritual evolution, woke us up to our relationships with the environment in her 1962 book *Silent Spring*. Carson helped us to become aware of how we impact the health of our environment and how our environment, in turn, impacts our own health. We now know that the air we breath, the water we drink, or even our proximity to Chernoble can all influence our health in a negative fashion. In like manner, the deep values that shape our lives—such as the "recent" adolescent anthropocentrism and self-centeredness—impact the health of the environment. We are inextricably linked with our environment, each influencing the other.

In *Sacred Eyes* and *Sacred Quest: The Evolution and Future of the Human Soul*, I showed the historical, scientific, political, and theological reasons that ours is a time in which the human Soul is reawakening to our connection with nature. I also spoke of how, after millennia of emphasizing the mind's rational abilities, we will be shifting our emphasis "twelve inches to the south," into the territory of the heart. From a virtually exclusive emphasis upon the head, we are now beginning to realize that our survival may depend upon the heart's loving capabilities. It is not my purpose here to rehash all that evidence but simply to point out that I believe the subject of this chapter integrally fits within that larger evolutionary context. It is the time, for humanity at large and for each of us individually to rediscover our ecological relationships, to open our hearts and to grow into a larger understanding and manifestation of love, the power of whole-making.

The heart is a good symbol for a discussion of ontological love for another reason. Loving in the way that I will be discussing it throughout the rest of this chapter takes courage; and, in Latin, *cor* is at the heart of the word *courage*, as well as literally being the root for the word *heart*. To be of good heart is to be courageous. Keep this in mind as we explore the ecology of the heart, for to love truly, one has to have the courage to be vulnerable. To open our hearts may be the most courageous move we ever make, as well as the healthiest.

We will explore the ecology of the heart precisely because an ecology has to do with our natural relationships. We live within an ecological web of relationships, a profound state of interdependency. Nothing is isolated and completely insulated from the rest of the world. Nothing. With every morsel of food we eat, every sip we drink, every breath we take—we are in constant exchange with the world about us. We all know that in the presence of some people we are energized, while others seem to drain us. We are also influenced by other subtle and unseen energies far more than we know.

Historically, in our attempts to understand health and illness, we have acted as if we could understand something better if we took it out of its relationships, took it apart, and focused upon pieces rather than the interrelated whole. So we concentrated upon genes or germs, blood or bladder, fibula or facial tissue, calcium or crania, tumor or trachea—a plethora of parts upon which we could, would, and should focus. We believed that, if we isolated parts from their original wholes, we could understand why that part was becoming a problem. Our favorite approach was then to declare war on the offending part.

Our medical paradigm of materialism and reductionism leads us to consider "the most fundamental part," namely, to identify the particular gene that we think might be *the cause* of any and every health problem. We presume that the skills we will develop in genetic engineering will solve all our health problems. Sounds so reasonable, doesn't it? True believers in the partial truly believe that knowledge of how the parts work, why they fail to work, and how to attack the failing part will carry us to a healthy heaven on earth. It is just not, however, that simple.

Of course, emphasis upon parts works some of the time. Three particular successes led us to exult over the focus on parts. First of all, in the nineteenth century, French scientist Louis Pasteur founded the science of microbiology by discovering that some diseases appear to be the result of germs attacking the body from the outside. Hence, Pasteur's "germ theory of illness" began shaping medicine's assumptions about what caused disease. Then, German physician Robert Koch, considered to be the founder of modern bacteriology, reinforced the biological notion of causation when he identified the tubercle bacillus as the single cause of tuberculosis. "Koch's postulate" of linking a single microbe to a specific disease won him the 1905 Nobel Prize. Third, as we considered earlier, the American scientists Jonas Salk and Albert Sabin, in the 1950s, were successful in developing vaccines that virtually eliminated polio from the lives of those who were immunized. The successes have been so dramatic. Why would we *not* be true believers in reductionism?

One problem is that success in *some* diseases led us to assume that there were single biological causes and solutions for *all* diseases. An answer that worked some of the time, we figured, must work all of the time. But worshiping at the Altar of the First Part blinded us to a very simple but important fact: not everyone who is exposed to viruses or bacteria gets sick. Not everyone with high cholesterol gets heart disease. Not everyone who smokes cigarettes develops cancer. Why not? Could it be that there is more to disease than the singular biological cause? Could it be that emotional, psychological, and spiritual factors are also part of the reason that people get sick or why some people stay well?

Why was it that not everyone exposed to the polio virus contracted polio? Could it be that my thirteen-year-old soil of soul was of such a condition to make me more vulnerable than some others who were also exposed to the polio virus? Could it be that my soul-self, at that time in my life, led me into such a constant stream of hyper-athletic activity that my immune system became exhausted and depleted? As legend has it, even Pasteur, on his deathbed, admitted a change of heart, saying, "The microbe is nothing; the soil is everything."

This is not a rant against reductionism or the attention to parts per se. Modern medical science has made wonderful advances precisely because of this methodology. The purpose here, however, is not to sing the praises of what we have accomplished in the past—the body politic already has a few strained shoulder muscles from patting itself on the back so frequently and so enthusiastically. The purpose here is to point out what our old habits of mind and addictions of spirit have overlooked. The full possibilities of miraculous healing will not be discovered simply by congratulating ourselves over the successes of our reductionistic past but by having the courage to explore beyond the known, beyond the boundaries of the dominant paradigm, beyond orthodoxy.

Part of the process of liberating miraculous healing will be in the willingness to understand the limitations of the dominate medical paradigm and the courage to explore a bigger picture of what enhances health and well-being, prevents illness and disease, and promotes healing. If we truly understand what has been overlooked in the past, if we can adequately consider all of what is involved in a larger paradigm of health and illness, we can cultivate miracle healings and spontaneous remissions that were thought to be extremely rare and beyond our capacity to cultivate. If we understand the soil of soul, we will know that it can be cultivated so as to sprout a miracle or two.

Unfortunately, the self-appointed protectors of the dominant medical paradigm are too often hostile towards those who venture beyond the boundaries of orthodoxy. Frequently, the greatest anger is directed at "their own," the courageous and innovative physicians. But the guardians of the gates are not paying attention to the movement of history. Nor are they being up-to-date scientifically.

The new and exciting implications emerging out of the sciences of ecology, wholeness, systems theory, relativity and quantum physics, and chaos and complexity theories are so well known that we need not document them here. Once the primary insights from those new sciences have become the dominant metaphors that business consultants and authors are using, as they now are, they have reached the mainstream.

David Bohm makes the defining statement. A protoge of Albert Einstein, and until his recent death, considered one of the world's leading theoretical physicists, Bohm said bluntly, "Science itself is demanding a non-fragmentary worldview."[7]

Medical science, therefore, if it wants to remain a scientific discipline *must* become more holistic. It *must* begin to understand the implications of quantum physics regarding a holistic and ecological reality. Not only is the "hip bone connected to the leg bone, and the leg bone connected to the ankle bone," but everything—everything!—is connected to everything else. From a scientific perspective, we can no longer assume that biological, sociological, emotional, psychological, and spiritual factors are unrelated. It would be bad or pseudoscience to continue down that familiar and narrow road.

The good news is that, as discussed earlier, the very soul of science is one that is "on the grow," and as we will see throughout the rest of this book, many studies now taking place within medical science verify the importance of the larger picture, the more holistic paradigm. Medical science is, without a doubt, on the grow. A very important and related question is whether we—you and I—are on the grow enough so as to realize the miraculous healing that is available for us across the emerging frontiers.

Miraculous healings can be cultivated by opening our hearts to a larger, more ecological, soul-self. Mine certainly has been.

Opening Our Hearts to the More-Than-Human World

The oldest healers in the world, the people our society once called "witch doctors," knew no other way to heal than to work within the context of environmental reciprocity.

THEODORE ROSZAK, PH.D.

We are human only in contact, and conviviality, with what is not human.

DAVID ABRAM

Civilized societies have had a several-millennia-long habit of ignoring, if not destroying, any sense of reciprocity and conviviality between humans and nature in general and humans and animals in particular. We have looked down upon the animal world from the "pinnacle of evolution" upon which we egotistically placed ourselves and arrogantly disdained those considered "primitive," "pagan," or "uncivilized."

We desacralized the world in the scientific revolution, conceptually transforming the Earth Goddess into a mechanistic Spaceship Earth. Animals previously viewed as messengers from God were converted, in our minds, into unfeeling automatons, moving targets, and disembodied trophies. The sacred Earth Goddess was reduced to a plethora of "resources." We objectified subjects, commodified the gifts of nature, and transformed many "thous" into "its." Superiority and domination, control and management, use and abuse leave little room for conviviality and reciprocity. In the process, we have lost a great deal in terms of a larger soul-self and many potentialities for healing to which we are just beginning to awaken.

One of the most valuable experiences in the past seven years for me has been the decision by Diana and me to move out of Boulder and live in the wilderness. Although more people are discovering our special mountain along the Front Range of the Colorado Rockies—and that will inevitably make more rare the extraordinary experiences we have had with wild animals over these seven years—we still feel very close to the wilds of nature.

In my previous book, *Sacred Quest,* I told of the dramatic and powerful experiences with a mountain lion and an enraged momma bear protecting her cubs, and many other stories. Suffice it here to simply state that I have learned something extremely valuable: humans can have a much more meaningful contact and conviviality with the wild, as David Abram put it, than my sixty previous years of being citified, civilized, and highly educated in our culture's prized "higher" educational systems ever taught.

I find a new and deeper meaning in the legends of a time before civilization when humans and animals spoke the same language and in the native and indigenous shamanic rituals of becoming one with the animals.

CAN WE SPEAK THE SAME LANGUAGE?

As an evolutionary theologian with an interest in the entire human journey, I am thoroughly aware of how we have spent the past ten-thousand years carefully developing the human mind and ego, a necessary "adolescent" phase in our evolutionary journey to become fully human. From the perspective of history, we can also see how, to accomplish that mental and identity maturation, we needed to emphasize separation and distinction. And—surprise, surprise—the developing ego not only needed to claim significant differences but also needed to claim superiority. Humans, we proclaimed, were not only different but special. *We* were made "in the image of God"; animals certainly were not! *We* were the pinnacle of evolution, the crowning achievement of God's creation. Our larger brain capacity in general and our left-brain rational, logical, and verbal capabilities in particular are precisely what makes us superior to the rest of the animal world. At least, that is what we rationalized.

Could it be that our adolescent pride and overly developed ego overlooked something very valuable? The famous Swiss scientist of the Soul Carl Jung believed that there are four valuable parts of the human psyche that had been repressed by the millennia of civilization: "nature, animals, primitive man, and creative fantasy."[8] Could Jung be right?

Could it be that since we are, in fact, animals, sharing almost all of our DNA with other species, that it is a delusion to think that we are totally distinct and separate? Has our "enlightened" development of the rational brain, what Jung called the "discriminating intellect," left us in the dark regarding an innate communion and communication with the animal world?

Could it be that compassion for wild animals and the ability to speak the same language are intimately connected? Could it be that if we expanded our capacity for compassion we would increase our capacity for communication?

Our subject here is an ecology of the heart: we are a participant in a complex, interwoven web of natural relationships. Science has been helping us to grow beyond the immature adolescent ego and to appreciate our incredible interdependencies. We are discovering, in the words of the famous ecologist John Muir, that we are "hitched to everything else."

To expand our understanding and our experience of life, we might do well to listen to those who were never citified and civilized away from their natural connections with the animal world. Ecological philosopher David Abram points out that many native and indigenous peoples hold that there was a time when animals and people spoke the same language. He quotes an Inuit (Eskimo) woman who explains that "in the very earliest time when both people and animals lived on earth. . . all spoke the same language."[9]

Similarly, anthropologist Mircea Eliade, writes, "The existence of a specific secret language has been verified among the Lapps, the Ostyak, the Chukchee, the Yakut, and the Tungus. During his trance the Tungus shaman is believed to understand the language of all nature."[10]

How can we learn this secret language, short of becoming experts in the shamanic trance? It may be that the very act of enlarging our soul-self to an ecological size is a starting point. Job's advice, in the Book of Job 12:7–8, comes down through the millennia to say:

> But ask the beasts, and they will teach you;
> the birds of the air, and they will tell you;
> Or the plants of the earth, and they will teach you;
> and the fish of the sea will declare to you.

Native American Dan George tells us, "If you talk to the animals they will talk with you and you will know each other. If you do not talk to them you will not know them, and what you do not know you will fear. What one fears one destroys."[11]

NATURE, ANIMALS, AND HEALING

What does all this have to do with healing? I know part of the answer to that question, but there are the parts that I'm still trying to figure out. Many native peoples believe that they can consult animals about the medicinal values of certain roots and herbs. The Pawnees of North America, for instance, grouped themselves in animal cults and became expert over the particular medicinal qualities of nature that were the particular province of that animal. For the Navajo, the bear is the medicinal plant guru who taught them all about healing plants. Why do we presume in the mainstream that their knowledge is lacking in value?

Although I do not intend to explore this area to any great extent in this book, I find it fascinating and significant that modern science has used its investigative techniques, rather than the shamanic trance, to gain the healing wisdom that nature has to teach us. Although I am choosing to focus primarily upon our relationships with the animal world, it would be just as legitimate to explore the wide-ranging and equally complex world of medicinal plants. For in spite of the invention of synthetic chemistry in the 1930s, there is a recent renaissance of scientific research into learning what nature has to teach us. Mark Plotkin writes,

> For almost twenty years, I've been combing the remote corners of the Amazon jungle searching for plants that heal. I am an ethnobotanist—a plant hunter, a shaman's apprentice—on the trail of natural compounds that can treat diseases for which modern medicine has no cure. . . . Mother Nature has been devising extraordinary chemicals for more than 3.5 billion years, and new technologies increasingly facilitate our ability to discover, study, manipulate, and use these compounds as never before. . . . *New*

> *technologies enhance, rather than diminish, nature's value as a source of healing compounds."*[12]

Consider how native and indigenous shamans, those who have special talents of gaining an "at-one-ment" with and speaking the language of nature and of animals, are called "medicine" people. David Abram, who spent a great deal of time studying with the shamans of Indonesia, suggests that the "medicine" person or tribal shaman

> acts as an intermediary between the human community and the larger ecological field, ensuring that there is an appropriate flow of nourishment, not just from the landscape to the human inhabitants, but from the humanity community back to the local earth. By his constant rituals, trances, ecstasies, and "journeys," he ensures that the relation between human society and the larger society of beings is balanced and reciprocal.[13]

Abram goes on to explain that precisely this reciprocity can address individual illness. The medicine person

> derives her ability to cure ailments from her more continuous practice of 'healing' or balancing the community's relation to the surrounding land. Disease, in such cultures, is often conceptualized as a kind of systemic imbalance within the sick person . . . commonly traceable to a disequilibrium . . . [with] . . . the larger field of forces in which it is embedded. . . .
>
> Only those persons who, by their everyday practice, are involved in monitoring and maintaining the relations *between* the human village and the animate landscape are able to appropriately diagnose, treat, and ultimately relieve personal ailments and illnesses.[14]

The word we use in English, *medicine*, means "power" in native or indigenous-speak. Specifically, it refers to the power that people can receive from a reciprocal relationship with nature. Sometimes, it refers to a specific "power animal" of the medicine person; thus, they may be known as the purveyors of "eagle medicine" or "bear medicine" or "serpent medicine," etc. The medicine person's power to heal comes precisely from her or his familiarity with the larger ecological web of relations within which we live, a larger soul-self that taps into a more comprehensive reality that is accessible for healing. If we would stop looking down our noses at such wisdom, an optical malady that inevitably leads to an arrogant, self-absorbed navel-gazing, perhaps we would have the vision to see the possibilities for miraculous healing that are generally unknown to modern scientific medical people. Even better, perhaps the day will come when scientific medical people learn to become "medicine people."

Lewis Mehl-Madrona is a "coyote medicine person"—*coyote* being the Mexican name for a half-breed. Mehl-Madrona is trained in both conventional Western scientific medicine, having received his M.D. degree from Stanford University, and in his traditional Native-American wisdom of healing. While in medical school, Mehl-Madrona began to feel deeply about the value of integrating ancient and modern approaches to illness. He is trained, therefore, in the best of modern scientific medicine but brings the perspective of a larger ecological soul-self inherited from his indigenous background. "For a Native American," writes Mehl-Madrona, "a healing is a spiritual journey."

> As most people intuitively grasp (except maybe doctors, who are trained to disbelieve the idea), what happens to the body reflects what is happening in the mind and the spirit. People *can* get well. But before a person can do so, he or she must often undergo a transformation—of lifestyle, emotions, and spirit—besides making the necessary shift in the physical body. . . . We all carry within our souls the capacity to heal ourselves.[15]

What is particularly instructive, however, is that the Native-American healing philosophies of "soul" include the larger soul-self that we are talking about in this chapter. Melh-Madrona explains:

> My training has been primarily in Lakota and Cherokee approaches to healing, but the key elements of a Native American approach remain consistent from tribe to tribe—the view of the

> suffering person as being simultaneously matter, spirit, psyche: a member of both a social and an ecological system; a cell in the body of God.[16]

I am suggesting that, if we would enlarge our soul-self to include nature and the animal world, we would be opening ourselves up to possibilities for healing that have been denied, overlooked, and trivialized for millennia in the dominant civilized cultures.

Becoming Native to This Place

Sam Keen was wrong.

I very rarely have thought or said that about the philosopher and theologian whose books have never failed to stimulate my mind and send my spirit soaring off into enjoyable flights of intellectual and spiritual discovery. He has a wonderfully incisive mind, a bold spirit, and the capacity to put creative thoughts into clear language. I have held Sam Keen in high regard for many years, but there was one particular advice he gave me in which he was dead-wrong.

I had invited Sam to address a conference at First Community Church in Columbus, Ohio. It was the late 1970s, and the topic of the conference was the new human potential movement. There were few people any better at articulating that movement than Sam Keen. At the end of the evening, I was driving Sam back to his hotel; and as I pulled up in front, just before exiting the car, Sam turned to me and said, "Bob, if you want to learn about human potentialities, you've got to move to California. You just can't do it in Columbus, Ohio."

I immediately sensed that Sam was wrong, as least as far as I was concerned, but for a long time, I didn't know why he was wrong. Certainly, the "human potential movement" was more prominent in California at that time.

Nevertheless, I had a vague sense that there was meaning and purpose to the fact that my roots were in Middle America, but it took many years before I could put very much intellectual specificity and clarity on that strong but amorphous intuition.

I now believe that there is an important indigenous component to our spiritual integrity. It certainly differs from person to person, and I am not suggesting that each of us finds our own indigenous factor in the geography in which we were born and raised. I do believe it is important, however, for each of us to find a place in which we are, or can become, native.

I travel far and wide to lecture, to teach, and to lead workshops; but I have found that there is something very "grounding" for me in the middle of this continent, the geography between and including Ohio and Colorado. My heart and soul are rooted, it would seem, in the heartland of North America.

I find spiritual sustenance in the land and the lakes of Iowa, Minnesota, and Wisconsin, and my soul is lifted when in the mountains of Colorado. My most nourishing and creative writing has been in a "dialogue" between our home on "Winged Spirit Mesa" in the Colorado Rockies and the waters and cliffs of Door County in northeast Wisconsin. Only an athlete, and perhaps specifically Michael Murphy, would understand when I say that my athletic soul is nourished when it is grounded on the beautiful golf course that overlooks the waters of Green Bay and that my spirit feels vividly reflected in the colorful spinnaker sails out in the bay, as I enjoy "golfing in the Kingdom of Door."

Yes, Sam Keen was wrong, at least as Middle America has to do with *my* human potential. Instead of seeking *the* Promised Land off in some "foreign" territory—foreign to where we can be our most native soul-self—perhaps we should take our clue from Moses's experience with the burning bush.

God, speaking to Moses out of the burning bush, told Moses to take off his sandals, for "the place where you are standing is holy ground." For the purpose of our healing, it may be important to take off whatever prevents us from feeling grounded, for it is that very place that can enable our health, wholeness, and holiness.

It may also be reciprocal. The land may be able to tell us where our "holy ground" is located. Perhaps the land of Middle America was telling me many years ago that I was native to that place. It may have been the land telling me, in ways that I could not rationally understand for a long time, that I am a "Native Middle-American." I'm not at all sure how to understand that fully, but my wife Diana suggests that it might be because I had previous lives, perhaps as a Native American in the Midwestern plains. She might be right.

I wonder. Could it be that the reason that, during my annual writing retreat into Door County, my soul feels nourished and my writing feels more creative because I spent a previous lifetime there? Could it be that several lifetimes before I picked up a golf club or typed away at my computer, I was a Winnebago (not to be confused with the recreational vehicle that co-opted the name) appreciating this special piece of land that was carved out by glaciers a hundred thousand years ago? Could it be that, in a later lifetime, I was a Potawatomi enjoying the immense embankments and the perpendicular cliffs of what is today the Peninsula State Park near Ephraim? Or could it be that, in another moment in time, I was a Huron, an Ottawa, or a Nipissing on what today is called Washington Island, off the tip of Door County? Could that be why I feel a special connection with that land? I wonder.

Going even further into this potential fantasy, could it be that I participated in one of those lifetimes in a common Native-American ritual wherein the placenta and umbilical cord that participated in my birth was buried in the land where I was born? Prince Modupe explains such beliefs:

> The placenta must be buried with ceremony in the compound with the witchdoctor present. As the navel cord ties an unborn child to the womb, so does the buried cord tie the child to the land, to the sacred Earth of the tribe, to the Great Mother Earth. If

> the child ever leaves the place, he will come home again because the tug of this cord will always pull him toward his own.
>
> When I go home . . . I shall speak these words: "My belly is this day reunited with the belly of my Great Mother, Earth!"[17]

The Australian Aborigines have their own special version of this ancient notion of becoming native to a particular place. They believe that a woman becomes pregnant when she passes a particularly spiritual spot in the landscape and the spirit of that land decides to enter her. The spirit is then born as a human being who in a very essential way is connected to that land—literally, an incarnate spirit of the land. Further, they feel that, to know that person intimately, you have to know the land from which her or his spirit came.

Could it be that I was conceived in some past life when my Native-American mother wandered past Wilson's Ice Cream Parlor along the Ephraim shores? Could that be why, today, when I pass Wilson's, I feel God calling me to go in and have a hot-fudge sundae? Well, maybe not!

Silliness aside, I have often wondered why Door County, Wisconsin, feels so special to me—not the people so much and certainly not the shops and tourist attractions, but the land and the water. And let's not forget the golf course.

Could some of the same reasons explain why I have come to feel so native to our little "Winged Spirit Mesa" atop Stone Mountain in Colorado? Would it have anything to do with the legend that, precisely on the spot where we live, Native Americans are said to have come to study the weather coming across the Continental Divide, so as to know what was heading their way?

Whether this is the explanation for my feelings, I do not know. But of one thing I am sure. Just because modern, academic, sophisticated, scientific, intellectual categories have no clear explanation for something does not make that something a "no-thing." The lack of conventional truth-giving does not make something not true!

"Unconventional" and "unreal" are not synonymous. "Unorthodox" and "unbelievable" are not the same—at least not for me.

Psychoneuroimmunologist Paul Pearsall recounts what an Apache shaman told him:

> Those in the Western world often forget that they too are indigenous peoples with roots to their original land and ties to their ancient ancestor's wisdom. The modern rational brain can also learn to think with its indigenous spiritual heart.[18]

I am stressing here becoming native to a particular place in a fairly narrow sense, but the bigger issue is this: perhaps by becoming native to one small place, we can be drawn into that "indigenous spiritual heart" wherein we become native to this planet. It is a deep heart-felt reunion with Mother Earth that is desperately called for today in the interest of healing all of us.

Diana takes a backseat to nobody when it comes to intellectual ability. Yet at the same time, she embodies, to an extraordinary degree, a balance of her able mind with an equally able "indigenous spiritual heart." She has, in fact, been my greatest teacher about our natural indigenous soul-self. I have seen time and time again that, when Diana brings her incredibly powerful feminine energy to focus in her medicine wheel rituals, spiritual magic happens. She, as I mentioned in the book's dedication, has been the single most powerful healing force in my life. And I have seen her do the same for countless clients who come to her as a psychotherapist—healing, as it were, as they sip from her special elixir of soul. A great deal of her power, I am convinced, comes from her extraordinary shamanic ecological soul-self.

I have seen Diana go through a fascinating and profoundly powerful process of becoming native to any land on which we have lived. After we purchased the land we came to call "Winged Spirit Mesa," Diana spent untold hours up on the land, even while we were still living in Boulder. The first thing she did was to walk our property until the mountain "told" her where her medicine wheel should be placed, indicating just the right spot of spiritual energy—in other words, the location of her ecological heart's spiritual rituals would be established *before* we decided where our house would be built!

She then built her medicine wheel with her own hands, conducted her rituals, walked the land, handled the stone, talked to the animals, and, in general, became at home, became indigenous, became native to that particular place. My tendency is to sit and look at the land, observe the animals, think, reflect, and meditate on becoming one with the land. Diana's style, however, is to embody and embrace the land—touching the land with her hands, her arms, her heart, and her soul.

That, in combination with Diana's being so "at home" with her femininity, is what gives her such extraordinary healing power. I have been a beneficiary of that healing power for more than a quarter century now, as have her clients too numerous to count.

One particular story that demonstrates how her indigenous heart is connected with the animal world involves the story of how an Australian Kelpie named Angel, a small- to medium-sized dog, came to live and heal with us.

THE STORY OF ANGEL

It was about 5:00 a.m., Sunday, January 14, 2001, when our beloved Belgium sheepdog Gypsy-Bear started to die. I was, as usual, up early and at my writing. Gypsy-Bear was, as usual, sleeping just behind me under my desk. When her breathing became labored, however, my attention was drawn to her. Sometimes, when she was dreaming, her breathing would change, her legs would twitch, and she would often let out some muffled yelps. But I could tell something was different this time. I turned around to look at her and knew immediately something was wrong. Her body was not moving at all, and her eyes were open in a glassy stare. She was unable to respond to any of my requests to come out from under my desk.

I awakened Diana, and we rushed Gypsy-Bear down the mountain and over to the emergency vet hospital in Longmont. A team of wonderfully sensitive veterinarians did all they could, but Gypsy-Bear had advanced cancer and massive internal bleeding. She was dead by 10:00 that morning. It was mercifully quick for Gypsy-Bear, but much too fast and unexpected for Diana and me. We had lost a great friend and companion, and we went back to a Gypsy-Bear-less home in grief.

Unfortunately, I had a two-week book tour scheduled to begin the very next day, so Diana and I had just one day to process and share our grief—much too little time to be together, and telephone conversations are an inadequate substitute at a time like that. I, at least, was out of town and busy with groups speaking about my recently published *Sacred Quest*—a schedule where I was not accustomed to having Gypsy-Bear along anyway. Diana, on the other hand, was living and sleeping daily in the very environment where Gypsy-Bear had been such a valued participant. Diana expressed the agony of her grief in her journal, as well as the story that unfolded:

> I've never felt so alone or depressed. Trying to take my daily walk on the mountain was more painful than words can express. I could feel her presence with me, but it did little to ease my aching heart.
>
> But, on Friday, January 26th (the day before Bob was to return home), I decided to meditate and call in a circle of angels to gather with me in my soul's temple. I asked for their assistance in helping me manifest (sooner rather than later) the right and perfect dog to join our family. I even spelled out what I meant by "perfect," namely, a dog who: (1) does not chase deer, (2) is obedient on and off the leash, (3) is able to handle being with me in my office at work when Bob is out of town, (4) gets along well with cats, (5) has a gentle and pleasant temperament, and (6) is infused with the spirit of our two previous dogs, Spirit of the Dawn and Gypsy-Bear.

> I knew that these requirements presented quite a challenge, and I expressed my willingness to be patient.
>
> Later that afternoon, I opened the paper and an ad in the classified section jumped out at me: "small, black, female dog available for adoption."
>
> The woman who answered my call said her name was Lauren and that she had come into possession of this "perfect" dog (she actually used that word) who had been abandoned in the Los Alamos, NM, wildfires.
>
> "What do you mean by 'perfect,'" I asked?
>
> Lauren began by saying that the dog does not chase deer, gets along well with cats, and proceeded to list almost all of my requirements. Lauren went on to say that she decided to put an ad in the paper for just one day, and had meditated that the right and perfect family would call. As it turned out, I was the only one who called.
>
> "And, what is the dog's name," I asked?
>
> "Angel," Lauren responded.
>
> My circle of angels had manifested our perfect little Angel within hours of my request, and two weeks to the day after Gypsy-Bear had died.

Diana and I bonded very quickly with Angel, and she has become an intimate part of our daily lives. I was not expecting, however, the extraordinary healing sensitivities that Angel has recently demonstrated.

My left knee has been presenting a substantial challenge in the last couple of years—torn miniscus surgically removed, extensive arthritic deterioration, and the recommended total knee replacement. Not having time for such surgery, however—given what I was doing and what I was wanting to do—I have been putting off the surgery and trying to keep the supportive musculature strong enough to continue my normal activity. One day, however, I overdid the exercising and was experiencing a great deal of pain.

I periodically iced the knee while sitting at my desk that evening, but the pain was still substantial by bedtime. I was able to doze off now and then after meditating, but the severity of the pain kept waking me up. After one such round of meditating, dozing off, and reawakening, I felt Angel climbing up on the bed—the first time she had ever done that during the night, for she prefers to sleep alone!—and cuddled up next to my left knee. She stayed there all night snuggling my knee. My pain subsided, and I slept more deeply and more restfully the rest of the night. There is absolutely no doubt in my mind but that Angel knew I was in pain and came to sleep with me specifically to lend some healing energy.

HEART-FELT HEALING BETWEEN ANIMALS AND HUMANS

I am privileged to have such a wonderful canine companion who can sense when I am in pain and who responds with such obvious love and healing compassion, but I am not alone. There is, in fact, a growing literature of stories and references to scientific research studies suggesting the healing capacities of animals, both tame and wild, in the United States and around the world.[19]

Susan Chernak McElroy, who credits her triumph over cancer to the love of the animals in her life, has written a book in which the following story is told.

It seems that, in India, a child fell into a river, and her mother was, understandably, panic-stricken. Responding to the mother's screams, a monkey on the opposite shore jumped into the river, grabbed the child, and swam to shore dropping the child safely at the mother's feet.

McElroy also tells the story of a a twelve-year old boy in Canada who, after his parents were drowned in a fishing boat accident, was alone and lost in the cold terrain. At night the temperature fell below zero and the boy, frightened, cold, and afraid, lay down on the ground and prayed for help:

> Suddenly he felt something furry against him. In the dark, he couldn't tell what kind of animal it was but it was warm so he put

> his arm around it and huddled close. Then, he cried himself to sleep.
>
> When he awoke the next morning, three beavers were lying against him and across his body. They had kept him from freezing to death.[20]

The world-renowned biologist Rupert Sheldrake, who created the innovative "morphic field" theory writes, "I am a great believer in the value of scientific inquiry, but I am more convinced than ever that the mechanistic theory of nature is too narrow. I have discovered that an increasing number of my scientific colleagues agree, although they are reluctant to say so in public."[21]

We are fortunate, however, that Sheldrake is not so reluctant. After several critically acclaimed scientific books, he has recently published a book in which he explores stories of humanity's relationship with animals and the possible meaning of those relationships. He reports that he has in his database "over two hundred stories about animals that comfort and heal." He references more than two thousand programs in the United States alone in which animals are used therapeutically in hospitals, hospices, and homes for the elderly, in what are generically referred to as PAT (pets as therapy) programs.

Dean Ornish reports a study of men and women who had sustained heart attacks and who had irregular heartbeats. During the study, some of the people died. An interesting but unexpected factor in those who survived, however, turned out to be that of having a pet dog: "Only one of the eighty-seven people (1.1 percent) who owned dogs died during the study compared with nineteen of the 282 people (6.7 percent) who did not own dogs—over *six times* as many!"[22]

Do yourself, and your animals, a favor—open your heart and be a lover. Expand your soul-self to include the rest of nature and find out how native you are to both place and pet.

CHAPTER SEVEN

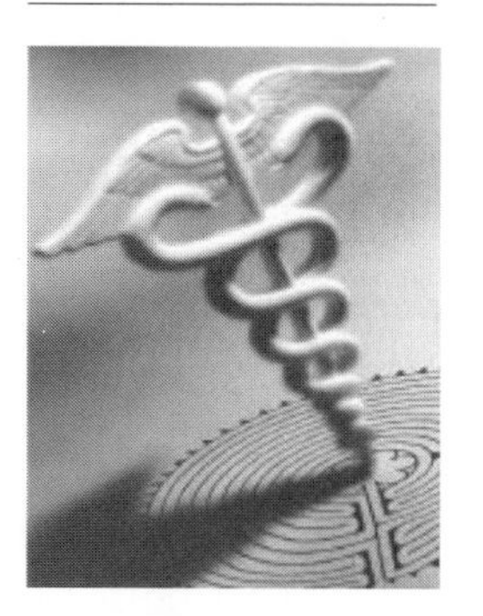

An ECOLOGY *of the* HEART: PEOPLE

Unconditional love will have the final word in reality.

MARTIN LUTHER KING JR., M.DIV., PH.D.

When it comes to calculating the power and reach of love, the mind is a pedestrian but the heart is a broad jumper.

SAM KEEN , M.DIV., PH.D.

I was writing this very chapter during October 2001, while living temporarily in Berkeley, California, and teaching at the Graduate Theological Union as a scholar-in-residence for the Swedenborgian House of Studies during the fall term.

On Friday morning, October 12, I had finished chapter six and titled this chapter when I realized it was time for me to leave for a meeting in Palo Alto, given the unpredictable traffic across the Bay Bridge into San Francisco and down highway 101.

I grabbed my cell phone, keys, and briefcase and headed out the front door to get into my car. Before I even closed the apartment door behind me, a young woman came running towards me frantically yelling, "Call 911—a child just fell from the third floor!"

I dropped my briefcase, quickly grabbed my cell phone, and dialed 911 as I ran, not more than sixty or seventy feet, two doors down to the west, to where an eighteen-month-old baby, unconscious and bleeding from the head, was lying on the cement driveway. Unbelievably, I got an automated voice telling me that all operators are busy!

The child's mother and I both arrived at about the same time, and someone yelled from across the street that emergency personnel were on the way. As I approached the unconscious child, I could not tell if she was alive or dead. The mother was in shock, glassy-eyed, and unable to say much of anything. She just kept pointing to the third-floor window from which her child had fallen, with nothing to break her fall until she had landed, apparently head-first, on the cement driveway. From the distance of that third-floor window, I wondered if there was any possible chance that the baby could survive that fall. I placed my hand gently on the child's back and discovered that she was breathing, although still unconscious, and told the mother to resist the temptation to move or pick up the baby. I tried to assure her that emergency help was on the way.

It was then that I experienced something quite extraordinary.

I was feeling a strong compassion for both the baby and the mother—what horrible and desperate sense of panic a mother must be experiencing at a time such as this. I don't recall thinking the rest of this through, but instinctively I put my right hand on the mother's back and kept my left hand gently on the baby and tried to send the greatest amount of love and healing energy of which I was capable into both of them.

I have never considered myself as having any special healing powers for anybody other than myself. Nor did I have any experience such as this in the past. In other words, I was not acting out of any previous experience, just doing instinctively what it seemed I should do.

Although I was vaguely aware of people gathering and heard someone tell someone else to get the baby's father, my total focus was on the baby and the mother. I don't know precisely how much time elapsed, but I felt a powerful sense of warmth in my left hand, the hand that was on the baby; and I turned to the mother and said, "Don't worry. She'll be O.K."

Later I reflected on how trivial and wishful-thinking that might have sounded to the mother—so perfunctory and so superficial—but, inexplicably, I was saying it out of a deep sense of *knowing*. In spite of all appearances, in spite of this child's fall from three floors onto a cement driveway, in spite of her bleeding and lack of consciousness—in spite of all that, I heard myself saying those reassuring words absolutely knowing they were true.

The little baby girl slowly regained consciousness, started to cry, and began moving a little just as the emergency vehicles arrived. I backed away to let the professionals apply their knowledge and skill in assessing the baby's vital signs and in getting her to the hospital.

I turned to one of the emergency personnel who was standing off to the side and said, "I think she is going to be all right." He looked at me incredulously and said, in a low voice so that the parents could not hear, "I wouldn't be so sure. With that kind of fall, the child may have massive internal injuries, no doubt a fractured skull, and death from brain swelling is a real possibility. She is definitely not out of the woods, in spite of the fact that she is conscious and moving."

They carefully strapped the baby to a small gurney, loaded her into the emergency vehicle, and left for the hospital, along with the mother, the father who had just arrived, and some of the parent's friends. I, finally remembering my meeting in Palo Alto and an evening lecture in San Mateo, got in my car and began the drive across the Bay Bridge.

The next morning, back in Berkeley, I was anxious to find out about the baby's condition. I was new in the neighborhood, however, a neighborhood in which a lot of student and faculty housing is crammed into narrow duplexes and triplexes. I did not know the name of the baby or her mother's or father's name. During the incident, I had not paid attention to which of the neighbors had gathered around. Consequently, I didn't know whom to contact to inquire about the child's condition.

My left-brain, no doubt having felt that it was ignored in the midst of the crisis, began to do the thing that left-brains do so well—regaining its favorite half-brained superiority by casting doubt and rationality across the waters of extraordinary experience. My memory of the event, therefore, began to get polluted. I questioned whether I had made up the part about the intense warmth in my hand. Was my reassurance to the mother simply my wishful thinking? Was I just trying to calm the mother? How could I possibly think a child could fall three floors, hitting her head on a cement driveway, and not be killed? Or at least very seriously hurt? "Get real, Keck," my left-brain warned, "be prepared for some tragic news."

So it was with the newly found, left-brain-created trepidation on Saturday that I asked my next-door neighbor, Andrea, if she knew the condition of the child. "Yes," she said, "we just came from the hospital. It's an absolute miracle. The doctors say that they are 90% sure that Naomi will recover fully with no lasting effects." That was the first time I had heard the baby's name. By Monday, the word was out across the campus that Naomi was recovering completely. Everybody just kept saying, "It's a miracle. It's an absolute miracle!"

The next day, on campus, I joined a group gathered around a bulletin board reading an announcement of Naomi's condition.The young lady standing next to me turned to me and asked, "Can you believe it? No broken bones, and the doctor's expect a full recovery. It's great, but it makes no sense. Did you see the window where the baby fell from and where she landed? Can you believe it?"

"Yes," I replied, "I can." The tears welling up in my eyes were from both joy and wonder. What an incredible privilege to be a close observer, perhaps even a participant, in that miracle. But how, I wondered, do I understand that miracle?

The miracle may have been that an eighteen-month-old child is light and flexible and remarkably able to survive a fall like that. On the other hand, the miracle may have been that powerful loving energy was shared from one human being to another through my hand placed gently on the baby's back, that my intentionality and focused love had miraculous power. Or perhaps the miraculous power may have come from an extended community of friends and strangers through their prayers; I discovered later that an email had gone out to the Graduate Theological Union community the next day asking for everybody's prayers on behalf of the baby. Maybe the parents themselves played important roles in the miracle. Perhaps it was a combination of all the above. Who knows? I cannot, with any degree of certainty, dissect that incredible event that combined potential tragedy, a great deal of love, and a miraculous outcome. But I do know this: love can be an incredibly powerful healing force and its scope, its capabilities, and its mystery far exceeds what our left-brain can comprehend. We would be foolish to underestimate the healing power of human connectedness, fueled by the energy of love. After all, the power of love is, itself, a miracle.

There is another piece to that story, for I too experienced a healing of sorts. During the event itself, I was totally focused upon the baby's health and the mother's feelings. I certainly was not thinking about the little problem I had been having with my left hand.

Six months earlier the middle finger of my left hand started sticking in a closed position—whenever I closed my left hand and then tried to open it, the middle finger would not open. I had to take my right hand and forcibly straighten it out. It is a rather common tendon problem, typically referred to as a "trigger finger." Needless to say, because I am a writer, the problem, albeit relatively minor, was especially bothersome.

The specialist I consulted first tried a cortisone shot into the tendon; when that was not successful, he said that the only way it could be corrected was by surgery. It would be a "very simple" surgical procedure, he said. I decided to have it done and, yes, my finger could then operate normally. The only problem was that the surgery would render my left hand eighty percent numb.

I was flat-out angry. To go in for what was described as a simple surgical procedure to correct a finger problem, without knowing one of the side effects could be a numb hand! I came out with a finger that works, but with no feeling in most of my hand. Writing then became even more difficult. Several consultations ended with my being told that nothing could be done, except possibly a more complicated surgical procedure. Wait a couple of weeks, the physician said, and maybe the numbness will go away. Several weeks drifted into six months and my left hand was still numb.

As that Friday morning's events unfolded, I understandably never thought about my hand. My total attention had been on little Naomi and her mother, until they were in the hands of the emergency personnel and on their way to the hospital. And, as mentioned, I then drove to Palo Alto for a meeting and to San Mateo for a lecture.

Late that evening, after all the events of the day were over, I was driving back across the Bay Bridge to Berkeley. In the middle of the Bay Bridge—I can almost point out the very spot where I was when it dawned on me—I realized that most of the feeling in my left hand had returned! Only a very slight amount of the numbness remained, perhaps five percent. And although an earthquake metaphor is not one wants to use typically while driving across the Bay Bridge from San Francisco to Berkeley, it felt as if my deep psyche had been quaked real good!

Could the experience of intensely attempting to send love and healing through my left hand into the injured child actually, serendipitously, have healed my own hand in the process? Could that powerful feeling of warmth that I experienced in my left hand, which was not matched in my right hand as it lay on the mother's shoulder, have been the power to heal *both* the child and me? I also wondered whether my anger at the surgeon had kept that numbness frozen in place, static and stable, only to be blasted away by the power of love. Could it be that I just learned something about the toxicity of anger and the healing power of love? I think so!

The Power of Love to Heal

There is a growing body of research that suggests that love, or the lack of it, is profoundly influential in our state of health and/or illness. Dean Ornish, who is familiar with that evidence sums it up succinctly:

> Anything that promotes feelings of love and intimacy is healing; anything that promotes isolation, separation, loneliness, loss, hostility, anger, cynicism, depression, alienation, and related feelings often leads to suffering, disease, and premature death from all causes.[1]

Love's power, or the consequences of not having love, have been demonstrated at the very earliest stages of life. In what has to be judged as one of the worst experiments of all time, the German Emperor Frederick II, in the thirteenth century, wanted to find out what language babies would speak if they were not taught a language by anyone. In order to find out, he had several newborn babies taken from their parents and given to nurses with the strict instructions that they were not to be touched or talked to. The emperor failed in both his humanity and his intellectual curiosity, for all the babies died before they could talk.[2]

In other more recent studies, babies died for lack of touching even though they were given adequate nutrition and were living in sanitary conditions. The babies in this case were not touched because their adult caretakers feared the spread of infectious diseases. So, instead of dying from a disease, they died from lack of loving, human contact. On a more positive note: "At the Touch Research Institute in Miami, premature babies given three loving massages a day for ten days gained weight 47 percent faster and left the hospital six days sooner."[3]

If we add to this what we now know about how massage can enhance endorphin production, it is not surprising that, in my own healing journey, I have found massage to be an extremely helpful modality. The larger issue, however, is that anything that honors and expresses a loving relationship with other people taps into the fundamental power of our participation in the whole.

Love is whole-making, and whole-making is healing and holy. When we recognize and utilize the connecting power of love, through intimacy, trust, compassion, touching, forgiveness, and altruistic service, profound healing can occur. Conversely, when we deny, denigrate, and deplete the power of love, through isolation, cynicism, loneliness, anger, and hostility, profound illness and premature death can result.

Professor James J. Lynch may have been the first to call our attention to the serious health consequences of loneliness. In 1977, when he was scientific director of the Psychosomatic Clinics at the School of Medicine at the University of Maryland, Lynch published his groundbreaking book *The Broken Heart: The Medical Consequences of Loneliness*. Drawing on a great deal of research, Lynch states bluntly, "The fact is that social isolation, the lack of human companionship, death or absence of parents in early childhood, sudden loss of love, and chronic human loneliness are significant contributors to premature death."[4]

Dean Ornish echoes that sentiment, stating that loneliness and isolation "increase the likelihood of disease and premature death *from all causes* by 200 to 500 percent or more, independent of behaviors."[5]

Loneliness is one way of cutting off the healing power of whole-making. Depression is another. It is certainly not surprising that there is a high risk of suicide among those suffering from depression. But the consequences of depression are far greater than that obvious link.

America's leading cause of death, coronary heart disease (CHD), kills about one million Americans prematurely every year. In one of the most impressive research surveys to date, covering some 1,200 studies and 400 research reviews, Harold Koenig, David Larson, and Michael McCullough state that "nine out of ten studies found increased cardiovascular mortality among the depressed." Further, they state that "in studies that examine subjects who already have ischemic heart disease, *outcomes* are decidedly worse if depression is present."[6]

Cancer is the second leading cause of death in America, killing more than a half a million American lives every year. "After controlling for age, smoking, alcohol use, family history, and occupational status, the likelihood of dying from cancer was twice as high among men with depression at baseline."[7]

Regarding the negative role that hostility can play in one's state of health, consider a few brief conclusions by a variety of prestigious researchers:

- "People high in hostility experience two to four times the risk of CHD of people who score low on this trait."[8]
- "Those who scored in the upper twenty percent of hostility when tested twenty years earlier had a forty-two percent increased risk of premature death *from all causes combined,* including heart disease and cancer, when compared to those who scored in the lower twenty percent of hostility."[9]
- "The effects of hostility are equal to or greater in magnitude to the traditional risk factors for heart disease: elevated cholesterol levels, high blood pressure, and so on."[10]

- Rosenman and Friedman, the physicians who first showed us that a personality type, what they called a "Type A Personality," was strongly associated with heart disease, have indicated that it is not simply being a workaholic that is the problem. The greatest risk factor appears to be that of hostility.[11]

My own interpretation of the Type-A research and the correlation of hostility and heart disease has, once again, primarily to do with our soul-self, our deepest identity. I suspect that the Type-A personality has a built-in propensity for a soul-self rooted in achievements and accomplishments. The more exclusively that condition exists, the more a quick temper and chronic hostility will accompany the life and death of a Type A.

As we have discussed earlier in this book, our primary identity is rooted in the deep soil of soul. If, in the case of a Type-A personality, that soul-self is nourished only by the next accomplishment, the next achievement, or the next prize, the person or the circumstance blocking the way to the victory stand is experienced as a direct attack on the very essence of self. With that set-up, the Type A cannot help but be hostile.

"Get out of my way, you S.O.B."

"The light's turned green, you blankety-blank. I've got things to do, people to see, and places to go."

Bordering on paranoia, the extreme Type A can feel that the anonymous "they" is doing such and such just to keep the overachiever from reaching the pinnacle.

Conversely, I would suggest that if our soul-self is "at home" in being-ness, rather than in the doing and the achieving, we will be far less prone to anger and hostility. The more our self-worth can just *be* and not need to be puffed up constantly by the next accomplishment, the far less prone to heart disease we will be. With apologies to Shakespeare—To be or not to be, that is the *answer!*

Love in the form of close relationships, a deep sense of community, and other manifestations of social support, such as one's religion, is turning up more and more in medical research as extremely influential in health, while at the same time, more and more evidence suggests that disease and premature death from all causes are the consequences of not having such social support:

- "The link between personal relationships and immune function . . . is one of the most robust findings in psychoneuroimmunology."[12]

One researcher who set out intentionally to *disprove* the notion that factors such as compassionate social support could influence cancer survival rates designed a research project with women with metastatic breast cancer and included weekly support groups as part of the research.

The researcher, Dr. David Spiegel, reported that "when I finally got around to looking at the data, I almost fell off my chair. Those women who had the weekly support group lived on average *twice as long* as did the other women who didn't have the support group."[13]

Typically, the medical approach has focused upon only physical causes of breast cancer—genetic propensity, smoking, or diet. But as Ornish points out, "there are no studies that prove that women with metastatic breast cancer can double their length of survival by quitting smoking or changing their diet."[14]

Dr. Spiegel's experience, in his approach to the research as well as its surprising results, graphically illustrates a very important point: historically, our medical paradigm in respect to cancer has been narrow, which may have contributed to its lack of success. The facts testify to the power of the paradigm and our stubbornness to creatively challenge the boundaries and to seek possibilities that lie outside the paradigm.

What might the advances and breakthroughs amount to if we invested as much money in researching potential metaphysical factors in cancer, as we do in the physical factors? For over a quarter of a century, the medical paradigm has been fed so many millions of dollars that we can't keep track of the actual investment! There have been, without question, some successes. The successes, however, too easily satisfy us and blind us to the probability that much greater success could be achieved if we had the courage to look beyond the boundaries of orthodoxy. Blind loyalty to the prevailing materialistic and reductionistic medical paradigm rarely considers the consequences of not investigating a larger range of influences. How many of the 1,500 Americans dying every day from cancer might be saved if we simply enlarged the paradigm and investigated potential mental, emotional, and spiritual causes of cancer with the same commitment as we do the biological and genetic components?

Physicians who have had the courage to venture out beyond the boundaries of orthodoxy have frequently been discredited and even demonized. The so-called "realists" have been looking down their hard noses at those who suggest some of the softer possibilities. But if cancer, or any other disease, is the result of a combination of factors, fighting just one—the strictly biological one—simply will not have maximum results. How many years and how many millions of dollars will it take before we understand that a primary problem in keeping us from the greatest potential success is the nature of the paradigm?

There is now a great amount of evidence suggesting that many social, psychological, and spiritual factors contribute to the onset and progress of disease, mortality rates, and the possibilities of healing. It is simply time that we wake up and address all of the potential causes and means of healing, not just the materialistic ones.

Larry Dossey is certainly one of the most influential and courageous physician pioneers exploring the territory out near the boundaries of medical orthodoxy and beyond. With all the conventional medical credentials, Dossey was unconventional enough to look into the efficacy of prayer:

> I found an enormous body of evidence: over one hundred experiments exhibiting the criteria of "good science," many conducted under stringent laboratory conditions, over half of which showed

> that prayer brings about significant changes in a variety of living beings. . . .
>
> Experiments with people showed that prayer positively affected high blood pressure, wounds, heart attacks, headaches, and anxiety.
>
> These data . . . are so impressive that I have come to regard them as among the best-kept secrets in medical science.[15]

Dossey goes on to say:

> If scientists suddenly discovered a drug that was as powerful as love in creating health, it would be heralded as a medical breakthrough and marketed overnight—especially if it had as few side effects and was as inexpensive as love. Love is intimately related with health.[16]

And, that brings me to my personal priority in terms of the healing power of love—the primary, intimate relationship.

The Power of the Primary Relationship

> *It may be more important to have at least one person with whom we can share open and honest thoughts and feelings than it is to have a whole network of more superficial relationships.*
>
> BLAIR JUSTICE, PH.D.

Judging from my own healing journey, I don't think there is any more powerful healing force than the unconditional love, support, and trust from the one primary relationship in one's life. To have at least one person with whom one can be totally intimate, at all levels of one's being, providing the opportunity to have a life of complete living, giving, and receiving of love, may be the single most important source for miracle healings. My testimony to how important Diana has been for my own healing journey is found throughout my writings and in the dedication to my books. My personal bias notwithstanding, it appears to be true for others as well.

- In research on people who had experienced medically inexplicable healings—generally referred to as "miracle healing" or "spontaneous remissions"—a surprising insight turned up: "More than half had been married over twenty years, and forty-one percent over thirty years, an unexpected finding for a sampling in this era of divorce."[17]
- Another study concluded that "married persons live longer, with lower mortality for almost every major cause of death, in comparison with single, separated, widowed, or divorced persons."[18]
- "One survey of ten thousand men with heart disease found a 50 percent reduction in frequency of chest pain (angina) in men who perceived their wives as supportive and loving."[19]
- There was one study which included 1,368 patients with heart disease who had undergone cardiac catheterization. Special attention was given to the differences between these patients regarding their marital status and/or the presence in their lives of a confidant. The study found that the risk of dying for those unmarried and without a close friend or companion, over the following nine years, was 3.3 times greater than those patients who were married or had a significant relationship.[20]
- Leukemia patients who were undergoing bone marrow transplants were asked about the amount and nature of emotional support they had from their spouse or close friends. Two years later the researchers checked in on the group and discovered that fifty-four percent of those with close and meaningful loving support were still alive, whereas only twenty percent of those with little or no support survived.[21]

There is an interesting testimony to the importance of the primary relationship from the timing of death when that relationship is severed. James Lynch, a pioneer in the research of loneliness, reminds us that "linkages between the loss of a loved one and sudden death are frequently reported in the medical literature."[22]

One of the more fascinating stories in this genre has to do with a particular set of twin sisters. The twins were rarely apart for any length of time, and neither married. At about 21 years of age, both began to have major problems psychologically—loss of sleep and appetite, a lack of any interest in socializing with people other than the twin, and a flattening of all emotional forms of expression. They both experienced delusions and increased suspicion of anyone other than the twin. Both became unable to function in the "outside world" and were institutionalized at age 31.

After about a year of continued deterioration, refusing all social contacts, their physicians decided to separate the twins into different wards so that they could not reinforce each other in their respective, and shared, pathologies. During the first evening of separation, the twins were checked at 10:20 p.m., 11:30 p.m., and at midnight—both were sleeping and checks of their respiration revealed nothing abnormal. At 12:45 a.m., however, both were found dead.

Although no one observed the actual dying of "Twin A," it seems that "Twin B" had a roommate who reported what happened in their room. The roommate said that "Twin B" got out of bed, went to the window and looked up at the room which held her twin sister, then sank to the floor and died.[23]

Given all the evidence, it is time that we begin to give greater attention to how love and compassion contribute to health promotion, disease prevention, and miraculous healings. Without question, there are kind and loving people in the medical profession, but it is also without question that love is *not* considered an essential part of the curriculum in medical schools. In light of the research we have been highlighting in this chapter, why shouldn't it be a priority in the training of all health professionals?

The other side of the medicine-spirituality partnership should also be challenged. Although it would be naive to suggest that, simply because people claim to be religious or spiritual, they are any better at loving than their more secular counterparts, it is time to give greater emphasis upon learning and practicing love and compassion as a part of any religion or spiritual practice. Does it get adequate emphasis in our graduate theological schools, which turn out the clergy leadership? I think not. Does it get enough attention in our churches, synagogues, and mosques—and I mean specifically *unconditional* love and compassion? I think not.

One place that tries to take the healing effects of love and compassion seriously is Commonweal, a retreat center for people with cancer, located in Bolinas, California. Its program involves yoga, meditation, imagery, poetry, walks along the ocean beach, and a lot of talking, hugging, and touching.

One marvelous story coming out of Commonweal involves Harry Rose. Rose had been diagnosed with cancer, believed that he could use his mind to heal, and enrolled in a program at Commonweal. He also happened to be Polish, a chemist, spoke with a deep accent, and was a Holocaust survivor.

The hugging and touching at Commonweal was a problem for Harry. As a twelve-year-old boy in Auschwitz, he had, understandably, become very circumspect about whom he could trust. He would not let himself get close to strangers, only family. Dr. Rachel Naomi Remen, the medical director at Commonweal, tells about Harry's protestations after he found himself in the midst of a hugging and touching session.

"Vot is this luffy, vot is this huggy, huggy, huggy, vot is this huggy the strangers, vot is this?"

On the final day of the retreat, it was time to tie up loose ends, and Dr. Remen turned to Mr. Rose and asked, "How are you doing, Harry?"

"Better," he replied.

"What happened that helped?" asked Dr. Remen.

"I took a valk and talked to God. It's better."

"What did God say?" Remen asked.

"Ah, I say to God, 'God, vot is this, is it OK to luff the strangers?" And God said, 'Harry, vot is this 'strangers'? You make strangers, I don't make strangers.'"[24]

Enlarging one's soul-self to include other people is critical in promoting health and well-being, in preventing illness, and in facilitating healing. Conversely, restricting one's soul-self to the boundaries of one's skin has pathological consequences. Coming out of an evolutionary epoch of ego and mental development, however, mainstream cultures tend to emphasize the individual as isolated from the community. Human ego development, no matter how necessary from an evolutionary perspective, leads inevitably to anthropocentrism and individualism.

As described earlier, Deep-Value Research clearly suggests that we are now embarking upon an evolutionary epoch with a spiritual purpose—thus, the value of the whole, the context, and the relationships in our lives will be rediscovered.

We have been created for wholeness, for relationships, and for the whole-making power of love. It is not coincidental that virtually all people who have had a mystical experience describe it as a profound sense of oneness with God and with all reality. Oneness, wholeness, unity—such are the words chosen to describe the divine and the human experiences that feel closest to the Divine. It should come as no surprise, therefore, that when we honor, participate in, and facilitate that wholeness, we are healthier—if we make strangers, we rend asunder that wholeness. When we do, we pay a stiff price in pathology.

To suggest that love, compassion for others, forgiveness, service, and altruism are good spirituality is certainly not a news flash. All religions say so in one way or another. The Upanishads say, "The Self is everywhere." Jesus said, "Love your neighbor as yourself." It turns out that good spirituality is also good for your biology.

Almost 3,000 men and women had their behaviors studied, along with their health, for nine-to-twelve years. In another example of how we appear to be created for love and whole-making, those who were engaged in a weekly activity of volunteer service to others were two-and-a-half-times less likely to die during the study.[25]

There was also the well-reported study of Harvard students who only *watched* altruistic service and had their immune system enhanced! The researchers had some of the students watch a documentary film of Mother Teresa serving the poor and dying in Calcutta's slums, while another group of students watched a more neutral film. Those watching Mother Teresa's compassionate love experienced an increase in their own immune systems protective antibodies, whereas the other students did not.[26]

If just watching love and compassion does our health a favor, consider how much better it is actually to help someone and do both of us a favor. What a marvelous testimony to both the ontological nature of love, as well as a profound demonstration of its power, if we can reach out and lessen someone's isolation and loneliness and help reduce his or her risk of dying prematurely, while we also enhance our own lives.

We conclude this exploration of the miracles that grow from within an ecology of the heart with an Hasidic parable, as told by Marc Ian Barasch:

> A man is vouchsafed a vision of the afterlife. He is first shown a great hall with a long banquet table filled with ambrosial delights. Each diner is equipped with a three-foot-long spoon, but no matter how much they contort their arms, thrusting their elbows into their neighbors' faces, their utensils are too long to maneuver even a singe morsel into their mouths. They sit together, opposite and side by side, in mutual misery.
>
> "This," says the man's otherworldly guide, "is Hell."
>
> The visitor is then taken to another place and sees an identical banquet table set with the same sumptuous viands and the same impossible silverware. Only here the denizens are well fed, utterly joyous, glowing with health and well-being.
>
> "This," pronounces his host, "is Heaven."
>
> The man is baffled. "What's the difference?"
>
> "In Heaven,"says the guide, pointing delightedly as a person

lifts his long-handled spoon across the table to the parted lips of a neighbor, "they feed each other."[27]

> *And then the day came when the risk to remain tight in a bud was more painful than the risk it took to blossom.*
>
> ANAÏS NIN

CHAPTER EIGHT

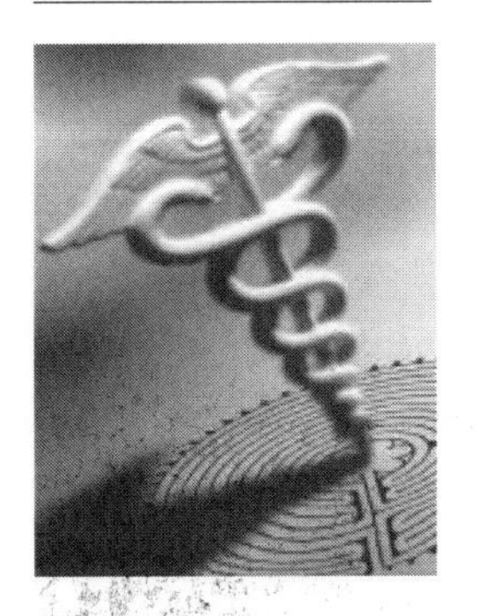

AWAKENING *the* HEALER WITHIN: CONSIDER *the* WHALE

We are standing on a whale, fishing for minnows.

ANCIENT POLYNESIAN SAYING

We have one whale of an inner potential for healing, but we have been taught that only minnows are medically proven and, by implication, are the only "catch" that is safe for public consumption. Don't believe it. Settling for minnows is disempowering. More importantly, the size of a minnow totally underestimates the power within us. In contrast, the next two chapters deal with awakening the sleeping giant of our inner healer, the slumbering whale of our inner potential for self-health, self-wholeness, and self-holiness.

A Bird Teaches Whale-ness

My cell phone's ring interrupted my meditation, as I sat on a precipice on the back side of Flagstaff Mountain, just west of Boulder. Spirit, our Wheaten Terrier, and I went up to this special view of the Continental Divide virtually every day as I was writing an earlier book, *Sacred Eyes*. It was a welcomed break for me in the middle of a day's writing, and Spirit sat at my side for virtually the entire time of writing that book—either beside my chair when typing in my study, in the back seat of my car, or beside me on the mountaintop. As I mentioned in the dedication to that book, "he would tolerate only so much work and head-tripping before he would demand play and heart-tripping—a therapeutic balancing."

It was unusual for my cell phone to ring, for only Diana had the number, and she would call me during the early afternoon hours only when it was absolutely necessary. So, it was with a touch of foreboding that I answered the phone.

On the other end of the line was an hysterical Diana, unusual behavior for her which, of course, set my heart pounding and my mind racing. "What is it, honey?" I asked, as I jumped to my feet, seemingly an unconscious preparation for whatever action or reaction was called for. She was out of breath from running and barely able to talk between her sobs but was able to tell me that our Cockatiel, "Feather," had escaped out of the house through a door that had been left ajar. She had chased Feather for some distance out through the open field just to the west of our home, but had lost him when he flew into the heavily treed neighborhood.

"I've run all over the place trying to find him, but I can't," sobbed Diana. "I can't stand the thought of losing him. The problem is—I've got clients this afternoon. I've got to pull myself together and get down to my office. Could you come right away?"

"Of course, I will, hon. You go on to work, and I'll get Feather back safely into the house." Spirit and I sprinted back to the car, all the while thinking that my total and completely confident assurance to Diana was speaking more about the level of my determination than it was about any realistic chances that I would have in even finding Feather, let alone being able to capture him and get him back into the house.

This was no small crisis. Diana is always extremely close to any and all of our animals, and in her marvelously mystical spirit, birds hold a particularly favored role as symbols of her soul. I knew how deeply disappointing it would be for Diana to lose Feather. My deep love for Diana sent a great ache through my heart for her and a firm determination throughout my soul that I simply had to find Feather.

As I drove down Flagstaff Mountain, faster than was either legal or safe, I kept imaging myself at a successful conclusion—knocking on Diana's office door to assure her that Feather was safely back in the house. I knew the size of the challenge, given the heavily treed neighborhood in which we lived and the nearby Wonderland Lake, but my love for Diana gave me absolute maximum motivation. I went into that zone of total and singular focus and concentration that had been so honed in my athletic years, but inexplicably, many years after any athletic application, still seems to be available when I need it.

It was about a half-hour later when I arrived at our home in North Boulder, sprinted into the house, told Spirit to "stay," and ran right out the back door and headed out to the open field. I surveyed the open space hoping that Feather might be perched atop one of the high weeds—but, no Feather. I walked rapidly along the tree-lined edge of the field looking intensely for Feather in the branches—but, no Feather. I pleaded with whatever intuitive capabilities I might have to direct me to Feather. I left the open space and went back to the southeast, through the many houses and the many, many trees, scouring every possible place where a bird might land—but, no Feather.

I had always resonated with eagle energy, loving the high and long view. So I asked if that eagle energy could enable me to see like an eagle—to be able to pick that little bird out of all the leafy treetops and branches.

When I am in that zone of single-minded purpose, I'm not conscious of the passage of time, so I don't really know how long it was—probably fifteen or twenty minutes into the search—before a small yellow movement out of the left corner of my vision caught my attention. There was Feather, flying from treetop to treetop.

I kept running, and Feather kept flying. All I could do was to keep track of him. After what was probably another fifteen or twenty minutes, Feather flew out of the area of the homes and began heading for Wonderland Lake, a couple of hundred yards to the north. I was sprinting along behind trying not to lose sight of him.

Feather proceeded to fly from treetop to treetop around the perimeter of Wonderland Lake. He was flying faster than I could run, would stop briefly on a treetop, and just as soon as I arrived at that tree, would take off for the next one. If I didn't know better, I would suspect that he was intentionally toying with me—in some tortoise-and-hare game—stopping periodically so that I would not lose track of him, yet taking off again so as to keep me at a steady sprint.

That process continued until he had flown and I had sprinted *twice* around the lake, which amounted to a total of about two miles. He then left the area of the lake and went back into the neighborhood. After several more trees, houses, and minutes, Feather, for the first time, landed on a low branch about ten feet off the ground, beside a fence. He stayed there as I approached, climbed the fence, and reached up to him. It may have been that he was getting tired or maybe he just felt sorry for the old man. In any case, he stayed on that limb while I slowly reached up to him, put my forefinger out by his feet, and when he stepped onto my finger, I placed my thumb on top of his feet clamping and securing him to my finger. Only then was I sure the chase was over.

I took Feather back home, placed him in his familiar cage. I knew, however, that my task was not over until I set Diana's mind and heart at ease. She does not answer the telephone when in a counseling session with a client, so I knew that the only way to reach her was going to her office and, as I had imaged, knocking on her door and informing her that Feather was safe. In what has turned out to be a common and regular spiritual serendipity of soul-synergy between us throughout our marriage, I was to learn later that Diana, even while counseling her client, had the image keep returning in her mind of my knocking on her office door and telling her that Feather was safe.

Only later did I began to reflect on the fact that my body was feeling no pain. *None*! Because of the late effects of polio and the broken back, I do not run *anywhere,* for *any distance, ever,* without having major consequences in terms of pain. My workouts consist of stationary bicycle exercise and walking, along with other low or non-impact exercises such as stretching and some minimal work with weights. Absolutely no running! If I try to run only a few yards, the pain level increases substantially. There is always a direct correlation—running equals pain and suffering. Usually the pain gets worse for two or three days.

So how do we understand that I had just run about three miles without stopping and had no experience of pain? I had absolutely no physical consequences as a result of what I had put my body through during that chase. Not then, nor during the following days. Little Feather had taught me about "whale-ness"—a lesson about the enormous capabilities that our inner healer has in reserve. More particularly, Feather taught me that love is the power needed to tap that reserve. It was my unqualified and uncompromised love for Diana, my absolute focus and determination not to have my lover experience a saddening loss, that apparently were the reasons I could sprint for about three miles without having any physical consequences whatsoever.

Remember my "big dream," my seminal life-defining dream of

the Architect in my basement that I shared earlier? It would seem that dreams of that magnitude just keep on revealing insight after insight, time after time, year after year. In this instance, it felt that the Architect (symbolic of God, the "designer" of my inner healer) showed me one more room in my "house" that I previously had not known was there. One more time I was taught that our innate capabilities, our "standard equipment," exceeds our previous awareness.

In that experience, Feather taught me about whale-ness, and the Architect introduced me to a new and larger soul-self—one that includes my inner healer. All of us have profoundly powerful and generally unrecognized healing capacities within us. What we will be exploring in this chapter and the next are the ways we have ignored, trivialized, or drugged that inner healer into a stupor, and the ways that we can begin to awaken to and facilitate that inner power.

In this chapter we will examine specifically the medical as well as the religious relationships with our inner healer, a past that worked against acknowledging such inner power, as well as glimmers of a new dawn and an emerging future of awakening to these previously untapped potentialities.

Slumbering in the Medical Slums

I have come to believe that [the] depreciation of the power of the patient is a symptom of a larger crisis in American medicine.

HERBERT BENSON, M.D.

You would think that any profession dedicated to healing would be open to anything that could promote health, prevent illness, and enable creative healing processes. You would be wrong. As with any profession, physicians have been prisoners of paradigms that can limit, constrict, and restrict, as well as sometimes liberate, their very purpose.

The inner healer has been slumbering in the medical slums—frequently out of sight and out of mind, ignored, trivialized, denied, denigrated, drugged, and told to stay out of the way so that the medical system could do its job. Some medical professionals act as if they, with their expert knowledge, technology, and pharmacology, are in charge. We are to be but passive receivers of their largess.

Before I get into this subject, however, I want to make an important qualifier. I am talking here more about paradigms than individual persons, more about the indictment of historical and cultural influences, than of particular physicians. Certainly, individual physicians are the ones who perpetrate the paradigm, but there have been many individual doctors who have transcended the paradigmatic box with unusually large hearts and minds.

I have been privileged to know and work with some exceptional physicians and want to applaud their courage. For many, in doing so, have suffered slings and arrows from outrageous professional paradigm protectors. So let's be clear about this: it is the *general influence of the medical paradigm* we are talking about here, not the exceptional individual physician. The former needs to be recognized for its deleterious and disempowering effects, the latter to be praised for her or his vision, courage, and compassion.

Consider, therefore, the historical, philosophical, and paradigmatic reasons that the institution of healthcare in general, and many in the medical profession in particular, have denied, denigrated, trivialized, and grossly underutilized our built-in capacities for health promotion, disease prevention, and self-healing.

M.D.'S AS FIELD GENERALS IN A WAR

Medicine favors the language and atmosphere of warfare, and we should not be surprised, given how physicians are trained. In a virtual boot-camp atmosphere, hospital interns, physicians-in-training, are tested with unnatural sleep deprivation. In order to earn their stripes as medical professionals, they have to be ready and able to treat the "wounded" for as many as forty-eight hours or more at a time and without sleep. It's akin to a battlefield emergency situation. Fatigued M.D.'s in white coats may not look like G.I.'s in battle fatigues, but the levels of stress may be similar. Is it any wonder that one medical student, in his graduation speech, said that "medical school felt like a family where the mother was gone and only the hard father remained at home.?"[1]

Being trained as if stress is the primary badge of courage and sleeplessness is the Holy Grail, is it any wonder that the United States "loses the equivalent of seven medical-school graduating classes each year to drug addiction, alcoholism, and suicide?"[2] Is it any wonder that the survivors of that stressful battlefield medical preparatory school become very familiar with, and have a preference for, battlefield terminology?

Cancer is probably the disease that receives the most declarations of war and warfare terminology. When our medical warlords determine that a tumor has "invaded" the body, like field generals they give orders, bring out their awesome technological weaponry, target the enemy, use radiation as nuclear bombardment, engage in chemical warfare, ask us to submit to surgical strikes, and search for the magic bullet.

As Herbert Benson of Harvard Medical School observes, "Doctors in Europe send patients to government-financed spas to relax and heal, a practice that's virtually unheard of in the States."[3] We should not be surprised. After all, relaxing in a hot tub is no way to fight a war!

The point is that, once war is declared, "civilians" are supposed to get out of the way and leave both the strategy and the execution of the war to the generals. Amateurs must move aside, for this is a job for highly trained experts! All of this tends to leave out, or at least to trivialize, the natural, internal, and innate capabilities for healing that each of us has.

Linda Quigley, however, a Pulitzer Prize-nominated journalist in Nashville, Tennessee, did not go along with the declaration of war when she was diagnosed with breast cancer:

> "War is hell," she said. "So, no, I don't think I'll enlist."
>
> Granted, the diagnosis of a life-threatening illness is tantamount to a draft notice, and to keep from joining the fight, you will probably need to reject some established medical thinking. . . .
>
> For me, treatment began with surgery, followed by six months of chemotherapy, then seven weeks of radiation.
>
> Was it a battle plan? Did it establish a line of defense? Would it be a fight to the finish?
>
> No.
>
> It was a rite of passage, moving into the next phase of a journey that would take me toward wholeness—minus a breast, but whole nevertheless. . . .
>
> I'm a conscientious objector and I won't go to war with you.
> But, hey, I'm always up for a picnic. Just let me get my hat.[4]

Another cancer patient in Nashville, Carol Matzkin Orsborn, an author and a public-relations executive, had a similar revulsion to the warlike terminology and searched for a more inspirational and life giving metaphor. "Could my breast cancer," she wondered, "be a spiritual initiation into deeper levels of understanding and experience, and not a battle to be waged against the enemy?" She, like her friend Linda Quigley, favored the metaphor of initiation:

> Unlike survivors who have battled their cancer to emerge victoriously unchanged, I have been cracked open to the very core of my being. But it is through these cracks, in the fertile ground of my vulnerable heart, that the tender sprouts of music, poetry, love, and friendship have taken root. . . . I was healing myself of cancer, not as a soldier, but as an initiate.[5]

Susan Kuner, with a doctorate in education and the director of Vanderbilt University's Virtual School in Tennessee, also liked the initiate metaphor better than the one of war:

> I did not feel like a warrior. I am naturally more curious than combative, more a student that a conqueror. I did not want to fight. I wanted to understand. . . . The initiate is poised to learn the language of faith and the science of the heart, to drown in unknowing and become transformed.[6]

In contrast to her friends, Karen Leigh Stroup, began her confrontation with cancer as a warrior. The ordained Disciples of Christ minister and spiritual guide, with a doctorate in religious studies from Vanderbilt University, recalls that:

> I bought into the military terminology for treatment at first. That is partly because that was all I had ever heard. I was a warrior, I told myself, fighting the cancer battle. I hoped to achieve victory on the battlefield and become a "survivor." I bought the video game "Doom" and visualized all the aliens I was killing as cancer cells. I read the psalms in which the speaker asks God to wreak vengeance on her enemies. For the first time in my life, I thought "Onward, Christian Soldiers" was an appropriate hymn. I found a picture of a breast cancer cell in a women's magazine and put it on a dart board. I was a warrior, no doubt about it. . . .
>
> But I realized one day that such language was doing me no good. The fact is that my cancer is not cured, it is not technically in remission, and I have a terminal prognosis. So I have "lost the war."
>
> In the wartime vocabulary of cancer treatment, I am a loser. I have been defeated.
>
> So why is it that I am a better person, a stronger person, a person who does not at all feel like a loser or a victim? I am a different person, but it is not because I have spent time as a soldier.
>
> It came to me slowly that battle imagery would not work for me. . . . I found my vocabulary, my way to speak about cancer treatment, in the world of faith, in the vocabulary of initiation.[7]

What all four of these women have in common, besides having breast cancer and living in Nashville, Tennessee, is that they are friends and co-authors of a marvelous book, *Speak the Language of Healing: Living with Breast Cancer without Going to War.*

With courage and creativity, each of them found her own way out of the medical paradigm of warfare terminology, as well as the cultural assumptions of being either a victim or survivor relying solely on technological and/or chemical interventions, and into an effective initiatory process with her inner healer. Whatever the future may hold regarding their cancers, they have transcended the options of victim or survivor—they have grown their soul-selves into a new level of meaning and purpose in life. They have engaged in a creative process with their inner healer.

M.D.'S (MAJOR DEITIES) TREATING P.P'S (PASSIVE PATIENTS)

> *The medical profession is unconsciously irritated by lay knowledge.*
>
> JOHN STEINBECK

There are two particular forces within the doctor-patient relationship that work against our inner healer's being fully empowered. One is the all-too-often arrogant attitude on the part of the physician. This, too, is encouraged by the very process of medical education. Recall the graduation speech by a medical student that was mentioned above? In that speech he went on to say, after reflecting on the boot-camp atmosphere with extreme sleep deprivation:

> [If] . . . we succeed in driving ourselves, keeping our performance up to snuff, then we begin to see ourselves as a separate breed, superior to the rest of humankind. This display of superhuman endurance . . . ultimately manifests as contempt for those patients who complain about their life and troubles on a cushy eight hours of sleep. In some of us it leads to arrogance.[8]

Interestingly enough, two different well-known physicians, in two separate books, use the same term in describing physician's "all-knowing" attitude. Harvard's Herbert Benson writes, "Too often, I'm afraid, an all-knowing attitude is cultivated in physicians,"[9] and

Christiane Northrup, former president of the American Holistic Medical Association writes, "As a physician, I was trained to be paternalistic, the all-knowing outside expert."[10]

The other half of a doctor-patient relationship that ignores the inner healer is the overly passive patient. There is an understandable tendency, when one is desperately ill or receiving a shattering medical prognosis, to return to a childlike state of wanting a paternal authority figure to take charge and to make it all right. Physicians may sometimes encourage dependency on the part of the patient, but it would not work if patients did not accept, indeed encourage, a subservient and passive role.

There is also the intimidation of an increasingly sophisticated mechanized, technological, and pharmacological emphasis within medicine. This all works to shift authority in the direction of the trained, knowledgeable, and skilled professional. The point, of course, is not to do away with beneficial knowledge and effective technology and medications—the point is an attitude of total control and authority on the part of the physician, versus total and passive submission on the part of the patient. That kind of relationship results in our standing on a whale fishing for minnows!

It is possible to have a productive teamwork between a knowledgeable physician consultant, who can advise regarding the technology and pharmacology that might be of benefit, and an empowered and awakened inner healer. Together, we can have one whale of a potential for health promotion, disease prevention, and utilizing our enormous healing capabilities.

THE SCIENTIFIC METHOD

I'm not going to get into any "M.D." machinations or wordplay on this subject. This is an even larger and in some ways a more insidious influence for ignoring unique individuality than what we have considered so far. It goes right to the very root of the process we have considered necessary in order to "prove" something medically and scientifically. Scientific proof has been the verification we have usually needed in order to consider something medically "true," "legitimate," or "safe." The problem is that it fundamentally ignores the individual, unique, "soul-print" of our inner healer.

I am not suggesting that we throw out the scientific method. Unquestionably, it has brought us great benefits. This discussion is not about having *either* scientific verification *or* the recognition of individual uniqueness. It is both. If we are not to be simply blind worshipers at the scientific altar, we should be able to consider carefully both the value *and* the limitations of the scientific method. In other words, we should be able to realize that science is good for some things, but it is not good for some others. Let's recognize and praise it for what it can accomplish, while being of clear sight and mind regarding what it, by its very nature, overlooks, underestimates, trivializes, and marginalizes.

Science is good at determining statistically significant generalities—it is not good at leading us into a high valuation of particularity. For example, science may establish that with such-and-such diagnosis, ninety-five percent of the patients will die within two years. What science cannot tell us is why the five percent live longer or why a few particular individuals have a total, apparently mysterious cure. It is perhaps understandable that medical science wants to focus upon what is "true" for the largest number, but that tendency fails to give adequate attention to the exceptional.

If your experience does not conform to the statistically significant group analysis, chances are you will be ignored or forgotten. Or worse, your experience will be thought, by some, to be illegitimate, made up, exaggerated, or simply misdiagnosed in the first place.

The scientific method also has a very strong bias for repeatability—validity of a given "truth" is based upon whether or not it can be repeated. This bias shows little interest in mystery, individuality, uniqueness, and novelty. The assumption is that if it can't be replicated, it is not "true."

My primary concern here has to do with our attitudes—attitudes that either affirm and awaken our powerful inner healer or attitudes that deny and constrict that power. In a culture that tends to worship science, tends to think that the scientific method is the be-all and end-all, we too easily slip into the assumption that only that which can be proven by science is actually "true," "legitimate," or valid." By definition, therefore, an individual's spirituality, which does not conform to any group, is untrue, illegitimate, or invalid. Consequently, when healing is exceptional, unique, novel, individual, and unorthodox, it is often discounted as "merely anecdotal." We almost never hear a scientist or physician speak of something as being "merely scientific." Yet medical science describes tendencies, not certainties, and it is only the "true believer," with the perpetual paradigmatic blinders on, who assumes the two are synonymous.

Something does not have to happen in a high percentage of cases, or to be repeatable, to be true or valid. One life in which an inexplicable and miraculous healing occurs has its own "proof" or validation. A life has been changed. A dramatic healing can happen only once and still be legitimate—certainly just as valid for that particular person as the healing of a thousand persons. We should not let our reasons for looking at generalities and replications, good though they may be, have us overlook the value of affirming and facilitating a very personal and, perhaps, a very singular experience.

Marilyn Koering is a case in point. She had been one of twenty women, all with "incurable" melanoma, participating in an experimental chemotherapy protocol. The other nineteen died rather quickly and proved to the researchers that the experimental drug was useless. Marilyn, however, lived on . . . and on . . . and on. Ten years after the others had died, Marilyn observed, "In these studies, people are treated en masse, not as individuals." Consequently, even though she defied the odds, the medical researchers were basically uninterested. "My care in the last few years has been zero. They've literally dumped me," she reports.[11]

Marc Ian Barasch and Caryl Hirshberg, as mentioned earlier, studied a large number of people who defied the medical odds and lived through what they called "remarkable recovery." Summing up Marilyn Koering's story along with the others they had researched, they concluded that "simply being treated as a unique individual, not a disease category or an errant statistic in a treatment protocol . . . [was] . . . the most frequently cited healing force we encountered in our research."[12]

Marilyn Koering was not only a cancer patient but also a professor of anatomy at George Washington University. She brought to her reflections, therefore, both a patient's and a scientist's perspective. One of the primary things she learned in her experience, and from her observations regarding others, was that ". . . the uniqueness of each human being may dictate their course."

Cultures that are overly worshipful of the scientific method value conformity over the exceptional, the group over the individual, commonality over uniqueness. All this tends to marginalize and trivialize the spiritual and the role that an individual's soul journey has in her or his health history.

Religions, by their very nature, emphasize commonality and conformity, just as does the scientific method. That is precisely why recent scientifically legitimate research has been possible in determining the link between religious activity—church attendance, prayer, etc.—and health or illness. But at its deepest realms, spirituality is very personal, particular, individual, unreproducible, unorthodox, unconventional, and unconforming.

There may be common elements to the physical, spiritual, religious, and psychological realms; but the really important stuff, the life-changing epiphanies, enlightenments, awakenings, conversions, or the deepest healings—*that* level is always personal, unique, unusual, and wonderfully anecdotal. By its very nature, it can't be replicated. Our souls are on the path, taking a journey, and each day that one lives, each step one takes, one is encountering new and different holy ground. It is the new and different holy ground of our beingness that, in part, is what makes some healings miraculous and unreproducible.

As Dr. Christiane Northrup reflects:

> Ultimately, I've found it enormously empowering to realize that no scientific study can explain exactly how and why my own particular body acts the way it does. Only our connection with our own inner guidance and our emotions are reliable in the end. That is because we each comprise a multitude of processes that have never existed before and never will again. Science must acknowledge truthfully how much it doesn't know and leave room for mystery, miracles, and the wisdom of nature.[13]

This entire chapter, and the next, are clarion calls for valuing, liberating, awakening, and facilitating the very idiosyncratic, eccentric, creative, maverick, novel, and potentially unrepeatable one-time-only experience of healing—those unique powers of the person that usually lie quietly and undetected in that whale of our inner healer.

Delightfully, there is growing evidence that the "new medicine" is awakening to that whale's existence.

Medicine Discovers the Whale

> *Each of us possesses an awesome healing power. . . . You are an authority on what will hurt or heal you. . . . Don't let any physician or healer, fortune-teller or card-reader, preacher or teacher, magazine story or medical book, friend or lover, therapist or support group impress something untrue upon you.*
>
> HERBERT BENSON, M.D.

The whale of our inner potential has been swimming in our depths all along, but medicine, generally speaking, has not been looking down there or in there. Nevertheless, and somewhat ironically, research that suggested the existence of the whale has been around for a long time—it's just that, until recently, too few researchers and/or physicians had any interest for looking into those watery depths.

Delightfully, however, we now have more and more medical graduates from the "James Ballard School of Medicine"—so named, in my frequently flippant mind, after the famous oceanographer and "aquanaut" who discovered life where there was not supposed to be any, at the bottom of the oceans. Increasingly, we have medical "psychonauts" who are intentionally plumbing the depths of the human psyche and discovering the whale of an inner healer that has been down there all along.

The whale is so huge, the medical deep-sea divers now so numerous, and the literature so vast that entire books are written on virtually each and every part of the whale's anatomy. We cannot and need not examine all the wonderful and relatively recent attention that has been given to the person's emotional states, personality traits, and energy systems. There is a fascinating literature dealing with miracle healings and miracle woundings (stigmata), just as there is seminal research throughout the important new science of psychoneuroimmunology, or PNI.

It has been only relatively recently that medicine realized that the psyche, the neurological system, and the immunological system of the human body were all interrelated. For a long time, medicine thought that the mind (psyche) and the body (soma) were connected only on a small portion of disease states. We, the general public, bought into that idea to the point that, if our physician told us we had a "psychosomatic" illness, we thought she was saying that it wasn't "real" or that it was "all in my head." We thought that "psychosomatic" meant that an illness was "caused" by the mind. Now we are learning that the appropriate definition of "psychosomatic" is the recognition that the mind, body, and soul are all interconnected in *every* state of health or illness.

Robert Ader, of Rochester Medical School and one of the leading researchers in psychoneuroimmunology, shows where we have come in our understanding of the body-mind-spirit synergy when he writes, "There's no such thing as psychosomatic illness. To say that there is suggests that there are some diseases that are not. All disease development is influenced by psychologic factors. The only question is how much; some are more influenced than others."[14]

As mentioned before, more research studies regarding the connection between religion and health have taken place in the past decade than in all previous decades put together. New attention has been given to the healing effects of forgiveness and compassion, as well as the deleterious effects of anger and hostility. A long history of research demonstrates how stress participates in virtually every disease and predominates in most. The estimates of illnesses that are stress related vary from sixty to ninety percent.

Nevertheless, the strictly materialistic way of thinking about health and illness continues. Consider the attention given the Human Genome Project, and the claim, sometimes implicit and sometimes very explicit, that our genes determine our experience of health or illness. Grandiose claims have been made about finding the gene that "causes" this or that disease—and if an expert says it, we tend to believe it.

The New England Journal of Medicine, however, recently published a study, the largest of its kind to date, that puts the materialistic paradigm in its place—a very small place, at that. It seems that Paul Lichtenstein, an epidemiologist at the Karolinska Institute in Stockholm, and his colleagues found that the idea that we will find a solution to our diseases primarily in our genes simply does not hold up to careful scrutiny. General estimates regarding the influence of genetics in cancer had been running anywhere from ten to forty percent. But in a study of almost 45,000 sets of identical twins, looking particularly for the connection between genes and cancer, Lichtenstein and his colleagues found that, if one twin developed breast, colorectal or prostate cancer, her or his genetically identical twin had only a eleven to eighteen percent chance of developing the same cancer before age 75.[15]

The point for our discussion is that our inner healer—all our psychological, emotional, and spiritual capabilities—plays a very substantial role in preventing illness and in the processes of healing. The physical aspects of health and illness have received most of the attention, but the metaphysical is profoundly influential.

It is probably obvious, given my personal history, as to why I would choose to illustrate this particular section with a focus upon the incredible power of mental imagery. Meditative imagery, as you may recall, was powerfully involved in my miraculous breakthrough while attending the medical conference in Park City, Utah. The power of mental imagery can be found in biofeedback research, clinical and experimental hypnosis, endorphin research, and stress research. I would submit that the research suggesting the healing power of "faith" is also verification regarding the power of the image held deeply, even unconsciously. I am particularly fascinated with the revelations in placebo research (from the Latin "to please") and nocebo research ("to harm").

As is commonly known, placebo research has been around for a long time; but as Howard Brody, M.D., one of the leading investigators of the placebo response, says, "The usual randomized, double-blind, placebo-controlled study is designed for one purpose only: to demonstrate whether or not the experimental drug causes patients to get better. What happens to the subjects in the placebo group, and why, is of no interest."[16]

The placebo group may not have been of interest to conventional medical researchers in the past, but it is precisely where my interests lie. For there we get a glimpse of the enormous power that resides in our inner healer.

If we go back to the 1950s, a time when the medical ethics code was not as developed as it is today, we can find a particularly revealing experiment. It was a time before today's techniques of coronary bypass surgery; and, in fact, most surgery directly on the heart and its vessels was impossible.

The idea that the mammary arteries in the chest might be diverting too much blood away from the heart fascinated some physicians. If this was the case, then the intervention called for would be to tie off those mammary arteries, thus, presumably, sending more blood to the heart.

The procedure was tried, and it appeared to work. In addition, the beneficial effects lasted for many months, and as Brody reports, "it seemed that this relatively minor surgery was going to be the miracle cure for angina." Brody tells the rest of the story:

> Then a few skeptical, and brave, surgeons began to have doubts about the procedure. They took advantage of the lax ethical standards of the day and didn't tell their subjects the truth about what was being done to them. Operations were performed on a number of patients in the same fashion that mammary artery ligation had always been performed, with one exception: They did not tighten the stitch placed around the mammary artery. The patients, waking up, had scars on their chests and pain from the incision, and thought that they had had the regular surgery; but in truth just as much blood was flowing through their mammary arteries as before. Yet these placebo-surgery patients reported almost exactly the same spectacular results as the previous patients, in terms of pain relief, increased exercise ability, and length of improvement. And just as many of them—two-thirds or more—seemed to get good results as in the "real" surgery group.[17]

Surgery is a powerful placebo, for you have every reason to believe that something *really important* has been done to you. The placebo response, of course, is tied to your positive expectation, the image you hold in your mind about what benefit you *expect* to happen. Brody, who holds a Ph.D. as well as an M.D., and who is one of the leading experts on the placebo response, points out that various investigators have found out some of what increases the power of that expectant image. Interestingly enough . . .

> capsules tend to work better than tablets; . . . injections tend to work better than drugs taken by mouth; and . . . injections that sting work better than painless injections. . . . [P]lacebos taken four times a day seem to be more effective than placebos taken twice a day . . . [and] . . . blue, green, and purple [capsules] seem to work especially well as sedatives and sleeping pills, while red, yellow, and orange seem to work best as stimulants or energy-boosters.[18]

What is particularly important for our discussion here is what placebo research indicates about the inner power we possess. That powerful inner healer appears to be awakened by what we expect. Importantly, that power can be tapped voluntarily and intentionally. In other words, we can learn something valuable from the placebo research and yet be able to utilize that inner power without having to be tricked into it. That is precisely what I do for pain management, and so can you.

I do not believe it was just a coincidence that I had read widely throughout the relevant medical literature and experimented with personal intentionality in both biofeedback and hypnosis training before I experienced my miraculous breakthrough in pain management. I had become convinced that to use some of my mental abilities I had to teach some other abilities to relax and get out of the way. Specifically, I had learned that my left-brained capabilities of rationality, the abilities of logical, skeptical, analytical, and intellectual engagement with a subject, so trained in the processes of "higher" and "graduate" education, would not be the abilities that would be most effective in pain management. Ironically, it was my left brain that eventually convinced me that, to be effective in pain management, I had to create the opportunity wherein I could rest the left brain and activate the right brain's imagistic wonders.

Specifically, I had been experimenting with, and practicing over and over, the meditation techniques of deep relaxation, deep slow breathing, and focused concentration on a selected image. The one I found most helpful for pain management was that of imagining that with each inhalation I was gathering all the pain in my body into my lungs, so that with each exhalation I was sending it out away from my body. I *believed* that my body would be freed of pain through that process. And it worked—then and now.

Interesting medical research in 1990s indicated the same basic insight—that expectant imagery can be powerful even when not tricked. That through intentionality and volition, one can focus an image that has powerful mind-body action. In one particular case, an experiment used a sham procedure on the now-common arthroscopic knee surgery for degenerative arthritis. In this experiment, however, patients had the benefit of full disclosure.

All of the patients involved in this experiment were told in advance that the experiment involved three kinds of "surgery" and that they would not know which kind they were receiving. One-third of the group would have the full surgery, involving inserting the scope into the knee and scraping down any cartilage that needed it. Another third would experience the scope inserted, but no scraping. The final group would only have nicks on the knee so that it looked as if it had been scoped, although it had not been.

All of the subjects had been fully informed of the fact that only one-third of them would get the actual surgery, which ostensibly was the only way to help their knees. In other words, they all knew that two-thirds of them would not receive any surgery that would be helpful; they just did not know which group they would be in. They all gave their consent. The results were, to say the least, interesting—"no significant difference in outcome among the three groups."[19]

Expectation and the image we hold in our minds and hearts are powerful and influential, whether that image is positive or negative. This power can work either way, depending on how it is directed.

One of the most fascinating stories of the negative placebo response—what is called a "nocebo" response—was experienced by the renowned cardiologist Dr. Bernard Lown. Early in his career, Lown was working under a distinguished professor of cardiology at Harvard, Dr. S. A. Levine. This particular story involved a women, simply referred to as "Mrs. S.," who had a non-life-threatening condition of the heart-valve, which in medical terminology is called "tricuspid stenosis," but among physicians often abbreviated to simply "TS."

Ms. S. was "a well-preserved middle-aged librarian" who was "able to maintain her job and attend efficiently to household chores." She had come into the hospital for some routine procedures but not because of any unusual complications. Dr. Levine, was conducting "class" for a number of visiting physicians, going from room to room, offering succinct bits of diagnosis and advice. Dr. Lown describes what happened when Dr. Levine and his visiting physicians entered Ms. S.'s hospital room.:

> Dr. Levine, who had followed her in the clinic for more than a decade, greeted Mrs. S. warmly and then turned to the large entourage of visiting physicians and said, "This woman has TS," and abruptly left.
>
> No sooner was Dr. Levine out of the door than Mrs. S.'s demeanor abruptly changed. She appeared anxious and frightened and was now breathing rapidly, clearly hyperventilating. Her skin was drenched with perspiration, and her pulse had accelerated to more than 150 a minute. In reexamining her, I found it astonishing that the lungs, which a few minutes earlier had been quite clear, now had moist crackles at the bases. This was extraordinary, for with obstruction of the right heart valve, the lungs are spared the accumulation of excess fluid.
>
> I questioned Mrs. S. as to the reasons for her sudden upset. Her response was that Dr. Levine had said that she had TS, which she knew meant "terminal situation." I was initially amused at this misinterpretation of the medical acronym for "tricuspid stenosis."
>
> My amusement, however, rapidly yielded to apprehension, as my words failed to reassure and as her congestion continued to worsen. Shortly thereafter she was in massive pulmonary edema.

> Heroic measures did not reverse the frothing congestion. . . . Later that same day she died from intractable heart failure.[20]

It is the power of the expectant or desired image that one holds within one's mind and heart, and particularly if powerfully concentrated and believed in, that we find substantiated in the recent prayer research. Perhaps no one has summarized that research as thoroughly and effectively as has Dr. Larry Dossey. But, precisely because the impact can be either positive or negative, Dossey points out that we should "be careful what we pray for." Dossey has been one of the most important pioneers in helping us realize that our imagery and words that express that imagery in prayer are powerful not only for ourselves but for others "at a distance." I will reflect momentarily on the theological implications for what he calls "non-locality."

We can see many ways in which contemporary medicine and an increasing number of courageous and pioneering physicians are recognizing the enormous power that each of us holds within. The materialistic and mechanistic paradigm, the conservative pace of medical change, and the all-too-frequently encountered arrogant physician have been easy targets throughout the past half-century when many times lay people were out ahead of the so-called experts. But to revisit a theme I touched on earlier, the saving grace is that medicine has an evolutionary soul accustomed to questioning and questing, challenging and changing. Thus, the changes in medicine have been real and substantive. I have serious concern, however, as to whether the religious and spiritual professionals and institutions will be able to change and grow similarly into the magnificent new synergy that is possible for health promotion, disease prevention, and for the processes of healing.

If we are to discover maximum human health and well-being, a courageous, growing, and changing medicine needs to be partnered with an equally courageous, growing, and changing spirituality. To do so, however, religions and spiritualities will have to throw off the shackles of their traditional commitment to stasis. The old assumptions that religious truth is static, that something decades old is better than a new vision, that centuries old is better than decades old, and better yet, millennia of stasis is the ultimate. As long as religions think that God was somehow more present two or five thousand years ago than is the case today, and as long as religions act as if spiritual truth is absolutely static and never-changing, religions and the spiritualities facilitated by those religions will miss out on an incredible opportunity that is presented at this time in history—a full understanding of how spirituality and medicine can create a powerful partnership in the interest of health.

Traditional chaplaincy and parish nurse programs have played important roles in the past, and do so today. We need, however, to increase the understanding and facilitation of the inner healer among those serving in these important capacities. There are powerful opportunities in the religious and spiritual aspects of healing that are not, as yet, being fully utilized. My hope is that this book serves to bring some of that into both discussion and effective manifestation.

Religions and the Whale

Hidden deep within the Hebrew Bible, just after Obadiah and just before Micah, is a brief story of just over two pages in length. Virtually all of us know it. It is the story of God, Jonah, and the whale. Consider its adaptation to the theme of this chapter.

The Call

The story begins with God's telling Jonah to go to Nineveh, for there is an important mission for him there. A significant point is that Jonah's call involved going somewhere. It was not a request to stand still on a soapbox and utter some proclamations—he was supposed to get up and go, to get moving, to pack his bags, and to head out for Nineveh.

I would suggest that there is an historic call from God, in our particular time in history, regarding a spiritual mission in health care. Medicine is beginning to hear it—but are the religious institutions who claim to be the primary cultural means of facilitating spirituality, or even all the individualized spiritualities, hearing it?

It is particularly baffling when we find Christian graduate theological education, clergy, and churches ignoring this call. After all, there is little debate that Jesus, the person around whom the Christian faith is ostensibly centered, had healing as a prominent part of his ministry. Yet, by and large, the clergy has left healing to the physicians. There are, of course, exceptions, but the point here is that they are still exceptional. It is not my intention to explore all the stories of Jesus' healing in any depth or detail, but one particular story illustrates two particularly relevant facts:

(1) Jesus was no kin to the Very Right Reverend Rigor Mortis. Jesus clearly had a spirituality "on the grow." He often remarked, "You have heard it said of old . . . but I say unto you," and then he would offer a new and a different perspective. He explicitly challenged the prevailing belief system regarding healing and consistently defied traditional religious law.

(2) Jesus appeared to have enormous trust in the innate healer within each of us.

The particular story to which I refer is found in the Gospel of John 5:1–9. Perhaps you recall how it went—a man had been sick for thirty-eight years, had found his way to the place where, as tradition had it, healing was available—the pool at Bethesda.

To understand the real significance of the story, we need to understand fully what the prevailing belief system about healing was at the time. The belief was that periodically the angel of the Lord would take a bath in that particular pool, and the evidence that that was taking place was when the waters were "disturbed." The first person who made it into the pool after the angel bathed, so the belief went, would be healed.

Jesus, who certainly would have known about the prevailing belief system regarding healing and this particular pool, came along and confronted this fellow. The story suggests that Jesus also knew that the man had been sick for thirty-eight years. How impudent on Jesus' part, therefore, to ask the man, "Do you want to be healed?"

Paraphrasing the guy's response, we can hear him saying, with considerable defensive energy, "Well, what do you think? Of course, I want to be healed! I've been sick for thirty-eight years, and I'm sick and tired of being sick and tired. I have come to where healing takes place, haven't I? But, you see, my problem is this—every time the angel of the Lord takes a bath, I try to get into the pool first, but someone else beats me to it. And, you know, only the first one in gets healed."

What is particularly interesting in this story is that Jesus did not buy into the traditional belief system at all. Had he done so, he could have acted in a wonderfully compassionate way by telling the man that he would stick close to him so that, the next time the angel bathed, he would help him get into the pool first. Jesus, however, ignored that option.

Instead of going along with a belief system that put the healing power outside the person, he apparently knew that the most loving and compassionate action was to empower the man with his own internal healing capabilities. Jesus knew that God had created within this man, and within all of us, one whale of an inner healer. According to the story, Jesus just told the man to get up and walk away. By implication, and the guy "got it," Jesus was saying, "You have the ability yourself. You don't need the external healing powers of the angel. Use what God has put within you—walk away from this place and this illness." The man did so, and he was healed.

Jesus was way ahead of his time. There was no judgment involved in his relationship with this guy—Job's friends were not his model counselors. Nor did he assume that healing comes primarily from the outside, as the modern medical model has emphasized. In this particular story, Jesus did not touch the man. He apparently, and simply, told the man that he had enormous healing capabilities himself. Get up, use those capabilities, and get on with your life.

Getting back to Jonah's story, the "call" today, to both medicine and religion, is to get on the move, for an important mission lies over there. And the "over there" is the Nineveh of the newest and best insights into the role of spirituality in healing—divine capabilities that are built into each and every person. That calls for both medicine and religion to make a move.

REFUSING THE CALL

The prominent part of the Jonah story is that he tried to refuse and reject the call. He tried to run from it. He set out for Tarshish, thinking he could "escape from the Lord." But I've got to tell you, Jonah, that is flat-out dumb. For if you knew that God resides within each of us, you would know that trying to run away just doesn't accomplish an escape. We take God with us whereever we try to run and hide.

So God sent a hurricane to show Jonah that his attempt at running away from the call was not a viable option. Trying his best not to hear even this message, Jonah goes down into a deep corner of the ship and tries to sleep through it.

The sailors, knowing that the hurricane had more to do with Jonah than the rest of them confronted him. Actually, in a rare moment of courage and responsibility, Jonah told the sailors to throw him overboard so that the hurricane would subside. They did so, and you know the rest of the story. A big fish—we usually interpret that to mean a whale—swallowed Jonah. In a curious parallel to the Christian metaphor of Jesus' spending three days in hell after his crucifixion before ascending into heaven, Jonah spent three days in the belly of the whale. The whale then "spewed Jonah out on to the dry land," and he finally answered the call and went to Nineveh to fulfill his mission.

We are currently at a time in history when religions have a tremendous opportunity to become a full partner with medicine in facilitating the role that spirituality plays in health and illness—if they do not refuse the "call" and try to sleep through the storm. There are, in particular, three ways that religions, if they stick with the prevailing belief system of the Very Right Reverend Rigor Mortis, are refusing to hear and are avoiding the movement necessary to respond to the "call" of our time.

Avoidance # 1—separating the physical and metaphysical: Throughout the history of today's major world religions, there has been the reductionistic propensity to separate spirituality and physicality, the so-called immortal soul and the mortal body, psyche and soma. After the Enlightenment, it became even more deeply entrenched.

This has led often to the feelings that the body is not really important and that it is only a temporary vessel for the really important stuff, the soul. It has resulted in the fear and rejection of sexuality and sensuality—that being part of the "depraved" human. It has let itself play the same game as did materialistic medicine—that physical illness is strictly a physiological matter and clearly distinct and separate from the spiritual or metaphysical. The result of both medicine's and religion's playing this game together has been a total disempowerment of our innate inner healer. Part of the challenging "call" today is seeing health and illness in a completely holistic and integrated fashion.

This story carries with it two subplots—one has to do with illness causation (the diagnosis) and the other with the process of healing (the prescription.)

If one comes down on either side of this simplistic separation of body and soul, one will never fully understand health and illness. In addition, a cop-out on the part of religious or spiritual people is that, if illness is strictly a physical matter, then we can leave it to the medical profession.

In reality, many factors usually contribute to our getting sick—including genetic, psychological, nutritional, environmental, geopolitical, economic, and spiritual factors. If we would get out of our intellectual need for simple and single answers, we would probably realize that the mix is very individual and personal. There is probably no way we can ever neatly break down the percentages regarding exactly how much of any illness is psychological, how much physical, how much nutritional, etc. One reason that we cannot is that the percentages would be different in every case.

The guild mentality—and the protection of professional turf—in both medical and theological graduate education works against overcoming this problem. The specialized disciplines in which the professors were trained have the momentum and the protective barriers. Until recently, you would seldom if ever find a theologically trained professor in a medical school. There have been a few pioneers, but very few. Nor would you find much medical knowledge among the faculty of a graduate theological school. But, and here's the rub, even if you did, chances are that he or she would have been trained in the old paradigm's categorical separation of physicality and spirituality.

Just as we saw earlier in this chapter, the discovery that genes control only a minor portion of disease causation brought the simplistic physicalists to their knees. Anyone familiar with those data cannot continue to claim that only physical factors are involved in someone's getting sick. So, too, must the overly simplistic spiritualists get off their high horse and stop asserting that spirituality is the one and only factor in disease. For a very long time, we have had religious people either leaving health and illness to the physicians or claiming that all illness is a result of the person's soul-level choice.

The prescription for regaining health and well-being obviously follows the diagnosis. What your belief is regarding why you get sick obviously leads to the way you think about getting well. If, for instance, you believe that your illness is of strictly physical causation and that your mind, emotions, spirituality, etc., had no role to play in it, then the only thing you can do is let the medical people treat the symptom. If, on the other hand, you believe that your illness is strictly spiritual in nature, then you would have no reason to go to physicians at all. Your prescription, in the latter case, would be to simply try to "get right with God."

The latter is what Job's friends did to him. "Your sickness and bad luck are clear evidence that you have sinned," they would say. "So, repent, and you will be well." But just because Job's friends did the personal responsibility thing poorly doesn't mean that all parts of us are not potentially involved in any or all illnesses. We must become more sophisticated in understanding the comprehensive factors in both causation and in healing, so as to be able to better facilitate people's inner healing capabilities.

If religious and spiritual people, as well as their institutions, continue to avoid this historic opportunity, they are missing a most important pastoral and compassionate opportunity. It involves claiming a degree of personal responsibility, however, and this has often been avoided because of fear about what is commonly referred to as "blaming the victim." It might be helpful for us to address that all-too-common barrier.

First of all, the issue of responsibility, at its best, is not about blame. Blaming and condemnation are simplistically arrogant, and the flip side of that, guilt, is not helpful in getting well. Secondly, it is usually not about victims, either. The entire issue of "blaming the victim" is wrong-headed and wrong-hearted. More importantly, it doesn't help us liberate and awaken our inner healer.

Just because Job's friends did it poorly, with all their simplistic association of sin and sickness, doesn't mean that spirituality is not involved in the causation of disease. We don't have to buy into judgment, guilt, and condemnation to accept what is becoming increasingly proven throughout the medical research literature—that spiritual issues such as love and forgiveness, hostility, isolation, meaning and purpose in life, all participate profoundly in our state of health or illness. And if we begin to shift from the simplistic "blame the victim" to an exploration of the ways in which we participate in getting sick, we will also discover new capabilities in how we can participate in getting well.

This is not to say that some people aren't victimized, with absolutely no personal participation in the causation whatsoever. The family on their way to church in Hawaii on December 7, 1941, did not "cause" the bombs to fly. The child who was incinerated on her way to school in Hiroshima had no responsibility for the dreadful decision to unleash the atomic bomb. The man who just happened to be living down-wind from Chernobyl did not cause his cancer. The woman raped in the night, the man on a flight to Cleveland on September 11, 2001, who looked out the window moments before crashing into the World Trade Center, or the woman rushing down the stairs in the World Trade Center on that fateful day when the entire building collapsed—these people were clearly victimized. The list could go on and on, for there is no shortage of people victimized by the actions of others or by being caught in a violent act of nature. That, however, is simply not what this discussion is about. What medical intuitive Caroline Myss calls "victimology" is what we are talking about—when we ignore or refuse to accept the responsibility we do have in getting or staying sick. "Woundology" is when we let our woundedness become our on-going identity, when our wound becomes our primary soul-self.

Only when we are freed up to explore fully the variety of ways that we participate in getting sick will we be able to explore fully the response-ability inherent in our inner healer. The former is linked with the latter—our awareness of why and how we get sick can lead our inner healer into the appropriate strategy for getting well. And the contrary is true—the extent that we refuse to consider our participation in getting sick is the extent to which we close off the opportunity for understanding how we can participate in getting well.

Avoidance # 2—a disempowering theology:

A second way religions avoid the current call of the Divine in the realm of health and illness is through the long habit of projecting the Divine up and away from ourselves. We discussed earlier the difference between the "theism" of a totally external God and the "panentheism" of an ever-present and thoroughly incarnated God. The point here, however, is that the former disempowers our inner healer, whereas the latter empowers us. Panentheism is the essential theology if we are to realize the full potential of our inner healer.

The idea that the Divine is incarnate within us is not new. Jesus said that God was in him and he in God. Unfortunately, most Christians think that "The Incarnation" has to do only with Jesus. Too many Christians for too many years thought that Jesus was of a totally different nature from the rest of us. Jesus was telling us what human nature was all about, and a lot of people thought he was just talking about himself, thus, tragically missing the point.

We hear an awakened incarnational theology that can liberate our inner healer being expressed by intellectual and spiritual giants, such as Emanuel Swedenborg, Sri Aurobindo, Alfred North Whitehead, Charles Hartshorne, and the man I consider to be one of the grandest living elder statesmen of theological genius, John B. Cobb Jr. In fact, the list could go on and on, for many of today's leading biblical and theological scholars, men and women alike, subscribe to such a panentheistic theology.

There is, I believe, a direct correlation between the extent to which we think of God as distant and the extent to which we disempower our inner healer. On the other hand, if we thoroughly know—I mean *really know*—that God permeates every aspect of our being, then we will know that the Divine has many miraculous healings awaiting us if we only explore that deep inner healer reservoir.

In contrast, when we project God on high and keep humanity distinct, separate, and on low, we then turn away from our highest and best capabilities. We fall into a kind of thinking that religions have all-too-often encouraged—that to think highly of one's own abilities is somehow blasphemous or irreligious. Religions, in the past, have often led us to believe that to affirm miraculous potentialities as being within, to believe we can tap into those potentialities without external mediation, is "not giving God credit." As a consequence, too many people have thought, tragically, that to be truly religious, they should deny, denigrate, ignore, and trivialize inner power.

The psychologist Abraham Maslow recognized this propensity to deny the best that we have within. He called it "The Jonah Complex."

> We fear our highest possibilities. . . . We are generally afraid to become that which we can glimpse in our most perfect moments, under the most perfect conditions, under conditions of great courage. We enjoy and even thrill to the godlike possibilities we see in ourselves in such peak moments. And yet we simultaneously shiver with weakness, awe, and fear before these very same possibilities.
>
> So often we run away from the responsibilities dictated (or rather suggested) by nature, by fate, even sometimes by accident, just as Jonah tried—in vain—to run away from his fate.[21]

Spiritual author Marianne Williamson also articulated this all-too-common yet spiritually toxic and disempowering self-deprecation:

> Our deepest fear is not that we are inadequate. Our deepest fear is that we are powerful beyond measure. It is our light, not our darkness, that most frightens us. . . . There's nothing enlightened about shrinking so that other people won't feel insecure around you. We are meant to shine. . . . We were born to make manifest the glory of God that is within us. It's not just in some of us; it's in everyone. And, as we let our own light shine, we unconsciously give other

people permission to do the same. As we're liberated from our own fear, our presence automatically liberates others.[22]

There is an interesting side note to Williamson's statement. This quote, for a period in the past, was frequently, and quite mistakenly, attributed to Nelson Mandela, who was then president of South Africa. It was such a persistent misattribution that *Common Boundary* magazine looked into it. Their research eventually reached Juan Henriquez, public-affairs officer at the South African Embassy, who set the record straight. "We have checked with the Office of the President, and they said [this quote] does not belong to the president."[23]

The existence of such a misattribution, and particularly its persistence, raises an interesting question. Could it be that the biblical writer of the Jonah story, as well as psychologist Abraham Maslow and author Marianne Williamson, all intuited and articulated something that was not only true but that holds such spiritual import that there is an unconscious desire for many people to attribute it to some high and lofty figure like Nelson Mandela? Could it be that, with all our fear of acknowledging inner power, that we think it would take some "larger-than-life" figure like Nelson Mandela, or an ancient biblical writer, or a dead psychological pioneer to challenge the traditional religious dogma?

Caroline Myss calls our time in history "the time of the conscious power of co-creation, the era of partnership between humanity and the Divine."[24]

In one very interesting study of 577 hospitalized patients, 55 years and older, it was found that those who conceived of God as a "collaborative partner" had better mental health than those who thought of God as distant.[25]

My not-too-distant neighbor, just a bit south along the Front Range of the Colorado Rocky Mountains, Joan Borysenko, indicates that studies conducted by the National Social Survey, based at the

University of Chicago, show that "people who have direct experiences of the sacred score at the top of the scale for mental health."[26]

A related theological issue to the disempowering notion of God on high and humanity on low is the consequential idea that humanity is inherently, thoroughly, and completely sinful and that our sin is so pervasive that we need saving from the outside. This issue is raised, by some, into being the very purpose of religion—to gain, from the outside, redemption from one's essential sinful nature. Salvation becomes the very purpose of religion for some, and it can only come from an external God or Savior, since, as this thinking goes, "there is no goodness within us."

There is no question but that this idea is losing credibility among many people, but there is also no question but that it has exerted a powerful influence for millennia. Like its theological parent of God on high and humanity on low, it has resulted in a devaluation of our inner healer.

Interestingly enough, although many Christians subscribed to the idea that salvation comes only from an external God and/or Savior, Jesus seems to have had a completely different notion of salvation. Jesus points to the territory of our inner healer: "If you bring forth what is within you, what you bring forth will save you. If you do not bring forth what is within you, what you do not bring forth will destroy you" (Gospel of Thomas 70:1–2).

Jesus' comment about salvation was echoed almost two millennia later, but from a psychological point of view, by the famous Swiss psychiatrist Carl Jung when he wrote, "The psychological rule says that when an inner situation is not made conscious, it happens outside, as fate."[27]

Avoidance # 3—hero worship:

The degree to which we worship an external hero, or an external Savior for that matter, is the degree to which we disempower, deny, and avoid utilizing the full potential of our inner healer. Once again, religious people have worshiped the spiritual giants around whom their religions were formed, even though that person spoke of how the spiritually advanced soul would do precisely the opposite. Personal veneration is not what Jesus or Buddha apparently wanted.

It is unlikely that either ever intended to start a religion and certainly did not want to be worshiped. Starting a religion that would venerate them as an external Savior or hero was the last thing on their minds.

Buddha, for instance, looked upon his own teaching as merely temporary assistance, to be eventually discarded, and certainly not as something to be worshiped. Karen Armstrong, in her great little book on the Buddha, points out how Buddha had no interest in his teachings being formed into dogma, doctrines, or creeds:

> To accept a doctrine on somebody else's authority was, in his eyes, an "unskilled" state, which could not lead to enlightenment, because it was an abdication of personal responsibility. . . . His own teachings must be jettisoned, once they had done their job.[28]

Buddha used a helpful teaching story to make his point. He told of a traveler who came to a river. To get across the river, he built a raft and rowed. Buddha would then ask his audience what they thought the traveler should do with the raft once arriving on the other side of the river—hoist it on his back and continue to carry the raft with him or leave it at the riverbank and move on? Buddha told the story in such a way as to make it sound rather ridiculous to carry the raft on one's back simply because it had been helpful in crossing the river.

> In just the same way," Buddha concluded, "*bhikku*s, my teachings are like a raft, to be used to cross the river and not to be held on to. If you understand their raft-like nature correctly, you will even give up good teachings *[dhamma*], not to mention bad ones!"[29]

Apparently, Jesus emphasized the same idea—a call, if you will, not to be a Son-worshiper but to discover the power that God has created within us. Recognizing the potential of hero worship, he spoke of how he needed to leave us in order for us to understand fully and utilize our capabilities. No egomaniac wanting to be worshiped would say that we will do even greater things than he, just as soon as he gets out of the way. "Truly, truly, I say to you, he who believes in me will also do the works that I do; and greater works than these will he do, because I go to the Father" (John 14:12).

Karen Armstrong, with her extensive research on Buddha, Jesus, and the prophet Mohammad, concludes that "all were trying to make human beings more conscious of themselves and awaken them to their full potential."[30]

It is encouraging to note, however, that we appear to be at a time in history when increasing numbers of people seem ready to awaken to those calls for personal empowerment.

Before I bring this section to a close, I want to make one thing clear. My criticisms of some of certain theologies, religious history, clergy or congregational propensities for stasis is in no way suggesting that I think religious, spiritualities, clergy, or congregations are irrelevant for the future of healthcare. Quite the contrary. I am pointing out what I believe to be critical stumbling blocks precisely because I believe they can and should fuldill important roles in healthcare. For maximum benefit, we need a fully empowered synergy between medicine on the one hand, and religions and spiritualities on the other. We need *both* to be at their best. We need both medical and religious professionals to be up-to-date and fully informed of their respective roles. I am critical of where either falls short precisely because I hold such a strong opinion of their potential role in the future.

As I emphasized in the previous chapter—and it was no mistake that I dealt with the health implications of relationships *prior* to dealing with our own inner healer—I believe the communal and relational aspects of life are critical for maximum healing potentiality.

A caring, sharing, and supportive community is absolutely a God-send, or more appropriately, a God-manifestation.

Institutional forms of religion can play extremely important roles *if* they begin to understand the enormous potential inherent within their calling; *if* they begin to enable empowering theologies; *if* they fully understand the influence of despair, depression, anger, hostility, or conversely, faith, hope, love, optimism, forgiveness; and *if* they begin to inform, educate, and enable their community about the powerful liberating roles of meditative prayer and dream work.

We must stop avoiding the divine call to "go to Nineveh," the place where the healing "summit" of medicine and spirituality will take place to negotiate dramatic new breakthroughs in miraculous healing for the twenty-first century.

CHAPTER NINE

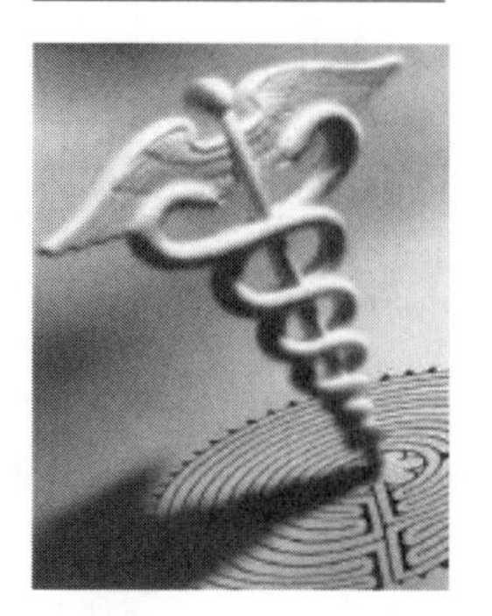

AWAKENING *the* HEALER WITHIN: *The* ULTIMATE "RULE"

The more we embrace the concept of an internal healing system, the more we will experience healing in our lives.

ANDREW WEIL, M.D.

Although healing is serious business, it helps to keep a little lightness in the discussion as well. So please allow me a little tongue-in-cheek fun with what I actually believe to be some seriously important principles by which to maximize our healing capabilities. We will consider four preceding rules before discussing what I believe is the ultimate rule for awakening our inner healer. (I actually don't like rules, per se, but we can treat them lightly in order to point to some heavy subjects.)

Rule#1: The "Have-an-Open-Mind, -but-an-Ear-for-Tall-Tales" Rule

Michael Murphy, the co-founder of Esalen Institute and the author of the voluminous *The Future of the Body: Explorations into the Further Evolution of Human Nature,* gave us wise words of advice when he wrote:

> We live only part of the life we are given. . . . To explore the further reaches of human nature . . . we must be open-minded but keep an ear for tall tales. . . . We need both prudence and imagination, both discrimination and a willingness to suspend judgment.[1]

To discover the full potential of our inner healer, we need not buy into every silly idea or unsubstantiated claim that comes our way. There are limits to our capabilities, and we need to be cautious regarding the tall tales that are spun out of minds that have no left-brained stabilizing influence. I often criticize a left-half-brained approach to life that rules out the wondrous and magnificent offerings of the right brain. But a half-brained approach on the right side is no better. It's half-brained either way.

What the whale and I are interested in here is the huge gap—and huge it is—between what we *think* are our limits regarding inner power and what truly *are* our limits. Just because we haven't experienced such and such before doesn't mean that it is impossible. If we close our minds too early, rejecting anything that has not previously been believable to us, we slam the door on a future of wonderful new discoveries and miraculous healings. If, on the other hand, we have no capacity for discernment, we will simply float around in woo-woo land with no rudder, no center-board, no compass, no direction, and simply demonstrate a huge capacity for gullibility. No, not everything is possible. But there is more that is possible than we have either thought or experienced before. Paraphrasing Shakespeare, there is more to life than is thought of in our philosophies, theologies, or even our common sense.

We simply cannot always trust common sense. For when it comes to the uncommon, our senses sometimes lead us astray. Any sensible person would know that the sun moves around the earth, contradicting scientific evidence. We can see the sun rising in the east and setting in the west. It feels as if we are on a stationary earth. But our senses cannot feel the fact that we are on a planet that is spinning at 1,000 miles per hour, making the illusion of earth's stasis seem believable. Modern science, however, from cosmology to quantum physics, has made it very clear that *most* of the universe is beyond our senses, common or otherwise. Most of reality, science tells us, is non-sense.

The time has come for medical science and spiritualities also to recognize that there are powerful possibilities for healing that lie outside our usual senses. Not everything within the inner healer can be touched, measured, quantified, or reduced to the scientific method for "proving" its reality. We tragically truncate our life if we limit ourselves to what has been proven scientifically. We must keep an open mind, curious about the mysterious, have the courage to quest, question, and challenge old answers, and yet wait for some actual evidence of validity before becoming a "true believer."

The whale of our inner healer can be awakened only if we are able to create a balance between careful skepticism on the one hand and a healthy dose of the queen's rule on the other.

Rule#2: The Queen's "Six-Impossible-Things-before-Breakfast" Rule

"There is no use trying," said Alice. "One can't believe impossible things."

"I dare say you haven't had much practice," replied the Queen. "When I was your age, I always did it for half an hour a day. Why, sometimes I've believed as many as six impossible things before breakfast."

LEWIS CAROLL

This rule is obviously closely related to the first rule, but there are some important nuances that deserve more elaboration.

The gentle, quiet, scholarly man in his late sixties, sitting at the end of the breakfast table, was not one you would immediately identify as having been a participant in one of the most dramatic accomplishments in the history of track-and-field competition. My daughter Krista and I were sharing breakfast with the other half dozen or so lodgers at a West Chester, Pennsylvania, bed and breakfast, and someone at the table knew of my athletic interests, and encouraged the man at the end of the table to tell me his story.

George Dole's humble and self-effacing manner underplayed the incredibly historic event in which he participated, so I had to supplement his comments with a bit of research of my own. It seems that Dole had been an outstanding middle- and long-distance runner while at Yale, but after graduating in 1952 had gone over to Oxford University to be a graduate student in Hebrew.

In March of 1954, Dole won the mile race in the Oxford–Cambridge track meet, in a time of four minutes and fifteen seconds. That was considered quite good, since it was widely accepted that it was humanly impossible to run the mile under four minutes. To be within fifteen seconds of what was considered to be the absolute barrier of human possibility was no small feat.

But while Dole gave primary attention to his studies and ran track primarily as an enjoyable diversion, there was a graduate medical student at St. Mary's Hospital in London by the name of Roger Bannister, who had been believing at least one impossible thing before breakfast—that he could run the mile in less than four minutes. And he was single-mindedly training to accomplish the impossible.

Ironically, Bannister was not even the most celebrated miler of his day. Earlier, as an Oxford University freshman, he could not even break five minutes in the mile. Nevertheless, he believed he was capable of the impossible. "Applying his medical research, he calculated precisely the amount of oxygen intake a runner would need to sustain a pace of 60-seconds per quarter-mile. He ran consecutive quarter-miles at a punishing pace, strengthening his heart and lowering his pulse rate from the low 70's to below 50."[2]

By 1950, Bannister had lowered his time to four minutes, 9.9 seconds. By 1952, he had qualified for the British Olympic team in the 1500 meters but finished a distant fourth in the Olympic Games.

But, on May 6, 1954, medical student Roger Bannister, Hebrew student George Dole, and several other top milers stepped onto the Iffley Road track in Oxford, England, to participate in what turned out to be an historic event. The "impossible" was about to be redefined.

It was a cold and blustery day, a Thursday morning, when Bannister left London, where he had been studying for final exams, boarded the train for Oxford, and began to mull over the challenge that was before him that day. The inclement weather led him to consider postponing the entire effort; but as track lore records it, "Bannister kept his eye on a flag at one end of the Iffley Road track; a few minutes before the start of the mile, the flag drooped, signaling a respite from the gusty winds. The race was on."[3]

It was a marvelous example of cooperation at the height of competition, for two of Bannister's teammates sacrificed their own best effort to play the role of "rabbits," the term used for runners who would run a lap or two faster than they could maintain for the entire mile, just to "pull" the best out of Bannister.

After one false start, the runners were off. As planned, "rabbit" Chris Brasher led Bannister through the first half-mile. Then, the second "rabbit," Chris Chataway, sprinted into the lead during the third lap, as Bannister tried to keep pace. Finally, Bannister was on his own during the final lap. He took the lead with 300 meters remaining, poured his heart and soul into an agonizing sprint, "his head thrown back and his face contorted in pain."

The modest George Dole, sitting at the end of the breakfast table in West Chester, Pennsylvania, some forty-five years later, explained how he witnessed the historic moment, "from across the field on the far side of the track," as Roger Bannister literally collapsed across the finish line in 3 minutes, 59.4 seconds. The supposedly insurmountable, impossible barrier was broken.

In a humble recognition of the teamwork involved, Bannister, in contrast to some of today's athletic egomaniacs, reportedly said: "We did it—the three of us! We shared a place where no man had ventured." Bannister retired from athletic competition in December 1954 to practice medicine and was knighted in 1975. George Dole went on to become a celebrated scholar, a translator of Emanuel Swedenborg's writings from their original Latin, and today is a Swedenborgian pastor in Bath, Maine. At 70 years of age, Dole still runs four miles, three times a week—almost amazing enough to make me wish I had studied Hebrew and Latin!

But there is another important point to this story. It is what has become known as "the Bannister Effect," namely, that once someone proves the impossible is possible, it opens up the flood-gates for others. That is precisely what happened in the mile run. Once Bannister had broken the barrier, others began to believe they could do it as well. It was, in fact, only seven weeks after Bannister did what no man had done before, that Australian John Landy ran the mile in three minutes, fifty-eight seconds. Then many did it. By 1964, a high-school student in Kansas, Jim Ryun, accomplished the feat as well.

We need constant examples of "The Bannister Effect" in the healing arts. All of us are drawn forward, all of us begin to realize the size of that whale of an inner healer, when someone has the courage to challenge the boundaries of the possible. Miracle after miracle occurs, proving the medically unproven, transcending paradigm-imposed limits, and even venturing into the somewhat corny translation of "impossible" to "I'm possible." Corny or not, tongue in cheek or not—it is seriously liberating stuff to have at least part of your day, perhaps before breakfast, dedicated to believing the impossible.

Rule#3: Keck's "Forget-the-Percentage-Stuff" Rule

> *We must assume our existence as broadly as we in any way can; everything, even the unheard-of, must be possible in it. This is at bottom the only courage that is demanded of us: to have courage for the most strange, the most inexplicable.*
>
> RANIER MARIA RILKE

You've heard people suggest that we are utilizing only ten percent of our mental abilities. You've heard other percentages tossed around—"It's three percent." "No, its five percent." Don't believe any of it! For us to guess any percentage presumes we know what constitutes 100 percent. We don't! Nobody knows the depths and profundity of the Divine that is within us. So, throw out the percentages altogether, and just keep exploring, with awe, wonder, and a deep sense of gratitude, the mysteriously huge whale of inner healer potentialities.

Rule #4: For Your Prayer Life, the "Don't-be-a-Half-Brained Fool" Rule

> *Love the Lord your God with all your heart, all your strength, all your soul, but only the left hemisphere of your brain . . . [just kidding]. . . . Love God with all your mind.*
>
> (BOB KECK PUTTING WORDS IN JESUS' MOUTH)

Virtually everybody now knows about Roger Sperry's Nobel Prize-winning discovery of the brain's hemispheric specialization, or what popularly is simply known as left- and right-brain propensities. It has been a useful metaphor, for as we explore more deeply into the subject, we realize how left-brained biased our culture has been in its value system. Schools, ostensibly in the business of training our brains, overemphasize the left-brain capacities of "reading, writing, and 'rithmatic." Scholarly activity is virtually all left-brained, and yet we consider scholars to be our experts in virtually every field of endeavor.

In the realm of pain management, I found my overly educated left-brain of little help. It was only after that my left-brain reading, thinking, and experimenting led me to realize that real pain management would come primarily through my right-brained capabilities. Only when I realized that I needed to have periods of time when I would let my left-brain "take a hike" for a while and allow the right-brain's deep imagery work to be my preoccupation did I experience real pain relief. I wrote a lot earlier about that experience, so I will not belabor it here.

What is important to elaborate on here, however, is how healing centers and institutions, including clergy and congregations, need to facilitate a whole-brained approach to spirituality and healing, if we are to liberate the miraculous from the whale of an inner healer.

Several of us invested considerable effort in the attempt to introduce "Meditative Prayer" into Christian churches twenty-five years ago. Some people were profoundly influenced, and their inner healer liberated. By and large, it appealed to a relatively small number of Christians. All too many, then and now, kept asking, "When did you leave Christianity and become a Buddhist?" Or "Aren't you giving yourself credit for your healing, and not God?" Or "Shouldn't we be focusing outside on God, rather than inside on one's self?" It would seem that the God within has a hard time in getting credit, as many people continue to separate human and Divine, heaven and earth, God's miraculous power and our sinful nature. It is time for increasing numbers of people to recognize the incognito God within and the whale of an inner healer that can provide some of those miraculous experiences.

Whole-brained spirituality need neither be limited to any one religion nor excluded from any. Indeed, it is a tragic denial of divine-human potentiality if we do. It is hard for me to imagine anyone's wanting to tap the enormous powers of the inner healer or any congregational setting that attempts to facilitate such empowerment that would not utilize some form of meditation and imagery combination. Not to do so is akin to standing on the whale and fishing for minnows.

If anyone wants to explore some extraordinary books that lay out many of the scientific studies having to do with the health benefits of prayer, as well as some wise advise regarding the potential pitfalls, Dr. Larry Dossey's body of work on the subject is as good as you can get. I would only add the encouragement of balancing the usual left-brain verbal prayer with some meditative form of prayer.

The Ultimate Rule: Living the Authentic Soul-full Life

> *I said to the almond tree, "Sister, speak to me of God," and the almond tree blossomed.*
>
> NIKOS KAZANTZAKIS

> *I always wanted to be somebody, but I now realize I should have been more specific.*
>
> LILLY TOMLIN

We, too, have got to be specific. We have to resist all the daily encouragement coming at us from our culture's biases, to live what it considers to be the generally good life. But specificity alone is not good enough. Your parents may have had a very specific life in mind for you, but the question is: is it really "you?" Your friends, teachers, spouse, spiritual advisors—anyone on the outside of you—may have a very specific life in mind for you, but again, the question is: is it authentically "you?" *You* may even have a number of very specific identities in mind: "If only I *would* have chosen the other fork in the road, I *could* have been really somebody, or at least I *should* have been that somebody." But specificity in the "woulda, coulda, shoulda" world is not what health and wholeness is all about. Specificity in authenticity is the ultimate means for awakening our inner healer.

The poet May Sarton says it, like all great poets, with an economy of words and a world of richness:

> Now I become myself
> It's taken time, many years and places.
> I have been dissolved and shaken,
> Worn other people's faces. . . .[4]

This entire book is about the role that spirituality can play in our state of health or illness, and a considerable role it is. But now we focus upon what I consider to be the single most important principle—our own unique and authentic soul-journey, *if* we but recognize it and live it. As poet David Whyte writes:

> We are the only part of creation that can refuse to be itself. . . .
>
> All of our great literary traditions emphasize again and again the central importance of this dynamic: that there are tremendous forces at work upon us, trying to make us like everyone else, and therefore we must remember something intensely personal about the way we were made for this world in order to keep our integrity.
>
> One of the distinguishing features of any courageous human being is the ability to remain unalterably themselves in the midst of conforming pressures.[5]

I would add to that, and stress as strongly as I possibly can, how personal the miraculous potential in our inner healer is and how much the authentic, soul-full life is the key for opening that treasure. Our inner healer is not an assembly-line product. It is not a carbon copy. It does not conform to any external orthodoxies or dogmas. It is our eccentric, creatively unique, individual, special-case, divine gift—an incredibly personal gift to ourselves, to the people with whom we share it in loving relationships, and to the world which we hopefully will serve. So let's think about real soul-level stuff. Like the almond tree, let's blossom precisely that which is truly and only ourselves.

To briefly consider the healing power of living authentically, we will explore (1) illness as a unique personal experience, (2) illness as a wake-up call, (3) a birth a new soul-self, (4) our body's own symbolic language, and (5) our dream's symbolic language.

1. Illness as a unique personal experience

Once again, we move from the either/or of the past to the both/and of the future. This is not to suggest that there are no general patterns to disease—of course, there are. The entire matter of medical diagnosis, research on the typical progression of a particular disease, potential benefits of specific interventions—all these are based upon generalities, and to a degree they work. The point is not to turn our back on whatever is generally helpful, but not to ignore the uniquely personal insights that are also helpful. The problem of the past is that the former has been emphasized to the virtual exclusion of the latter.

You may be diagnosed as a "cancer patient." You may have many characteristics of the disease that are similar to those of other cancer patients. But *your* illness—all the aspects of causation, development, pace, and direction of the disease, your internal emotional and spiritual experience with the disease, your expectation regarding your future, what interventions might be most efficacious—these elements are very personal. That very personal part is what we are addressing here. You may be a "cancer patient" in general, but the unique "you" can play a very important part.

I contracted polio, but part of the reason that I stayed completely away from the "post-polio syndrome" literature and support groups for many years and still keep them at the distant periphery of my life today is that I did not want conventional expectations or other people's experience to influence my own. I have recently checked what has been learned in the medical research regarding PPS, and found that it generally confirmed my own experience. But I did not find anything that would suggest a radically different process of dealing with it than what I already do.

What we are talking about here is the individual process of "gathering medicine," as the cultural anthropologist Angeles Arrien would put it. Fundamentally, "medicine" for indigenous peoples tends to be interpreted as "personal power." Arrien explains that the shamanic way for indigenous cultures to "gather medicine" is to reconnect with yourself at the very deepest and most personal levels.

As I have mentioned before, Marc Ian Barasch is one of the most insightful and helpful thinkers and writers about the healing process that I have come across in all my reading. The absence of the official "health professional" academic degrees were not only no barrier to Barasch's insights, but actually might have given him the creative freedom to think "outside the box." He has been particularly helpful on the subject we are dealing with here. Barasch, and Caryle Hirshberg, engaged in an extensive investigation of people who had miraculous healings, or what they called "remarkable recoveries."

> We spoke to a large number of remarkable recoveries, many of them verified in the medical literature. It made sense to try to determine what, if anything, they might have in common. In our search for similar threads within the different stories, we had considered mechanisms of biology, aspects of the mind-body connection, even spiritual beliefs. But the more interviews we conducted, the more we were struck by the sheer force of individual personalities, by how people's approach to healing had been a reflection of their own unique selfhood. . . .
>
> Over and over we took note of a certain quality that we came to call "congruence"—an impression that these people, in the midst of crisis, had discovered a way to be deeply true to themselves.[6]

Another investigator, psychologist Paul Roud, interviewing eleven so-called "incurable" patients who had inexplicably recovered, said that he found in common that they all had learned to "follow their heart's passions." People who experienced miraculous recoveries, as Barasch observed, "stopped trying to please others, and began to live according to their deepest inner biddings."[7]

Barasch and Hirshberg also observed that people's attention to authenticity, which had been critical in their healing, often marked the beginning of a person's most creative work. The two, I would suggest, are importantly integral to one another. We may understand much more about healing when we see it as a creative opportunity than when we think that we are simply returning to the previous state of "health." We may be much more likely to experience the miraculous when we are creatively fashioning a new soul-self, a new life, a new experience of being, than when we are interested in simply returning to a place where we had been before.

When we begin to look beyond the disease generalities we share with others and have the courage to explore the most personal, individual, unique, and creatively authentic aspects of our illness, we may find a path into healing no one could have predicted. Creative authenticity may lead one into unconventionality, but it may be the most effective and the most thorough healing of which we are capable. One particular means of doing that is to consider illness as a personal wake-up call.

2. Illness as a Wake-Up Call

Kafka once said that a good book should be as an axe for the frozen sea within us. The same may be said about a "good" illness. An illness may be good—that is, it may serve us well—if it awakens us to what has been frozen within us, alerting us to the life energy that is stuck or calling attention to a soul-self that has outlived its usefulness.

Psychiatrist Jean Shinoda Bolen writes in close proximity to the spirit of this book. She writes about the value of story, of the need to author our own unique healing narrative, and about how serious illness can be an important soul-level wake-up call. What I have referred to as the importance of getting to the depths of our soul-selves she refers to as being "close to the bone," but I think we are pointing to the same reality. "When an illness is truly a turning point," Bolen writes, "it is not merely a return to what was before, but a life-altering passage."[8]

Another extraordinarily sensitive soul and author, Dawna Markova, wrote a poem the night she witnessed her father die "with a shrug." She entitled the poem, and then a book by the same title, "I Will Not Die an Unlived Life." Her father's death was a wake-up call to Markova, to not live or die "with a shrug." She began to see her own challenges with cancer as creative opportunities to live more clearly, more authentically, and as a way to "find the very ground of my being." She says that the poem she wrote "is a candle that my soul holds out to me, requesting I find a way to remember what it is to live a life with passion, on purpose. There is only enough light to take the journey step by step, but that is all any of us really needs."[9]

> I will not die an unlived life.
> I will not live in fear
> of falling or catching fire.
> I choose to inhabit my days,
> to allow my living to open me,
> to make me less afraid,
> more accessible;
> to loosen my heart
> until it becomes a wing,
> a torch, a promise.
> I choose to risk my significance,
> to live so that which came to me as seed
> goes to the next as blossom,
> goes on as fruit.[10]

If we are willing to let an illness take us into our depths, we may discover a whole new life. We may not see our entire future with any degree of clarity, but all we need to begin a new life is the wake-up call to live, as Markova reminds us, "with passion, on purpose."

3. A BIRTH OF A NEW SOUL-SELF

I have emphasized throughout that I believe our deepest identity, or what I am calling our soul-self, may be a very important ingredient in any illness, as well as in our healing. I have suggested that, in fact, the need for a new soul-self may even be the primary lesson to learn from an illness, that the illness itself may be a critical catalyst to a dramatic healing. A breakthrough in what may appear to be an intractable illness may lie in our willingness to jettison a soul-self that has outlived its usefulness and to creatively grow a new and more appropriate identity.

Illness may, in fact, be the manifestation of an organic principle of life—to die to the old so that the new may be born. The soul-self that participated in creating our dis-ease or disease may need to get out of the way, so that a newer and healthier one might create the genius of our "next" life, our new incarnation of spirit.

The word *genius* in its original Latin meant "the spirit of a place." The genius of authenticity arises when we are able to live into the spirit of our deepest soul-self, and there is genius in knowing when the spirit of our deepest authenticity has changed or needs to change. To continue to be authentic, in other words, means that we must be able to be born again and again and again—who knows how many times?—into the most authentic soul-self for today and tomorrow.

The very process of becoming new, always becoming more authentic, never ends. It is the essence of life that we are continually "on the grow." We will address the perpetual process of becoming in the next chapter, but suffice it here to say simply—as long as we are alive, the genius of who we are will always be birthing a soul-self that is more authentic to the moment than was the one before.

God, the divine within-ness of the universe, has given us a plethora of rich symbols by which we can ritualize the birthing of a new soul-self. Everything in the universe is constantly changing. The cells of our body are forever dying and giving birth. Every twenty-four hours we are blessed with the symbols of the end of one day and the dawn of a new one. The natural within us calls us into new beginnings.

Many native and indigenous peoples have known how valuable the process of becoming new is to health. Psychologist Richard Katz studied the Kung hunter-gatherers of the Kalahari Desert and found that "a transformation of consciousness is at the core of the Kung experience of healing." It is a transformation of one's deepest identity, reports Katz, that brings them to a fuller sense of themselves, which is precisely at the core of their healing.[11]

There is a marvelous line in T. S. Eliot's *Four Quartets* that speaks of "the life of significant soil." Jean Shinoda Bolen interprets that line: "Having a life of significant soil means being both the soil and the organic gardener. We become fertile soil when the seeds within us develop and grow, when we 'compost' past experience, dig deeply, and attend to this piece of earth that is ourselves. Life has meaning when we birth and tend to new life that comes out of our bodies or minds or souls."[12]

The life of significant soil, for me, is when I have the courage to cultivate the soil of my soul in order to allow my most significantly authentic soul-self to grow. Like anything else having to do with organic life, it doesn't mean it will happen overnight. It takes time. It also means that we sometimes have to eliminate the weeds that may choke the life out of new sprouts. It takes time, and it takes attention. But if we do cultivate and blossom a most unique and personal soul-self, to personalize and paraphrase the Kazantzakis quote at the beginning of this section, I suspect that the Divine Gardener within will be pleased to say, "Now *that* is significant soil!"

4. Our body's own symbolic language

Every wound, as Angeles Arrien is fond of saying, has its own wisdom.

In a culture that is preoccupied with simply eradicating the symptom, however, we seldom listen or watch for the wisdom.

If instead of taking a spiritual perspective on our illness, we worship the god of commercialism, then we will believe that there is a "product" for every problem. We will believe that the drug store provides the heavenly dispensation of exactly what it is that we need to get well again. If we do that, we will ignore the wisdom of our wound.

If instead of listening to the language of our depths, we listen to the commercial promises of "quick relief" or ask our physician for a "quick fix," we will ignore the wisdom of our wound. That wisdom seldom comes in superficial and literal language. It usually comes to us in the symbolic language of our body. Physical symbols may be giving us wisdom about the cause of our cancer, heralding a message about our heart disease or articulating an insight about our arthritis.

A related issue has to do with the recurrence of disease. Recurrence may, in fact, be the signal that we have not listened to the wisdom of the wound the first time around. Recurrence may be a message from our soul, telling us, "This illness has an important message, and you did not get it the first time around, so here it is again. Pay attention." We may "get" the same illness over and over, until we "get" the message. It is very important, therefore, to learn to "hear" or "read" symbolic language.

In the very spirit of unique individuality, however, it is not for me or anyone else to tell you what the symbols of your physical illnesses may mean. Throw out the dictionaries of "disease messages." Throw out the "friends" who think they know the cause of your disease better than you do. Throw out the arrogant gurus or overly simplistic spiritual authors who presume to know more than they can possibly know about your unique depths. Listen, instead, to your own inner healer, and perhaps your true friends who may assist you with loving questions—not judgmental know-it-all questions, but simply gentle and prodding questions. You can ask the questions yourself. Questions like:

- If the immune system is the biological process of distinguishing the "me" from the "not-me," are there identity issues involved when my immune system goes haywire? Does the weakness of my immune system mean that I need to strengthen my sense of "self?" Does an over-reactive auto-immune disease suggest that my "self" is attacking myself? Is my immune system telling me something about my need to grow a new soul-self?
- Is there a symbolic wisdom message in the location of my cancer?
- Does my throat cancer have anything to "say" to me? Have I not been speaking my truth? Is my stomach cancer telling me that I need to deal with whatever I cannot "stomach" in my life? Is my bladder cancer telling me that I need to deal with my anger—that something is, in today's slang, "pissing me off?" Does colon cancer have a message about elimination? Eliminating a "pain in the butt?"
- Are my heart problems suggesting that I have been by-passing my heart's important symbols of compassion, love, or feeling life in all its glorious nuances? Is my heart attacking me simply to get my attention?
- Does my back pain suggest that I been trying to "carry the world on my shoulders?" What is the emotional message in the pain?
- Is my arthritis symbolic of my resistance to "move," emotionally, psychologically, or spiritually?

The questions are as numerous as all the potential messages that each of us individually need to hear. Each one of us must have the courage to ask the questions that best apply to our own organic propensity for the creative processes of becoming, for the necessity of authenticity, and then to listen to what our inner healer has to tell us.

Disease may be a physical and visible symbol of a spiritual and invisible dis-ease. It may be that whatever is deep inside the visible—the in-visible—is reflected in the visible. A very prestigious and wise physician reflected on the visible and the invisible, while explaining what he thought made a true physician:

> The physician should speak of that which is invisible. What is visible should belong to his knowledge, as he should recognize the illnesses, just as everybody else, who is not a physician, can recognize them by their symptoms. But this is far from making him a physician; he becomes a physician only when he knows that which is unnamed, invisible and immaterial, yet efficacious.[13]

One might think that the physician uttering such words would be one of today's "New Age" physicians, a bit ahead of his time. One also might think that few of today's "mainstream" physicians would agree with his criteria for being a physician, that of being attentive to the invisible and immaterial.

No, it was not one of today's far-out physicians although, yes, he was ahead of his time. And, yes, many of today's physicians disagree with him. But, interestingly enough, the physician who wrote those words was the sixteenth century's so-called "father of modern medicine," Paracelsus. He was, indeed, ahead of his time, and to some extent, ours. But, he was pointing to the holistic future, a future when we know that body, mind, spirit, inside and outside, visible and invisible all participate in our state of health or illness, even if that future has yet to arrive.

If that which is generally unconscious and invisible has any validity in our state of health or illness whatsoever, consider its role in prevention. Currently, orthodox medicine encourages us to think of prevention primarily through physiological "early warning signals." We run tests on the body trying to catch any early indications of physical symptoms.

But what if the psyche—the spiritual, the invisible, the immaterial—is, in fact, the earliest source of "wisdom warning." What if the earliest indications of what will eventually manifest in physical problems are, in their earliest hints, metaphysical? And what if, when we don't pay attention to the metaphysical, that wisdom finds the only language we are accustomed to "hearing," namely, physical symptoms? If that is the case, then it is to the psyche that we should look first for "early warning signals." That brings us to the subject of dreams.

5. Our dream's symbolic language

> *The closer I look, the more my dreams seem to insist upon the same spiritual onus:* You must live truthfully. Right now. And always.
>
> Marc Ian Barasch

I was up early, as is usual for me on a day of writing. I had literally just finished typing in the above quote from Marc Barasch, when Diana awakened and called for me. She had just experienced what felt to her as a very profound dream, and she wanted to share it with me. The timing as well as the content felt very significant. She recorded the dream in her journal, as well as her next day's actions in light of the dream, as follows:

> I dream I am choking on something caught in my throat. I reach with my fingers into my mouth and feel several long human hairs extending from my throat cavity. I begin to pull on the hairs knowing that they are attached to something. Much to my amazement, a round, white, cotton filter pops out of my throat. As I examine it, I realize the long hairs were mine dating back to the '70's when I wore my hair long and straight. I'm intrigued by the fact that this filter has been at work within me for all of these years.
>
> As I awaken from the dream I ask, "What have I been filtering for so many years, and why did I need a filter?"
>
> I immediately began to sense a larger pattern of meaning. For

> just a few days earlier, on New Year's Eve, Bob and I walked the labyrinth at First United Methodist Church in Boulder, as a ritual of releasing that which was old and of welcoming in the energy for new beginnings.
>
> My walking meditation to the center of the labyrinth had been very powerful and rich in imagery. As I reached the center, I felt I had released patterns my soul had carried for many lifetimes. My prayer, as I walked out of the labyrinth, was to become conscious in this new year of any remaining issues needing release.
>
> As I worked with the dream imagery, I imagined myself as the filter in Diana's throat. My job was to filter all she took in from a perspective of thirty years ago, not an easy task as she is now approaching sixty.
>
> My imagery described the constant disappointment of trying to hold on to the past, and the impossible task of physically looking the part. Although intellectually I know I cannot compete with how I looked in my thirties, emotionally I am still grieving the loss. I loved the attention I so easily received as an attractive young woman when all I had to do was show up.
>
> My soul essence was showing me the total waste of my precious time and energy trying to maintain a soul-self that should have been outgrown years ago. The filter had been working to the best of its capacity for years, but it was now time, as the dream symbolically described, to pull it out and discard it.
>
> I returned to the labyrinth the morning after this dream and walked to the center in honor of the woman I want to continually become. I asked to be empowered to express my newer and more authentic soul self with a timeless beauty and grace that transcends all filters.

Through all the years of our marriage, I have witnessed Diana's soul, through the medium of her dreams, move her step by step into greater wholeness and integrity. What are crucial ingredients in that process, however, are the degree to which she trusts this deep level of spiritual enlightenment and the courage she has always shown to make the changes her soul suggests.

Although I periodically have very significant and life-enhancing dreams, I must admit that dreams are a befuddling part of my life. Although having had experiences that convince me that dreams are an absolutely incredible gift from the divinity of my inner healer, I nevertheless find them to be maddeningly elusive. I am married to a woman who can remember every night's dreams in glorious and rich detail and who understands the spiritual import of her dreams like a scholar of inner spaces—if scholar and inner wisdom are not oxymoronic. Yet, in contrast, I feel, most of the time, as if I am an absolute dream-dunce! How can there be such a difference between us regarding dreams when both of us take the spiritual life so seriously? More importantly, how can there be such a difference between how influential *some* of my dreams are, yet how infrequently I remember any of them?

It may be that there is just a natural wide range of differences between one person and another when it comes to dreams, just as there are in other areas of our lives. Perhaps it is just one more signal of how unique and individual our soul journey in general and our inner healer in particular really is.

This much I know—our dreams can be an absolute treasure of wisdom from our inner healer. And dreams are incredibly versatile; they can be precognitive and predictive, they can show us what are our "early warning signs" of pathology, they can point in the direction of greater health and well-being, and I am sure they can do things that I haven't even thought of. Most importantly, they can speak to us at many different levels simultaneously.

My seminal Architect dream has continued to reveal deeper and deeper meanings, even thirty years after it first arrived. It provided a meaningful symbolism to how little I know, at any given time, regarding the capabilities that have been created within me, as well as the continual process of discovery. I have no doubt that it predicted my healing, but that it did so in a very indirect way—that it would be the *very process of discovery itself* that would play a major role in my healing path.

An 86-year-old retired barber in Massachusetts had a very direct and specific dream about his healing, a dream that had immediate results. The medical literature does not record his name, but tells us that he was a patient who "suffered a massive stroke that left him with a sudden, severe right hemiplegia, making him completely bedridden and unable to move his right arm or right leg."

> Neurological consultation determined that, because of the patient's age and history of hypertension, there was little or no chance for neurological recovery. . . . On the fifth day of hospitalization, the patient greeted his doctor with excitement, saying that he had just dreamed the night before that an angel dressed as a nurse stood at the foot of his bed and told him that he would be able to move his arm and leg when he awoke. The patient easily raised his right arm and right leg off the bed. This is the only case we could locate in the literature of a religious healing involving a stroke deficit.[14]

Marc Barasch, whose dreams predicted symbolically his own cancer well before medical science could find any "early warning signals," spent fifteen years exploring what he calls "healing dreams" and then wrote a wonderful book with that title. I have used this quotation earlier, but I feel that it is particularly apt here also:

> I have coined the term *Healing Dreams*, because they seem to have a singular intensity of purpose: to lead us to embrace the contradictions between flesh and spirit, self and other, shadow and light in the name of wholeness. The very word for "dream" in Hebrew—*chalom*—derives from the verb meaning "to be made healthy or strong." With remarkable consistency, such dreams tell us that we live on the merest outer shell of our potential, and that the light we seek can be found in the darkness of a yet-unknown portion of our being.[15]

We discussed earlier how spiritual messages, if not heard in their initial physical symbolic form, may remind us of the same message in the recurrence of disease. Here we take it one step farther back in the chain of early warning signals. If we are not attentive to the metaphysical messages, such as in our dreams, they may come with a greater sense of urgency—through a nightmare. Nightmares might be our inner healer telling us that there has been a message sent frequently that has not been "caught," so it is coming again, but this time with more energy. Then, if we still don't "get it," it may keep trying to get our attention, in the form of recurrent nightmares. A nightmare may, literally speaking, come as a way to "scare the hell out of us," before that hell gets manifested in physical pain and/or disease.

Several years ago, I had been going through a particularly rough time in trying to help a nonprofit organization work its way into financial solvency. I was working long hours in raising the money that was needed but feeling more and more frustrated with the internal pathology that was threatening to tear the organization apart. One central and trusted employee had been actively undermining the effort. When her dishonesty came to light, she came to me in tears and told me I should fire her. I didn't. I asked only if she would begin to correct the problem, act more honestly in the future, and I went back to my external focus on raising money. It happened again and again, and I was getting increasingly angry. I bottled up my anger and repressed it. She had been a longtime friend, and I was aware of what a rough childhood she had experienced. I did not want to add to the trauma in her life. I tried to explain how the organization could not survive with that kind of internal destructive behavior, but I could not bring myself to fire her. Then, I had a nightmare.

The dream was of a huge mountain of a man who was beating me up, and each fist was about the size of a big boulder. I remember thinking in the dream that I could out-run this guy—why don't I simply run away? But I didn't. I just stood there taking a beating and getting real bloody in the process.

I awoke in the middle of that nightmare, in a cold sweat. I had a visceral feeling of getting clobbered with those enormous fists. I couldn't figure out why I just stood there taking the beating. Then, the biblical truth came to mind—if you can name the demon, it loses its power.

I went back to sleep and back into the dream. Once again, the giant monster was beating me bloody. In the midst of the beating, I asked, "What is your name?" (I know this sounds silly in the light of day but, believe it or not, that's what I did in the dream.) To my amazement, the guy immediately stopped hitting me when I asked the question. He calmly replied, "My name is Real Kind."

"Right!" I thought in the dream. "You are beating me to a bloody pulp, and you tell me that your name is Real Kind." And then I woke up.

It helps to be married to a dream therapist, for in our morning's walk around Boulder's Wonderland Lake, I asked Diana's help in understanding what in the world that nightmare could possibly mean. Like a good therapist, she simply asked me questions, most of which I had no clue regarding an answer. But then she asked me, "What are his initials?"

"R. K.," I answered.

"And, Robert Keck," Diana continued, "what are your initials?" (You may recall that I admitted to being somewhat of a dream dunce.)

"O. K.," I responded, "so what's that supposed to mean?"

"Could it mean," Diana continued, "that there is something very personal for you about his name?"

And it was with that question that a whole flood of "Ah, ha's" came washing over the soil of my soul.

I realized that a very strong influence within the family atmosphere in which I grew up was that of being "nice" out in public. I was so passionate about life in general and sports in particular, and in my adolescence such passion often erupted with a temper tantrum. My parents worried about my losing my temper during a ball game and bringing disgrace upon our "nice" family. They stressed repeatedly how important it was for me to control my temper. The programing worked. I *never* lost my temper in the heat of a ball game. I repressed any anger I felt when in the public eye, was always "nice" and "real kind."

Then, as an adult, during my years as a United Methodist minister, the same behavior was reinforced. I did not believe that expressions of anger were appropriate for a minister out in public. So, again, I bottled up the emotions, repressed any anger, and continued to be "real kind."

What the nightmare was telling me, during that challenging time with an employee who was being dishonest and destructive, was that such repression of anger was unhealthy for me. My soul was making it crystal clear that my habit of being "Real Kind," in this case not taking the strong action that would have been appropriate, will clobber me from the inside out. In this particular case, the nightmare likely saved me from having some major illness, for it was an extremely stressful time, and I was repressing strong emotions—not a healthy combination.

I don't know how many times that message had been trying to get through to me throughout the years, since I do not remember dreams easily. Perhaps the severity of this particular situation forced my soul to communicate in a manner that would get my attention. The nightmare was telling me that I needed to jettison that "real kind" soul-self and grow a more balanced, healthier self-identity. I'm not aware of that particular nightmare's ever returning, and it may be because I have tried to find appropriate ways to deal with my strong emotions rather than to repress them. I have tried to let that old soul-self die, so that a more integral, honest, and authentic soul-self can grow. Health promotion and disease prevention, and certainly pain management called for my having a more authentic correspondence between my interior state of being and my exterior patterns of behavior.

An illustration of recurring nightmares comes from the professional practice of a Jungian analyst, Dr. Hal Stone. Back in the earlier years of the holistic health movement, Dr. Stone founded and directed the Center for the Healing Arts in Los Angeles, and it was there that Diana and I came to know Hal and his wife Dr. Sidra Winkelman. Together Hal and Sidra had originated the psychological technique known as "Voice Dialogue," which is now used by therapists throughout the world.

My particular interest in Hal's work at the time, however, had to do with the fact that cancer patients, who were engaged in medical treatment, were often referred to Hal by progressive physicians for his dream work, as it might be helpful to their patients in their healing. Hal's approach was to explain to the patient how helpful dreams can be and then ask them to begin recording their dreams so that they might, together, look for any healing insights.

One patient was a woman being treated for stomach cancer. After suggesting to the patient that she begin recording her dreams, she replied, "Oh, I've been recording my dreams for years." With the availability, therefore, of past dream journals, Dr. Stone and his patient began to look for patterns in the past, as well as revelations in the present.

To the patient's surprise, for the meaning of it had never occurred to her, they discovered a recurring nightmare that began about two years prior to the clinical diagnosis of stomach cancer and had stopped when she began to work with Hal on her dreams. The recurring nightmare was of a dog tearing at her stomach! There is no scientific proof that there was any connection between her dream and her cancer. No statistically significant controlled double-blind studies. But it certainly does raise some questions.

Could it be that, if the woman had paid attention to the symbolism in her nightmare when it first occurred—some two years before a medical diagnosis—she could have prevented getting stomach cancer? What would have been the result if she had asked the symbolic questions—what does the dog represent in my life?—what is it that is tearing at my gut?—what is it about my life that I cannot stomach? We cannot know the answer to that. But one would have to have an incredibly naive belief in "coincidence"—the timing of the nightmares and the nature of her cancer diagnosis—not to at least begin to explore those questions.

As I mentioned earlier, dreams can be the medium through which our inner healer accomplishes many things. Sometimes they are suggestive of a life-long path, as was my architect dream. Sometimes they are an early warning signal, such as was Marc Barasch's "big dream." Sometimes they are indicating something quite immanent, such as with the 86-year-old stroke victim. Sometimes they can be pointing us to a spiritual, emotional, or psychological pattern that might, if not dealt with, become a physical problem—such as Hal Stone's patient or my "Real Kind" dream.

While in the process of writing this book, I experienced a very powerful dream that both eased a considerable anxiety I was experiencing, as well as predicted what actually was about to happen.

Throughout the forty years since that life-changing mystical experience in the Cornell chapel, my top priority in life's decisions has always been clear and without doubt—to follow my soul's purpose. Many times that has meant choosing a direction that carried with it a great deal of financial uncertainty. Certainly, the redirection that came out of that spiritual experience—ministry rather than professional athletics—carried a substantially different financial future.

After *Sacred Quest* was published, I was again faced with one of those critical decisions. Do I invest all my time in marketing that book, in teaching and lecturing, or do I forge ahead with this book on healing? The former made more economic sense than did the latter. Once again, there was considerable soul searching, prayer, and meditation. What, I wondered, was God wanting me to do next?

The answer was clear and unambiguous. I knew that I was supposed to write this book—right now—but with all the research and writing time demanded, I was anxious about finances. As I worried about how I make the practicalities work—research and writing time—I had what felt like a very powerful dream.

As the dream began, I was Stephen Hawking, in a wheelchair, unable to talk, and concerned about how I was going to get across the busy street. Since I had no voice, nobody seemed to know how desperate I was to get across the street. (Stephen Hawking is the celebrated Cambridge University physics professor who is afflicted with ALS, amyotrophic lateral sclerosis, or what is popularly known as Lou Gehrig's disease. He has lost his voice and is confined to a wheelchair.)

Hawking is a symbol of someone who has something significant to say, yet he has lost his voice. He wanted to get somewhere, in this case across the street, but could not do so on his own. He needed help.

What felt powerfully relevant to me was that I feel that I have something helpful to say and write about the deep ingredients of healing. I was not sure, however, that I would be financially able to spend the time researching and writing, in order to get it published. In other words, I was worried about having my voice heard and to get across the "publishing" street.

As the dream continued, I sat there at the curb feeling enormous frustration. Even without my asking, a man came up behind me and began to push my wheelchair across the street. Then to my amazement, as we got about half way across the street, I regained my voice. By the time we reached the other side of the street, I was getting up out of the wheelchair and walking along beside the friend who had given me a hand. The dream ended with the two of us walking along in animated conversation. I don't recall the particular content to the conversation, but we both had an energized and excited manner in our walk and in our talk.

I awoke feeling like a huge weight had been lifted off my psyche; and, indeed, shortly after that, some good friends came forward to provide the assistance I needed, friends whom I mention by name in the "gratitudes" at the end of this book. Several supported my research and writing time, one created a web site as a gift, and another donated the design of the web site.

Such messages from my soul, my inner healer, from the divinity within, remind me of how blessed I am, and at the same time, remind me of what little faith I sometimes have. Several wonderful friends enabled the dream to come true, literally and symbolically. For that I am extremely grateful. I just wish I could always hold the faith and trust the process. Too often, I don't.

Of this I am sure, however: we incarnate an amazing divinity that "speaks" to us in symbols and synchronicity, and comes from the divinity incarnate in others. If we can live spiritually "with passion and on purpose," growing anew out of the soil of our souls, if we have ears to hear, eyes to see, and hearts to love, we will, indeed, experience the miraculous.

Thus, it feels to me that the most appropriate way to conclude this chapter is by way of that Hindu salutation, "*Namaste.*" With hands together in front of me in a prayerful pose, and my head bowed, I celebrate the incredible healing powers that have been created within each of us, and I give voice to the word that means "the God within me honors the God within you."

Namaste

CHAPTER TEN

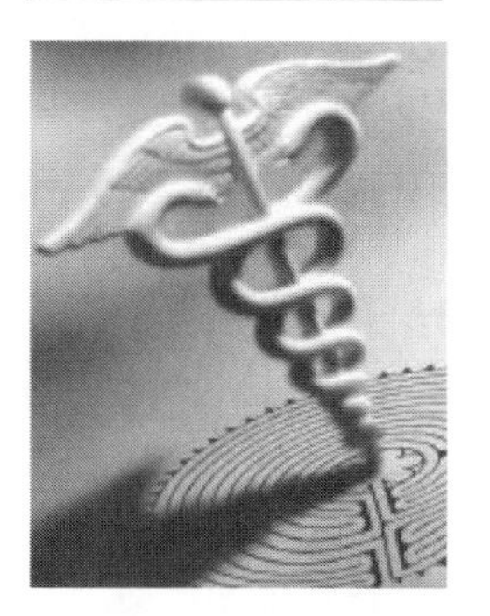

MIRACLES-*in*-PROGRESS: *It's about* TIME

We are now experiencing that exciting moment when our new meaning, our new story is taking shape. . . . This new story has as its primary basis the account of the emergent universe . . . from a sense of cosmos to a sense of cosmogenesis . . . where time is experienced as an evolutionary sequence of irreversible transformations.

BRIAN SWIMME AND THOMAS BERRY

Swimme and Berry, a mathematical cosmologist and a cultural historian, respectively, have put into words what science has been revealing about the universe, what many of us intuit—that we live within a wonder-filled universal story of evolutionary and transformational change. Ours is a universe on the grow, where every moment is filled with potentiality and possibility. We have the privilege to participate in a very becoming universe. Within such a universe time is real, not an illusion. In fact, time is an essential ingredient. Time means there will be changes and, vice versa, change means time is real. You can't have one without the other. It is time, therefore, to get our healing processes in tune with the timeliness of reality. It is time to become user-friendly with change.

What we will attempt to clarify in this chapter is that optimal healing is more available to us when we learn to live our healing as a sacred path, when we learn to live our healing as a miraculous process, and when we learn to live comfortably within the realities of time.

In contrast, for instance, consider how we have habitually approached healing as if the goal were to restore or return to a previous state of health. We have acted as if we previously had a static ideal condition we called "health." Illness interrupted that condition, and the medical, surgical, or pharmacological interventions that we turn to are for the purpose of restoring that previous condition. The dictionary definition of health, unfortunately, is based upon that former notion. It is wrong for our time. It does not liberate our full potential for healing. Healing, at its best, is not a restoration project. Nor is it a maintenance project where the status is quo. Healing is a journey into the next phase of our life.

Restoration, return, stasis, predictability, or certainty are simply not possible, in life in general or in healing in particular. To think they are is simply a denial of reality. The assumption that one can experience a once-and-for-all-time miracle, as if the miracle then becomes static, is delusional. All life is a process. All miracles, even though the onset may come very suddenly, are lived out over time, within process. Life and healing include many unpredictable, creative, and innovative miracles-in-progress—potentialities awaiting us in our emerging futures. It is all about time.

We will discover new possibilities for healing when we move from "cosmos to cosmogenesis," from a desire for stasis to the quest of creating and birthing the new. The full potential of health and well-being is found within the very processes of time, which we now know is irreversible. There is no such thing as going back to a previous state of being. Healing, rather, is a transformational process of becoming.

The cliche that "there is nothing new under the sun" is simply wrong—*everything* under the sun, including the sun itself, is new every moment. It doesn't stay the same, and it certainly cannot return to a previous state of being. The sun had a beginning about five billion years ago, we are presumed to be about mid-way through the sun's life, and it will have a death. Every second the nuclear burning of hydrogen that takes place at the sun's core releases energy equivalent to 100 billion one-megaton hydrogen bombs. And it continues to do so in the next second, the next, and the next.

Stasis is an illusion. Stasis is a pipe-dream. Absolute stability is absolute nonsense. Yogi Berra was a very gifted catcher for the New York Yankees, and I love the humor in his manner of thinking and speaking. Yogi, however, was wrong on the matter of time. It was funny, but simply not accurate, when he said, "it is *deja vu,* all over again"—*deja vu* being French for "an impression of having seen or experienced something before."

Every moment is a new experience. Time makes everything different, all the time. Time is synonymous with change, uncertainty, mystery, process, aging, dying, novelty, creativity, and becoming. Therefore, becoming user-friendly with the processes of time is absolutely critical if we want to have a comfortable relationship with life, let alone understand our full potentiality for health, wholeness, and holiness.

It takes only a moment's reflection to realize the extent to which we have historically been uncomfortable with change, desirous of certainty, covetous of dogma, enamored with simplistic black-and-white answers, and amazingly fearful, particularly in America, of aging and dying. We often give high-sounding spiritual praise and lip-service to mystery, novelty, creativity, transformation, being born-again, or experiencing a new heaven and a new earth; but we have typically experienced a soul-level sticker-shock when we discover what becoming new really costs.

Becoming user-friendly with time means that we become accustomed to leaving the past behind and welcoming a new future. We let go of the need for certainty and control, of stasis and dogma, of complete familiarity and habitual ways of seeing, thinking, and doing. It means that we find the courage to live into the unknown, the uncertain, and the flow of the miraculous. It is not to suggest that these challenges are easy. It is only to suggest that it is necessary if we want to "get real," and if we want to fully absorb the miraculous in life and in our process of healing and becoming new.

In this chapter, we will, first of all, summarize how science, over the past couple of centuries did a complete turn-around regarding time. From "cosmos to cosmogenesis," as Swimme and Berry put it, from a steady-state universe to an ever-expanding and evolutionary one, from a preoccupation with certainty and predictability to the creative processes of chaos, complexity, novelty, change, possibility, and uncertainty.

In my previous book, *Sacred Quest,* I dealt at some length with what I believe to be a similar challenge to the world's religions and spiritualities—namely, to grow out of the illusion of stasis, stability, dependability, and dogmatic certainty, and into the creative reality of process and change. I won't repeat that entire discussion here; but suffice it to say, as I have indicated earlier in this book, the optimal partnership between medicine and spirituality will result only when *both* take time and change seriously and when *both* operate out of an evolutionary and transformational paradigm.[1]

Secondly, in this chapter we will consider how the medical research regarding the deleterious effects of stress, and our own personal experience of stress, all have essentially to do with our comfort or discomfort with the changes and challenges that time brings our way.

Thirdly, we will explore what I believe to be the spiritual essence of stress management—namely, learning to live within the critical balance of being and becoming. That discussion, once again, involves a theme on which we have touched periodically throughout this book, that of living through changes in our essential soul-self identity. A spiritually mature person can plumb the eternal depths of being in the "now," while at the same time, always living into the divine challenge of becoming, of living a life on the grow, of transforming an out-dated soul-self into a newer and deeper soul-self. Such persons will have a better chance of living a miracle-in-progress.

The "being" side of that balancing act is to know the depths of the eternal now, whereas the "becoming" side is to know the promise of potentiality in all its verb-ness, its aliveness, its possibility of miraculous healings.

Finally, we will revisit the theme of our deep, fundamental, identities out of which we live—what I have been calling soul-selves. We will explore how it is a crucial issue in a great deal of health and illness, as well as in our comfort or lack of comfort with aging and dying—namely, learning to live posthumously, developing comfort with the process of dying and being born anew, soul-self after soul-self.

Since we are accustomed to thinking about healing within the context of medical science, let's begin with science itself, for science has been going through its own transformational crisis regarding time.

Timely Lessons from the New Sciences

We are at an important turning point in the history of science. . . . We are observing the birth of a science that is no longer limited to idealized and simplified situations but reflects the complexity of the real world, a science that views us and our creativity as part of a fundamental trend present at all levels of nature. . . . Time is our basic existential dimension.

ILYA PRIGOGINE, PH.D.

Lesson #1: The essential role of time itself

René Descartes, as one of the primary philosophical fathers of modern science, thought that the very purpose of science was to gain certainty. Science followed his lead, but to do so meant that time became the enemy. Time means change, and classical science needed the universe to hold still, so that measurement and predictability could take place. It conceived of the universe, therefore, to be in a "steady-state," with no fundamental changes taking place. But, wouldn't you know it, the universe wasn't listening to Descartes and it just kept expanding, changing, and evolving anyway, as we were to eventually discover it had been doing for some fifteen billion years.

When we began to listen to the universe itself, rather than Descartes, we discovered that *nothing* is static, *nothing* is stationary, *absolutely nothing* holds still. *Everything* is evolving. *Everything* is changing. *Everything* is affected by the passage of time.

Even the greatest minds, however, had difficulty with making that transition from a certain and predictable universe where time was irrelevant to a changing, uncertain, and unpredictable one where time was central. Albert Einstein, for example, the very name we associate with intellectual genius, was one such reluctant scientist, and he wrote that ". . . for us convinced physicists, the distinction between past, present, and future is an illusion, although a persistent one."[2]

Einstein so much wanted a stable and dependable universe that he actually fudged his mathematics and inserted a "cosmological constant" into his equations. "He developed a timeless static model," Nobel Laureate Ilya Prigogine writes, "in accord with his philosophical views."[3] Later, fellow physicists challenged him on this, pointing out that his own theory of relativity predicted an expanding universe. Prigogine writes that, "at the end of his life, however, Einstein seems to have changed his mind."[4] In fact, many other science writers report that he actually admitted that that was "the biggest blunder" of his entire scientific career.

Prigogine, understanding both the emotional attachment to a stable, certain, and predictable universe, yet knowing what science has now discovered, says that "to deny time may be a consolation . . . [but] it is always a denial of reality."[5]

LESSON #2: ORDER ARISES OUT OF CHAOS, "FAR FROM EQUILIBRIUM," BUT WITHIN "THE STRANGE ATTRACTOR(S)"

Chaos theory is such a wonderfully intriguing subject, yet one within which we don't want to get bogged down—after all, our interest here is primarily in how the new sciences provide a dramatically new conception of reality, as well as providing helpful metaphors regarding miraculous healing. The new sciences use some strange language, however, so perhaps we should start with a few simple and brief definitions.

Chaos theory

is the new scientific discovery which demonstrates that even very small changes can have enormous results, as they tend to build upon themselves. What may appear at first as inconsequential or minor changes can have huge and dramatic effects. Thus, absolute and certain prediction is impossible, precisely because not all the small influences can be considered.

An ancient Chinese proverb states that the flap of a butterfly's wing can be felt on the other side of the world. It was an apt analogy for Edward Lorenz, one of the founders of chaos theory, because he was a meteorologist. He was testing a model of weather prediction and, to double check his earlier results, he took what he thought was a minor shortcut, introducing an error of only one-tenth of one percent. He thought, as a result, the final calculations would be only slightly off. How wrong he was.

Nonlinear systems, he discovered, take small differences in initial data and magnify them in ways that are totally unpredictable.

Thus, Lorenz found himself considering the meteorological truth in the Chinese proverb, "Does the flap of a butterfly's wings in Brazil set off a tornado in Texas?"[6]

"Far from equilibrium"

means that when fluctuations and chaotic changes become so great that they take the system far away from the stasis of equilibrium, that is when a reordering and self-organization takes place. In the old mechanistic approach to life and matter, we considered fluctuations, disruptions, disturbances, disequilibrium, and disorder as problems to be eliminated. But, as the new sciences are showing us, living systems use disorder, particularly when it is far from equilibrium, as a means to reorganize, to transform, and to change for the better.

"Strange attractors"

is the curious phrase that chaos and complexity science gives to the boundary that contains the chaotic activity. In computer models, it is the "strange attractors" that demonstrate the inherent order within the chaos. To use Margaret Wheatley's words, "the [chaotic] system never lands in the same place twice, yet it never exceeds certain boundaries."[7]

There is a rich metaphorical relevance in the new sciences for our discussion on healing. Illness can certainly create a great deal of chaos within our previously well-ordered life. Most of all, it *feels* as if we have been thrown into a chaotic situation. An illness may even take us to our limits, far from equilibrium. Illness, to borrow Erich Jantsch's term, is an "equilibrium buster." It shatters our comfortable patterns of life, frequently changing virtually everything about our life. Nevertheless, it is solid science now to say that disorder, by itself, can be the very process that creates new order, breakdown can lead us into a breakthrough, disorganization can be the precursor to reorganization, apparent self-destruction (a soul-self identity being destroyed) can create the conditions for self-reconstruction (constructing a new soul-self identity).

Too often, however, our immediate response to the chaos and disequilibrium of illness is to want a quick fix, a strong and bold, if not heroic, action that will restore order and equilibrium to our lives. And, we want it *now, right now!* The sooner the better, for chaos scares us. Disequilibrium is uncomfortable. So, we rush out and purchase some drug that will "dampen the fluctuations," that will eliminate the symptoms of disorder, and that, we hope, will restore us to "health" and return us to the prechaotic state.

Make no mistake about it, there are times when allopathic medicine, with its powerful drugs and sophisticated surgical procedures, is necessary—and welcomed. But the question here is this—do we too often rush into too quick and too powerful a response, so that we miss the best possible transformational healing? By wanting desperately to return and restore, do we miss the opportunity of creating a new and a better state of health and well-being?

The suggestion from the metaphors of the new sciences is that to interfere with the chaos, to simply want to stabilize our lives with a quick fix, to attempt to return or restore, may not be the path into maximum healing. The chaos of illness may, rather, be the message that deep and fundamental changes in our lives may be precisely what is called for, in the interest of health, wholeness, and holiness.

Sometimes trusting the passage of time, patience itself, will show us the way through the illness to a new soul-self. "In chaos theory," Wheatley writes, "it is axiomatic that you can never tell where the system is headed until you've observed it over time."[8]

Understandably, we have some fear and trepidation that we might get totally lost in the transformational process. We may want transformation but fear obliteration, and in the midst of chaos it is not always easy to tell which it may be. We may be willing to become a new soul-self, but we fear losing all remnants of "self" in the process. Science, however, has an answer to that as well.

It seems that, within the natural processes of chaos and order, there is both change and a measure of stability. Jantsch, one of the earliest and best interpreters of Prigogine's Nobel-Prize-winning work writes: "The characteristic of living systems is to continuously renew themselves, and to regulate this process in such a way that the integrity of their structure is maintained."[9]

That's where the "strange attractors" come into play. We are wondrous living beings that have an incredible capacity for maintaining an integrity of a healthy self by constantly renewing ourselves. It may be precisely the desire to maintain stasis and equilibrium that contributes to disease, whereas it may be the courage to go with the flow of chaos, trusting that there are boundaries of the self that will create order out of the chaos, that will enable us to ride the rapids of life in a healthy manner.

Integrity and change become two sides of the healthy coin, as it were. "Caterpillar and butterfly," as Jantsch explains, "are two temporarily stabilized structures in the coherent evolution of one and the same system."[10] For, just as the Greek word for soul is the same word for butterfly, we as individuals can be a coherent and integral system, while periodically transforming our deep soul-selves. A healthy lifestyle is in having frequent chrysalis experiences, allowing the caterpillar soul-self to dissolve and a new butterfly soul-self to resolve. It is the new order that emerges out of the current chaos.

In a book dealing with the role of spirituality in healing, I cannot resist the temptation to bring a bit of theology into the discussion of "strange attractors." Is it not God, or whatever term you may use to refer to the ultimate divine power of the universe, who is the boundary of Being-ness itself? Our theologies, down through the ages have certainly had some very strange iterations and permutations, but we should never forget that our capacity for thinking about God does not, and cannot, define the nature of God. God is not reduced by or limited to the small capabilities of the human mind, in spite of how often we have arrogantly assumed that God and our ideas about God are synonymous.

We do, however, see a commonality throughout the world

religions in conceiving of God as love. If that intuition is correct, and I believe it is, then the love of God might be the "strange attractor" that "holds" us within the boundaries wherein order arises out of chaos and the phoenix of health can arise out of the ashes of illness.

A very important quality remains in our consideration of the metaphorical meaning of chaos theory—that of uncertainty and unpredictability. Of such is our very definition of miraculous healing in this book—the notion that wondrous transformations are possible, transformations that lie outside and beyond the dominant paradigm, outside and beyond the scientific capacity to predict or control, and sometimes outside and beyond science's ability even to research or "prove." It is also precisely that which discredits our spiritual attempts to insert "theological constants"—ostensible timelessness and dogmatic rigidity—into our ideas of God, heaven, and eternity.

LESSON #3: QUANTUM LEAPS

Management consultant Margaret Wheatley has written what is both a wonderful and a hugely popular book on how the new sciences provide important insights for leaders in organizations. She was ahead of the curve in seeing how the new sciences had important implications for the business world, and her visionary writing caught a wave of interest among the more intuitive business leaders. Although she was writing primarily for business executives, her words are applicable for our discussion here. Consider the following, relative to the subject of miraculous healing:

> The quantum leaps that we speak of so glibly also teach about quantum interconnectedness. Technically, these leaps are abrupt and discontinuous changes, where an electron jumps from one atomic orbit to another without passing through any intermediate stages. Exactly when the leap will occur is unpredictable; physicists can calculate the probability of a jump occurring, but not precisely when it will take place. What is at work here, though we cannot observe it, is a whole system creating the conditions that lead to the

> sudden jump. Because we don't know and can never know enough about the whole movement, we can never predict exactly how its influence will be manifest.[11]

As we have discussed in various ways throughout this book, in a comprehensive and holistic approach to health and illness, more relationships, influences, and interconnections are involved than we can possibly know, measure, or predict. The era of thinking that health or illness can be confined to precise and predictable pieces of information is over. We, as it turns out, are miraculous wholes, and chaotic uncertainty is fundamental to our nature precisely because, to use Wheatley's words again, "the *wholeness* of the universe resists being studied in pieces."[12]

As with the quantum leaps described in the new sciences, miraculous healings cannot be predicted, but their possibilities are inherent within the system's interrelationships. We may have coveted order, certainty, and control. We may have lusted after return and restoration. But, if we are willing to go with the essential flow within natural systems, miraculous quantum leaps in our state of health and well-being can occur.

Quantum leaps, transformational shifts, self-reorganizations, and miraculous healings, in fact, *do* occur. They occur precisely because more is involved in healing than we have thought of in our medical or theological paradigms. The picture of the possible is almost always larger than what we can think of, influences far more extensive than we can conceptualize.

LESSON #4: LIVING WITHIN THE ART OF THE POSSIBLE

> *[Science now] . . . requires a new formulation of the laws of nature that is no longer based on certitudes, but rather possibilities. In accepting that the future is not determined, we come to the end of certainty.*
>
> ILYA PRIGOGINE, PH.D.

The art of living in the realm of the possible is no longer seen as simply uncritical wishful thinking. It now has a solid, scientific basis. The new sciences present a world that is uncertain and unpredictable, full of surprises, miracles, potentialities, and possibilities. The suggestion here is that the more we become user-friendly with that high-altitude attitude of living, the greater our chances will be of experiencing miraculous healings.

For too long now, we have praised the cynic and the skeptic. We have called them "the realists," as against "the idealists." The former are "down to earth," whereas the latter have their "heads in the clouds," hungering for the "pie in the sky." However, just as we saw in earlier chapters, one's expectations tend to be lived out biochemically. To a great extent, both the skeptic and the idealist are "realists." They will both, in all likelihood, experience precisely what they are expecting.

If we want to participate in miraculous healings, we might want to practice, as we discussed earlier, the habit of believing at least six impossible things before breakfast. Classical science worshipped certainty, and it praised tough-minded cynics who honed the skills of debunking. The new sciences recognize a world of change and uncertainty, and they trust the emergent actualities at the edge of chaos. John Briggs and David Peat, among the best science writers helping us understand the new science of chaos, write:

> Chaos helps free us from these confines . . . [of classical science.] By appreciating chaos, we begin to envision the world as a flux of patterns enlivened with sudden turns, strange mirrors, subtle and surprising relationships, and the continual fascination of the unknown. . . . Chaotic systems lie beyond all our attempts to predict, manipulate, and control them. Chaos suggests that instead of resisting life's uncertainties, we should embrace them.[13]

Stress—Time's Good News/Bad News

The so-called "fight or flight" syndrome, what more scientifically is referred to as the "stress alarm response," is a major physiological response that is triggered by the mind—the mind's *perception* of a threat or challenge. The mind sees what it interprets as a threat or a challenge, and the body responds in a wonderfully complex and comprehensive way, so as to prepare us to meet that threat or challenge.

We all know it well. Whether or not we have thought much about it, it is a very democratic process—virtually everyone's body shifts into the "stress alarm response," whenever they perceive something threatening or challenging. Think about anything that you feel is rather challenging. You fear getting up to speak in front of a large audience, so you get a "nervous" stomach, your hands sweat, your mouth goes dry. Or you fear flying in an airplane, and your entire body and mind go into a panic mode.

Remember what you felt like just after you were involved in an automobile accident, or even a close call when you expected or anticipated an accident. In all likelihood, you were not the same calm self immediately afterwards, as you were a few moments before. It is the stress alarm response that increases muscle tension, raises blood pressure, secretes adrenalin and other stress hormones, gives you greater strength, quicker reflexes, sharper thinking; and your body prepares for more rapid blood coagulation so that you don't bleed to death if cut.

Our capacity for such extraordinary physical capabilities when caught in a crisis is a wonderful survival resource. It is rapid, it is automatic, it covers a wide range of potential emergency needs, and it is all triggered by the perception of a threat or a challenge. It is incredibly good news that we have such a responsive body-mind-spirit. It is good news that we are able to meet emergencies with greater abilities. It has been an important ability for our survival.

There is also good news in how this stress alarm response can be utilized by performers—musicians, dancers, athletes, etc.—in a more intentional and voluntary fashion. The Olympic games are a case in point.

Last night I watched the opening ceremonies of the 2002 Winter Olympics in Salt Lake City. The former athlete that resides in the vestiges of my former soul-self could sense the thrill that those athletes must be feeling as they face the critical moments of performance for which they have been training for years. They all know—when that special moment comes, they need to be "psyched up" to just the right pitch, to just the right degree, and for precisely the right duration, so that they can call on the very best of their abilities. They are, in effect, calling on the stress alarm response—meeting the challenge by intentionally "psyching up."

All of the athletes competing in the Olympics have exceptional physical abilities, or they would not have worked their way through the competitions that enabled them to reach this pinnacle. In most cases, extremely small differences separate the athletes in terms of their physical abilities. What will determine the difference between winning the gold medal or finishing far down the competition is the subtle but important skill of honing and controlling the stress alarm response in precisely the right degree at precisely the right time.

The good news of the stress alarm response, therefore, is that it can happen automatically when facing a threat or impending danger, and it can be called forth voluntarily when it is desired in order to meet a challenge of reaching maximum human performance. The good news is in the immediate and short-term appropriation of superhuman physiological and psychological capabilities.

There is also bad news.

The bad news enters when we fall into the habit of treating every day as if it were an emergency. If we habitually perceive virtually everything that happens to us throughout the day as a threat or challenge, our capacities for superhuman responses are overused and we begin to wear out and break down. Stress research reveals that constantly living within a state of emergency can have severe deleterious effects on our body, mind, and spirit.

Experiencing all of life as an emergency is a habit that leads to dis-ease, and eventually to disease. A failure to become user-friendly with the changes that life presents may, in fact, be *the* most significant factor in the onset of disease. As we saw earlier, genes determine only a small percentage of disease. It is time we shift our old habits of thinking about disease as soley physical and recognize the enormous role that our mind and spirit play.

The more we learn about stress and its impact on our body, mind, and spirit, the more it seems that it is not only a large component, but one over which we can exert some considerable control. To a great extent we can manage our health and well-being by learning to manage our perceptions of life's changes and challenges.

I should at least mention in passing that there is, of course, a variety of stresses that impact health and well-being—environmental stresses, our choice of foods, lack of sleep, etc. The kind of stress that is relevant to our discussion here, however, is that which is triggered by the perception of a threat or a challenge. And the point that we are making here is that, if we fear time and change, everything about the future will be perceived as a threat or a challenge. We will constantly be preparing to either fight or run from the emerging future. The stress alarm response that is helpful in an acute situation becomes chronic. Acute stress is the good news of the stress alarm response—chronic stress is the bad news.

There is now a great deal of medical research linking chronic stress with a variety of illnesses. Relative to our two major killers, for instance, chronic stress creates excessive blood clotting and can participate in heart attacks and strokes, whereas the stress hormone cortisol can weaken the immune system making us more susceptible to tumor growth.

Drs. Harold Koenig, Michael McCullough, and David Larson, in the massive survey of fifteen hundred research projects and reports in major medical journals that we referred to earlier, show the widespread evidence that chronic stress is involved in a wide range of diseases,

> including asthma, diabetes, gastrointestinal disorders, myocardial infarction, hypertension, cancer, viral infections, and autoimmunity . . . elevated blood pressure, accelerated atherosclerosis, osteoporosis due to inhibition of bone formation, cognitive impairment due to damage to hippocampal regions of the brain, and impaired cellular immunity.[14]

Herbert Benson and his colleagues at the Harvard Medical School's Mind/Body Medical Institute have contributed a great deal to our understanding of both the deleterious effects of stress and of the substantial benefits of stress management, focused primarily on the meditative discipline that Benson calls "the relaxation response." In addition, Benson points out a very important finding:

> Studies indicate that between 60 and 90 percent of all our population's visits to doctors offices are stress-related and probably cannot be detected, much less treated effectively, with the medications and procedures on which the medical profession relies almost exclusively. In other words, the vast majority of the time, patients bring medical concerns to the attention of a healing profession that cannot heal them with external tools or devices.[15]

Run those words through your mind again and again. Pause for a moment to consider the implications of what this prestigious Harvard physician just said—that the vast majority of doctor visits are stress-related and that the complaints cannot be *detected or treated* by the training, tools, or devices of the physician. Doesn't this begin to raise some questions?

- If this is so, why do we keep taking our complaints to those who can't help us?

- Why don't we either learn to empower ourselves to reduce our chronic stress or demand that the physicians we are going to be trained in ways that can help us?
- Isn't it time that we awaken to the self-help capacities that we have explored in the previous chapters?

We are, indeed, standing on a whale of a lot of inner capabilities, while we still go fishing for minnows. We are, indeed, capable of developing, cultivating, and savoring the interpersonal relationships that can play such a crucial role in health promotion, disease prevention, and healing. We are, indeed, capable of learning more about how to live, give, and receive love. We are, indeed, capable of managing our attitudes and expectations in ways that benefit our health and well-being. We are, flat-out, capable of cultivating miracles!

We all have within us enormous potential to promote health, prevent disease, and participate in the processes of healing. So why do we continue to refuse that responsibility and response-ability, and look to some external expert? When will we learn what our medical professionals are really good at and truly value their skills and knowledge, while, at the same time, learn what it is that we should do for ourselves?

Regarding chronic stress, whether it is Benson's "relaxation response" or the guided-imagery and meditative synthesis that I have come to use, we have a whale of a huge capacity to relax deeply, to choose our perception of the threats and challenges that come our way, and to use the stress alarm response when it is appropriate or when it can add to our enjoyment of life, and to refuse it when it is inappropriate or deleterious. Those inner capabilities are substantially aided or hindered by our internal relationship with, and our perceptions of, time and change.

If we can more skillfully manage our propensities of perception and our habitual ways of reacting to change and challenge that are deleterious, we can walk the sacred path away from a chronic experience of stress and into miraculous healings. The central spiritual issue on that sacred path may be that of discovering the appropriate inner balance between "being" and "becoming."

Being and Becoming: The Essential Balance

To live in an evolutionary spirit means to engage with full ambition and without any reserve in the structure of the present, and yet to let go and flow into a new structure when the right time has come.

ERICH JANTSCH, PH.D.

Balance is an important principle in virtually all aspects of health promotion, disease prevention, and the processes of healing. Throughout this book, we have discussed the value of a balanced cooperation and partnership between science and spirit, medicine and spirituality. In chapters six through nine, we considered the power of relationships balanced with the full utilization of our inner potential. Now we turn to the balance that is necessary for living a life that is user-friendly with time and the stress of change and challenge—being and becoming.

As with any of the important balancing acts of life, there is always a tendency to emphasize one over the other, or in some cases, to slip totally into an either/or choice of opposites. We want simple and singular answers, so we decide that the answer is "all in what we eat," or "all in physical fitness," or "all in our spiritual life"—all in this or that. We seem to like either/or, simplistic, categorical answers. We think it makes life easier.

Being and becoming have often fallen prey to separation and oversimplification, of taking the kernel of truth in just one of them and blowing it up into a total philosophy of life. There is great value for us to just "be here now." There is, indeed, great value in "the power of now." But it is not the whole picture. If it is oversimplified, it is inadequate for a philosophy of life or a path into health and well-being. In and of itself, it is a truncated spirituality.

The same oversimplification sometimes is found on the becoming side. If we focus only on becoming better, achieving more, accomplishing additional goals, of righting the wrongs of the world, of working for justice and equality—all wonderful values—life can get out of balance and "become" unhealthy.

A balance between being and becoming is incredibly important. The full potentiality of health and well-being is found within a both/and, not an either/or. We will briefly consider them separately, so as to be able to focus upon the richness of each; but in the final analysis, at their best and for our best, they work in harmony.

BEING: THE ETERNAL NOW

Eternity has been misunderstood for a very long time, and we probably do not fully understand how much that misunderstanding has disempowered us. Out of a soul that was uncomfortable with change and time, we fashioned religious concepts—God, heaven, nirvana, eternity—that were outside of time, i.e., timeless. At a deep unconscious level, we wanted the really important stuff to hold still, to be dependable, predictable, and stable. Time and change, therefore, threatened our need for stasis. Our level of spiritual maturity was unable to handle, in the realm of the really important spiritual matters, change, novelty, surprise, creativity, innovation, emergence, evolution, or the new.

At least as far as the Christian tradition was concerned, Jesus was evidently about two thousand years ahead of his time. Even though his followers would continue to conceive of eternity as being in a timeless hereafter, Jesus apparently thought of eternity as something available here and now, right in the midst of time and change. His disciples, reflecting the traditional view, asked him about when they would enter eternity. Jesus replied, "What you look forward to has already come, but you do not know it" (Gospel of Thomas 51).

On other occasions, Jesus indicated that he believed that heaven was within people—obviously, therefore, part and parcel of time—and that eternity was spread out upon the earth.

If we define the eternal as the *spiritual depths available within time*, available within every moment, we need but eyes to see, ears to hear, and a soul open to those depths in order to experience eternity. There are at least four important qualities within the eternal now—love, grace, forgiveness, and faith—and I would submit that each and every one of the four can have a direct impact on our health and well-being.

Virtually all religions, in some way or another, recognize that love is one of, if not *the* primary quality of God, the very nature of God, and the universal power capable of bringing us into an at-one-ment with all—with nature, animals, and other people. Love, therefore, is in the eternal now. We also discussed earlier the substantial medical research that reveals the healing power of love, as well as the serious consequences of disease when one does not feel loved.

Grace is a quality of the eternal now when we internalize the fact that we do not have to earn that essential and ontological love of God. Eternal grace is eternal love recognized, accepted, and absorbed within the deepest parts of our soul-self.

Closely related to love and grace in the eternal now is forgiveness. Forgiving our faults and mistakes seems to be God's nature. It is freely given, and we need only to be receptive to it. In other words, forgiveness is available even before we are capable of receiving it—it is a fore-given.

Faith, however, is perhaps the most misunderstood of the four qualities within the eternal now. It has been misunderstood primarily because it has been associated with "beliefs." Belief systems, doctrine, and dogma are the result of our fear of time and change—faith is the quality of living spiritually within time and change.

Faith, therefore, is actually quite the opposite of belief. Faith is not a set of intellectual certainties, defining that which we believe is stable and predictable and dependable. Faith, rather, is an inner intuition that is comfortable with the grand mystery of life, a knowing that we cannot believe our way into the ultimate truths of the universe. Faith is trusting in the love of God, *in spite of* our inability to figure out all the apparent inconsistencies.

Because faith is not based upon a set of beliefs, it has no need to convince others of its existence. Faith has no missionary zeal for accomplishing cookie-cutter conformity or counting "converts." Faith is more a right-brained knowing than it is a left-brain believing. Faith is more of a feeling than it is an intellectual certainty. Faith is comfortable in resting, rather than having to work at spouting concepts or gaining advantage. Faith is noncompetitive. Faith is at home in the deep mysteries of the eternal now.

Love, grace, forgiveness, and faith—the spiritual qualities of living in the eternal now—are marvelously summed up in the following, which was discovered by anthropologist Angeles Arrien on the door of a coffee shop, written by a little old lady who comes in every Monday morning for her cup of coffee. It is entitled, "Anyway."

> People are unreasonable, illogical, and self-centered.
> Love them anyway.
> If you do good, people will accuse you of ulterior motives.
> Do good anyway.
> If you are successful, you win false friends and true enemies.
> Succeed anyway.
> The good you do today will be forgotten tomorrow.
> Do good anyway.
> Honesty and frankness make you vulnerable.
> Be honest and frank anyway.
> People favor underdogs but follow only top dogs.
> Fight for some underdogs anyway.
> What you spend years building may be destroyed overnight.
> Build anyway.

People really need help but may attack you if you help them.
Help people anyway.
Give the world the best you've got and you may get kicked in the teeth.
Give the world the best you've got anyway.[16]

There may be no more substantive stress management than being fully in the eternal now, of resting in and being fully absorbed by the profundity of eternal love, grace, forgiveness, and faith. Chronic stress simply cannot find a soil of soul in which to plant its weeds, to take root, and to choke off the quality of a healthy life when we are totally present in the eternal now.

Boredom, however, can sometimes be the greatest barrier to experiencing the eternal now. We get bored, our life gets very superficial, when we lose track of the eternity that is available within every now. Some of us seemed trapped in lives and activities that cultivate "boring." For instance, how boring it would be, we might think, to be a tollbooth attendant? How destructive to an exciting experience of the now it would be to spend day after day standing there before an endless parade of cars with anonymous drivers, simply taking money and making change? A tollbooth attendant and the passing motorist must have one of life's great non-encounters. How boring!

Psychologist Charles Garfield, however, encountered a very unusual tollbooth attendant several years ago, one who has found in the eternal now a way of conquering the innate boredom of his job. Garfield tells the story as follows:

> I have been through every one of the seventeen tollbooths on the Oakland-San Francisco Bay Bridge on thousands of occasions, and never had an exchange worth remembering with anybody.
>
> Late one morning in 1984, headed for lunch in San Francisco, I drove toward one of the booths. I heard loud rock music. It sounded like a party, or a Michael Jackson concert. I looked around. No other cars with their windows open. No sound trucks. I looked at the tollbooth. Inside it, the man was dancing.

"What are you doing?" I asked.
"I'm having a party," he said.
"What about the rest of the people?" I looked over at other booths; nothing moving there.
"They're not invited."
I had a dozen other questions for him, but somebody in a big hurry to get somewhere started punching his horn behind me and I drove off. But I made a note to myself: Find this guy again. There's something in his eyes that says there's magic in his tollbooth.
Months later I did find him again, still with the loud music, still having a party.
Again I asked, "What are you doing?"
He said, "I remember you from the last time. I'm still dancing. I'm having the same party"
I said, "Look. What about the rest of these people. . . ."
He said, "Stop. What do those look like to you?" He pointed down the row of tollbooths.
"They look like . . . tollbooths," I replied.
"Noooo . . . imagination!"
I said, "Okay, I give up. What do they look like to you?"
He said, "Vertical coffins."
"What are you talking about?"
"I can prove it. At eight-thirty every morning, live people get in. Then they die for eight hours. At four-thirty, like Lazarus from the dead, they reemerge and go home. For eight hours, brain is on hold, dead on the job. Going through the motions."[17]

Garfield met the man later for lunch and for more conversation. He was impressed at how this man, in a job in which most of us would be bored to death, had discovered eternity in one tollbooth, while in the other sixteen attendants were just passing the time, waiting for the day to end, waiting perhaps for eternity in the hereafter. Garfield asked the man how it did it:

"I knew you were going to ask that," he said.
"I'm going to be a dancer someday . . . [and this job is] paying for my training. . . . I don't understand why anybody would think my job is boring. I have a corner office, glass on all sides. I can see

> the Golden Gate, San Francisco, the Berkeley hills; half the western world vacations here. . . . and I just stroll in every day and practice dancing."[18]

In my opinion, he was practicing more than dancing. He was practicing the experience of the eternal now, daily, in a tollbooth. And, if we look closely, we can see that wonderful balance of the eternal now and the eternal potentiality. He was celebrating the magical depths of each day, while at the same time he had his eye on the future for which he was practicing—he was enriching his daily activity with dance, while he was preparing for a future of dance.

The power-filled spiritual life has the eternal now in balance with a becoming future. And a becoming future means action—love in action, grace in action, forgiveness in action, and faith in action. Regarding health and illness, a great deal of medical research now points to the extent to which these eternal qualities impact health and well-being, particularly as they are manifested in support groups, loving and forgiving friends, and lives dedicated to service, improving and brightening the lives of others.

I am not aware of anyone's researching that tollbooth attendant's future health as compared to those who spent their days in the "vertical coffins" down the row of other tollbooths. But, if I were a betting man, I'd lay my money on the future of *his* health, as compared to someone who finds his or her job boring.

BECOMING: THE ETERNAL POTENTIALITY

Who of us can say that we can sit within the eternal now and that we fully understand and manifest the power of love? Nobody, of course. Every one of us can learn more about love in the next moment than we knew before. Every one of us can give grace and forgiveness to someone today, more fully and more magnificently than we did yesterday, and tomorrow more fully than today. The possibility of becoming is the eternal gift of potentiality.

All the qualities of eternity can become more incarnate in our lives in the future than they were in the past. The spiritual life, and the healthy life, is a very becoming life, or it is less than it can be. Time is a blessing—it is our opportunity to become more loving, more graceful, more forgiving, and more faithful. Time provides us the privilege of growing, developing, maturing, evolving, changing, and transforming. Time enables us to live into another soul-self, and then another, and another.

What a wonderful gift time is for us. What opportunities it provides. In the eternal now, I can feel my soul calling me to learn more about love and to live love more fully, but I need time to do that. In the eternal now, I can feel my soul calling me to try to figure out what is happening in our world at this extraordinary hinge of history and to write about it, but I need time to do the research and the writing. In the eternal now, I can sense the grandeur of being a parent, but if it were not for time, I would not be able to savor the process by which every child grows into a very special, unique gift to the universe. The same can be said, of course, about the pleasure of having grand—yes, so marvelously grand—grandchildren. If it were not for time, none of us could experience the miracle of a grandchild's being born and growing into a special, unique incarnation of spirit.

On the other hand, where there are enormous gifts, there are also great challenges. Personally, my greatest challenge in the balance between being and becoming lies in too easily becoming preoccupied with the latter. Whether it was because of my early preoccupation—compulsion might be more accurate—of becoming an accomplished athlete, I became accustomed to setting goals and devising the strategies by which I could accomplish those goals. It has been a life-long personality trait—I was probably born a "Type-A" personality. I think I might have come out of the womb with a long-range plan in mind and impatient to hit the ground running—

people to see, places to go, things to do, goals to accomplish, heights to achieve, battles to fight, wrongs to be made right, and injustices to correct. It has been a life-long habit. But a personality trait tilted toward the becoming side of this balance can easily get out of balance. Becoming can become an obsession, either magnificent or malignant.

If one becomes too habitually "Type A," one can transform time into the enemy. "I can accomplish anything," a typical Type A will say, or at least feel, "if I just have enough time." My friend Bill Reichart used to say, if I was lucky enough to beat him in a handball game, "I didn't lose; I just ran out of time."

An excessive obsession with goals and accomplishments can lead to a soul-self that identifies itself with the goal or the next accomplishment. That can lead into what Larry Dossey has called "hurry sickness," and it is strongly implicated in heart disease. If our very identity is dependent upon our next achievement, then we *need* that achievement—desperately! The anger and hostility that are frequently found to be the most toxic factor in the link between Type-A behavior and coronary heart disease are a result, I suspect, of when someone or something gets in the way of our path towards that which we *need* to accomplish. Chronic stress can easily become the consequence when one's identity, one's deepest soul-self, is tied to achieving a particular goal and when the path to that goal is littered with stumbling blocks, another person's agenda—indeed, another person's needed achievement—and various and sundry other frustrations.

In life and in our work rarely can we control all the variables. Things that we cannot anticipate mess up our well-made plans. The chronic stress of feeling out of control, of being frustrated, of getting angry—all can be the result when our deepest soul-self has its identity wrapped up in that next accomplishment. The part within any one of us that borders on the Type-A personality trait has a particular need for balancing the eternal now with the eternal potentiality.

The essential point here is that there are soul-selves that outlive their usefulness or their ability to contribute to health and well-being. Or sometimes we grow into an exaggeration of a soul-self that gets us out of the critical balance of being and becoming. Then, precisely then the soul-self can contribute to dis-ease and disease. Then, and precisely then, the ability to be a shape-shifter regarding soul-selves may be our most effective sacred path into healing.

Dreams often come to tell us when we are getting out of balance. Like a typical Type A, my dreams usually send the message via the symbol of a car or some other method of transportation. Our cars, after all, are what many of us use to get where we want to go. If our soul-self is trying to get somewhere and if there is some imbalance involved in the "getting," our dreams will often use symbols of transportation to tell us what we need to hear.

For me, cars in my dreams are frequently running out of gas—not very subtle symbolism there! Or my brakes won't work, and I am out of control—pretty obvious what that means! One particular car dream had me baffled, however; but it does help to be married to a dream therapist. In this dream, I was driving my car and ran out of gas—that part I understood. But when I got out of the car to go after some gas, I realized that I did not have any clothes on. The nudity was the part I did not understand at first.

In the dream, I jumped back into my car and sat there with the frustrating dilemma—do I sit here out of gas, or do I run naked down the street to the gas station? With Diana's help, I came to realize that the nudity was symbolic of an ego problem. I would not be comfortable in exposing the fact that I was out of gas. My self-image was more self-reliant than that. I was not comfortable in revealing my lack of self-sufficiency. I like to relax, but *needing* to take a rest was not part of my Type A personality—and there is a big difference between the two. My dreams were telling me that I was not only getting very fatigued in my rush to accomplish whatever was the goal de jour, but that I needed—just for the health of it—to learn to be more comfortable in admitting the fact that I periodically need to rest.

As I was writing this last chapter, I was feeling the crunch of deadlines, I was bordering on "hurry sickness." The publication timeline had already been set, and to deliver the manuscript on time meant that I had a lot of work to get done in a relatively short period of time.

Because of my travel schedule for speaking engagements, the days of writing were limited. On those days, however, I was getting up at 3:00 or 4:00 a.m. to begin my writing, often working straight through the day until I "hit the wall." I found myself, when friends and family would ask about my progress, using words like—"It's going fine, but I am having to sprint to the finish line." After weeks of such "sprinting," I would get so fatigued that I knew I was not doing good work. I was having to rewrite and rewrite, over and over again. But I kept trudging away. Then, I had two dreams, two nights in a row, that were both very revealing.

The first dream:

> I am driving my car down a very narrow and rough dirt road through a jungle. All of a sudden, I see that the road is blocked by an enormous black panther. The panther is not making any hostile or aggressive moves; it is just lying there across the road, blocking my way, and calmly looking at me.
>
> I realize that my desire for him to move is not going to cause him to move, and I will not be able to proceed until the panther itself decides I can go on. I have no real choice in the matter. I simply have to take a deep breath, relax, and wait. [I then woke up.]

The next night I had a very similar dream—brief but to the same point:

> I am walking down a sidewalk and that same big black panther is lying across the sidewalk, blocking my path. Once again, it is neither hostile nor aggressive. It is just lying there calmly, looking at me as if to say, "You are not going to pass this way until I decide it

is time to move." [Again, I woke up before I knew when, or if, I was able to go on.]

Two such similar dreams two nights in a row moved me to read up on the nature of black panthers. What is the panther symbolizing in my dream? In book after book, panthers are referred to as being powerful animals whose power is manifested in short sprints. It is not a long-distance runner. So, the panther sprints, and then rests, sprints and then rests.

I remembered how often I had used the sprinter metaphor to describe my rush to the finish-line on this book. My problem was that I sprinted day after day, going weeks without a rest, and then becoming overly fatigued. This time, however, I listened to the panther, took a day off, and found renewed energy for my writing.

It is not easy, however, to change long and deep habits. I find myself continually falling off the same end of the being–becoming balance. Time and time again I get preoccupied with what I want to become, what I want to make happen, what I want to accomplish. I am by nature a sprinter, but I keep forgetting to take the necessary periodic rests. The panther came to remind me of that. The panther, just as in Diana's constant advice to "stop and smell the roses," was a reminder of the eternal gifts inherent in being in the now.

I have confessed where my challenges are in the balance of being and becoming—so, where are your greatest challenges? Each of us has his or her own unique degree and manifestation of challenges in this critical balancing act. Perhaps your gifts are in understanding and wanting to savor the depth of beingness in the eternal now, while your challenges are with getting attached to one way of being, wanting to hold on, and resisting change. Or perhaps you are enamored with the processes of becoming new, and your challenge is that you too easily pass over the depth of eternity that is available in every here and now.

It is not an easy balance to discover, but it is one that has enormous implications for managing the stress of life and for gleaning the potentiality of living a miracle-in-progress. The eternal now has a profound depth, but it does not stand still. Each "now" becomes the next "now." Each state of "being" is in the process of becoming the next state of "being." Miraculous living and healing can be so wonderful that we are tempted to want them to stand still; but just like breathing, a healthy existence is found in experiencing each breath deeply and then letting it go so as to experience the next. In a more profound sense, each soul-self can provide a deeply meaningful experience of life, but there are the appropriate times to let go, to hone the skill of non-attachment, expiration following inspiration, and to become the new soul-self that continues the miracle-in-progress. It is learning the miracle of living, dying, and being born anew, at a soul level of being and becoming.

Composing a Life That Lives Posthumously, Soul-self after Soul-self

> *Only to the extent that man exposes himself over and over again to annihilation can that which is indestructible arise within him. In this lies the dignity of daring. Thus, the aim . . . is not to develop an attitude which allows a man to acquire a state of harmony and peace wherein nothing can ever trouble him. . . . The more a man learns wholeheartedly to confront the world that threatens him with isolation, the more are the depths of the Ground of Being revealed and the possibilities of new life and Becoming opened.*
>
> KARLFRIED GRAF VON DURCKHEIM

I am indebted to the Jungian psychologist Roger Woolger for calling my attention to the extraordinary wisdom of Karlfried Graf von

Durckheim, the great German psychologist and Zen teacher. The words above from Durckheim, written over thirty years ago, describe not only a fundamental insight into human psychology, which he also shared with Carl Jung and others, but speak precisely to what I have considered a central theme when healing is viewed as a sacred path—becoming more and more familiar with the sacred Ground of Being through the processes of transforming our deepest soul-selves.

What may feel like a tragic accident or illness at one level may be the catalyst—perhaps even a call—for a deeper and more meaningful soul-self. In other words, what our current identity, our primary personality, and our style of life may consider to be a major problem—a substantial interruption or a stumbling block—could very well be the soul's process of change, growth, and development. It may be that our previous identity was the problem, that the interruption in our lifestyle was for the purpose of redirecting us into another style of living, and that the stumbling block prevented our movement on that path precisely because we need to use it as a stepping stone into a higher path, a more exalted experience of living, a becoming into eternal potentiality.

If our life is going well, we usually want it to remain so. We prefer stasis. We would like to know that tomorrow will be the same as yesterday and today. But our soul-level life, like all other organic, natural, life-affirming dimensions of this existence, is accustomed to movement—a constant process of birth, life, death, and rebirth. Our soul's business is spiritual growth, maturation, and transformation—thus, it's very nature is that of living posthumously, again and again. Whether we like it or not!

The matter of previous or future lives is not within the scope of this book, although I am extremely curious about the larger and more extended reality in which we have participated for billions of years and will probably participate in for more billions of years. What is of primary interest to us in this book, however, is whether we try to live *this* life with a soul-self that is rigid and presumably static, or whether we try to resonate with the growth and changes in our soul, that which is inherent in anything organic and living. The equally large and complex subjects of aging and dying are not the purpose of this book, but they, too, are challenges for resonating with spiritual growth, maturation, and transformation.

What is integral to our discussion here is that becoming user-friendly with a life-long process of practicing posthumous living—living through soul-self changes, time and time again—is a critical ingredient in health promotion, disease prevention, and the processes of healing. Throughout this book, I have been suggesting that there are three crucial components when considering the spiritual role in healing—an ecology of the heart with nature and other people, awakening our inner healing potentiality, and the natural, organic, processes of transformation. It is the latter that has so much to do with our comfort, or lack of comfort, with time.

The famous Swiss psychiatrist Carl Jung, who provided what I consider to be perhaps our best understanding of the human mind, particularly in its spiritual manifestations, put it bluntly: "There are spiritual processes of transformation in the psyche."[19] One particular thirty-five-year-old woman was paying attention to those transformational energies in her deep psyche when she shared the following dream with her psychotherapist Murray Stein.

> I am walking along a road, feeling depressed. Suddenly I stumble on a gravestone and look down to see my own name on it.
>
> At first I am shocked, but then strangely relieved. I find myself trying to get the corpse out of the coffin but realize that I am the corpse. It is becoming more and more difficult to hold myself together because there is nothing left to keep the body together anymore.
>
> I go through the bottom of the coffin and enter a long dark tunnel. I continue until I come to a small, very low door. I knock.
>
> An extremely old man appears and says: "So you have finally come."
>
> (I notice he is carrying a staff with two snakes entwined around

> it, facing one another.) Quietly but purposefully he brings out yards and yards of Egyptian linen and wraps me from head to foot in it, so I look like a mummy. Then he hangs me upside down from one of the many hooks on the low ceiling and says, "You must be patient, it's going to take a long time."
>
> Inside the cocoon it's dark, and I can't see anything that is happening. At first, my bones hold together, but later I feel them coming apart. Then everything turns liquid. I know that the old man has put one snake in at the top and one at the bottom, and they are moving from top to bottom, and back and forth from side to side, making figure eights.
>
> Meanwhile, I see the old man sitting at a window, looking out on the seasons as they pass. I see winter come and go; then spring, summer, fall, and winter again. Many seasons go by. In the room there is nothing but me in this cocoon with the snakes, the old man, and the window open to the seasons.
>
> Finally the old man unwraps the cocoon. There is a wet butterfly. I ask, "Is it very big or is it small?"
>
> "Both," he answers. "Now we must go to the sun room to dry you out."
>
> We go to a large room with a big circle cut out of the top. I lie on the circle of light under this to dry out, while the old man watches over the process. He tells me that I am not to think of the past or the future but "just be there and be still."
>
> Finally he leads me to the door and says, "When you leave you can go in all four directions, but you are to live in the middle."
>
> Now the butterfly flies up into the air. Then it descends to the earth and comes down on a dirt road. Gradually it takes on the head and body of a woman, and the butterfly is absorbed, and I can feel it inside my chest.[20]

As this woman's dream indicated, transformation often takes time. My sudden and dramatic transformation as a college senior, from an athletic soul-self to that of a spiritual seeker, was immediate, yet it has taken a lifetime to understand even partially and to grow into the processes of practicing the posthumous, of being willing to be transformed when it became necessary or helpful. My seminal Architect dream occurred within a few moments in a night in the early 1970s, yet it has been living itself out and revealing more and more insights to me for the subsequent thirty years.

Time is on our side, if we have a priority for spiritual growth, evolution, development, maturation, and transformation. The depth of time, as in the Eternal Now, when combined with the becoming of eternity's potentiality within the processes of time—they are the sum and substance of why we have the marvelous privilege, and necessity, of becoming user-friendly with time. Time can be our helpmate when healing becomes a sacred path. And it is about time we discover and incarnate that reality.

If we resist those deep transformational energies, that may be one of the primary causes of disease, for it is denying an essential, natural energy that is fundamental to each one of us. If, on the other hand, we learn to move, to change, to resonate with those deep transformational energies, and grow into a soul-style of living posthumously, that may be a powerful factor in preventing illness and in creating a healing.

To transform literally means to pass over from one form to another. It is the miracle that is within us, the miracle-in-progress, that can enable us to pass from meaninglessness to meaning, from purposelessness to purpose, from chronic stress to the wonderful balance of the Eternal Now and the Eternal Becoming, from "vertical coffins" to having a party, and from illness into wellness. So, transform, live posthumously, discover a deeper soul-self, be well, and become healthy, whole, and holy. It's about time.

CONCLUSION

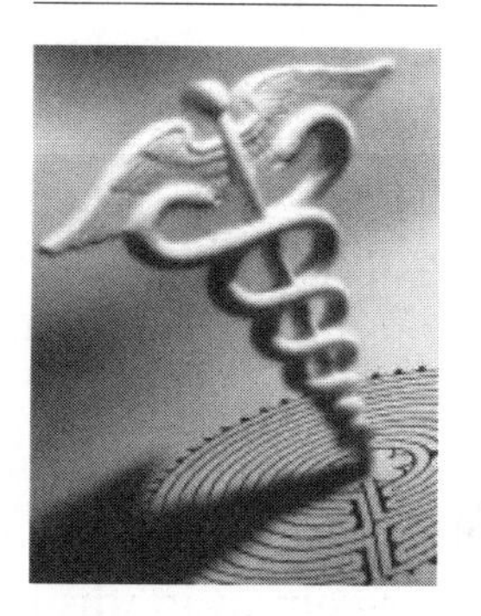

AUTHOR-IZING *Your Own* STORY *of* HEALING

Preserving the soul means preserving a desire to live a life a man or woman can truly call their own.

DAVID WHYTE

Our soul wishes us—to embark on the journey without knowing the destination. It is not given to us to arrive without ever departing. Perhaps the path, a sincere striving to understand more, is the goal. In the end, the task of an examined life. . . is ours alone to reject or embrace; which way we choose makes all the difference in the world.

MARC IAN BARASCH

Anthropologist Angeles Arrien tells of an Inuit legend that says, "The Great Spirit must love stories, because the Great Spirit made a lot of people." In the same vein, the Great

Spirit made you and wants you to live your own very special and unique story of healing. You are one of a kind. Being authentic to your own soul journey is crucial, for real healing does not come in carbon copies.

That is why I don't believe in formulas or dogmatic prescriptions for healing—guarantees that if you do such and such, you will find your maximum healing. To do so would be to ignore the mystery of the Divine that permeates all of reality. To suggest that there could possibly be one strategy or a single best path for everyone would violate all of what we have been talking about in this book regarding individual uniqueness. I don't believe in recipes when it comes to spirituality and/or healing—we are not cookie-cutter miracles in waiting. As Sam Keen so appropriately wrote, "You are unique. Your life is a once-told tale, an unrepeatable drama."[1]

So, too, is your illness, and so, too, can be your miraculous healing. Consequently, although I have shared my personal experiences throughout this book to illustrate some basic principles, I am in no way suggesting that my experience is a model or guide for what is right for you. There are, I believe, some general principles or guidelines that can be helpful, but each of us needs to find the nuance, the shading, and the texture of how those guidelines work best in our own lives. So, my wish for you is that you . . .

ACTIVELY CULTIVATE YOUR OWN MIRACULOUS HEALING

Contemplate, cogitate, ruminate, and meditate. Use all of your capacities intellectual and intuitive, conscious and unconscious. Ask your dreams for your inner wisdom. Walk a labyrinth, a moving meditation about what it is that you need to let go of as you journey into the center, an empowering awakening at the labyrinth's center and in the center of your being, and walk out moving into a new life, a new soul ID, and into a miraculous healing.[2]

If each of us approaches healing as a sacred path and if we have the courage to enter the adventure on our *own* unique and original path, exploring our own special version of illness and healing—while encouraging and supporting one other—the miraculous will come to deepen and enrich our lives. Health and well-being, the miraculous, mysterious, and marvelous feeling of wholeness, and the serendipities of holiness may be found in the next soul-self that you will uncover and discover.

Until now, you may have been sick and in pain.

Until now, you may have been in despair and depressed.

Until now, you may have felt empty and unfulfilled.

Until now, you may have resisted being changed and transformed.

Until now, you may have felt disconnected from your spiritual depths.

If, however, you now choose to engage your healing as a sacred path, this may be your moment of demarcation, your opportunity for embarking on a new life, your discovery of a new soul-self, and your experience of a miraculous healing—all of which has been waiting for you "until now." Perhaps you will find yourself becoming a miracle-in-progress and, in the words of poet David Whyte, traverse

This opening to the life
we have refused
again and again
until now.

Until now.[3]

NOTES

An Invitation

1. Maya Angelou, *Wouldn't Take Nothing for My Journey* (New York: Bantam Books, 1993), 29–30.
2. Jean Shinoda Bolen, quoted in *Publisher's Weekly*, May 26, 1997, 33.

Chapter One

1. Elaine Scarry, *The Body in Pain* (New York: Oxford University Press 1985), 40.

Chapter Two

1. Marilyn Ferguson, *The Aquarian Conspiracy: Personal and Social Transformation in 1980s* (Los Angeles: Tarcher, 1980), 417.

Chapter Three

1. See websites www.nins.nih.gov/health and www.medical/pubs/post-polio.htm.
2. Elaine Scarry, *The Body in Pain,*13.
3. Marc Ian Barasch, *Healing Dreams: Exploring the Dreams That Can Transform Your Life* (New York: Riverhead Books, 2000), 18.

Chapter Four

1. Richard Tarnas, *The Passion of the Western Mind* (New York: Harmony Books, 1991), 169.
2. For a more thorough discussion of the Deep-Value Research which examined 35,000 years of spiritual evolution and the causal influences that determined why certain values became dominant, why we think and act as we do, and why we create and run our institutions as we do, see my earlier books, *Sacred Eyes* (Knowledge Systems, Inc., 1992) and *Sacred Quest: The Evolution and Future of the Human Soul* (West Chester, Pa.: Chrysalis Books, 2000).
3. Barbara Tuchman, *A Distant Mirror: The Calamitous 14th Century* (New York: Ballantine Books, 1978), xix.
4. See Norman F. Cantor's book, *In The Wake of The Plague: The Black Death*

and the World it Made (New York: The Free Press, 2001) for a good discussion of how recent scholarship speculates on the destruction actually being the resulting combination of bubonic plague and anthrax.

5. Tuchman, xiii.
6. Cantor, 6.
7. Tuchman, 123.
8. Tarnas, 319–320.
9. Carolyn Merchant, *The Death of Nature: Women, Ecology, and the Scientific Revolution* (New York: HarperCollins, 1980), 193.
10. The Institute for the Future, *Health and Health Care 2010* (San Francisco: Jossey-Bass Publishers, 2000), 187–188.

Chapter Five

1. Larry Dossey, *Reinventing Medicine* (HarperSan Francisco:1999), 22.
2. *Research News* 1, no.1 (September 2000): 12.
3. Ibid, 2.
4. Ibid.
5. Ibid.
6. Louise Levathes, "At GWU, a Healing Spirit," *Washington Post*, 7 August 2001, HE01.
7. Ibid.
8. Larry Dossey, *Healing Words: The Power of Prayer and the Practice of Medicine* (San Francisco: HarperSan Francisco, 1993), 25.
9. *Research News*, 3.
10. James S. Gordon, *Manifesto for a New Medicine: Your Guide to Healing Partnerships and the Wise Use of Alternative Therapies* (New York: Addison-Wesley Publishing Co., 1996).
11. Ibid., 17, 18.
12. *Health & Health Care 2010*, 198.
13. Kathleen A. Brehony, *After The Darkest Hour: How Suffering Begins the Journey to Wisdom* (New York: Henry Holt & Co., 2000), 75.
14. Emanuel Swedenborg, *The Universal Human and Soul-Body Interaction*, trans. George F. Dole (New York: Paulist Press, 1984), 58, 87.
15. Joel Davis, *Endorphins: New Waves in Brain Chemistry* (New York: The Dial Press, 1984), 53.
16. Ibid., 115.
17. Ibid., 158.

18. Candace Pert, *Molecules of Emotion: Why You Feel the Way You Feel* (New York: A Touchstone Book, 1997), 186.

Chapter Six

1. Marc Ian Barasch, *The Healing Path: A Soul Approach to Illness* (New York: Tarcher/Putnam, 1993), 60–61.
2. James Hillman, Foreword, "A Psyche the Size of the Earth," in *Ecopsychology*, edited by Theodore Roszak (San Francisco: Sierra Club Books, 1995), xvii.
3. Dean Ornish, *Dr. Dean Ornish's Program for Reversing Heart Disease* (New York: Ivy Books, 1996), 49.
4. Gail Godwin, *Heart* (New York: William Morrow, 2001), 18.
5. Dean Ornish, *Love & Survival: 8 Pathways to Intimacy and Health* (New York: HarperCollins, 1998), 2.
6. Ibid., 3
7. David Bohm, *Wholeness and the Implicate Order* (London: Routledge & Kegan Paul, 1980), 1.
8. Barbara Hannah, *Jung, His Life and Work* (New York: Putnam, 1976), 150–152.
9. David Abram, *The Spell of the Sensuous: Perception and Language in a More-Than-Human World* (New York: Pantheon Books, 1996), 87.
10. Mircea Eliade, *Shamanism: Archaic Techniques of Ecstasy*, trans. Willard R. Trask (Princeton: Princeton University Press, 1964), 96.
11. Quoted in Michael W. Fox, *The Boundless Circle: Caring for Creatures and Creation* (Wheaton, Ill.: Quest Books, 1996), 5.
12. Mark Plotkin, *Medicine Quest: In Search of Nature's Healing Secrets* (New York: Viking Putnam, 2000), xv. The emphasis is Plotkin's.
13. Abram, 7.
14. Ibid., 7–8.
15. Lewis Mehl-Madrona, *Coyote Medicine: Lessons from Native American Healing* (New York: Fireside, 1997), 16–17.
16. Ibid., 247–248.
17. Prince Modupe, *I Was a Savage* (n.p.: Museum Press, 1958), 72.
18. Paul Pearsall, *The Heart's Code: Tapping the Wisdom and Power of Our Heart Energy* (New York: Broadway Books, 1998), 10.
19. Some of the books that cover stories and research studies about the animal and human healing bond include: Susan Chernak McElroy, *Animals As Teachers and Healers* (New York: Ballantine Books, 1997); Howard

Clinebell, *Ecotherapy* (Minneapolis: Fortress Press, 1996); Rupert Sheldrake, *Dogs That Know When Their Owners Are Coming Home and Other Unexplained Powers of Animals* (New York: Three Rivers Press, 1999). Articles dealing with this subject include: Larry Dossey, "The Healing Power of Pets: A Look at Animal-Assisted Therapy," *Alternative Therapies* 3, (1997): 8–15; A. T. B. Edney, "Companion Animals and Human Health," *Veterinary Record* 130 (1992): 285–287; A. Rennie, "The Therapeutic Relationship between Animals and Humans," *Society for Companion Animal Studies Journal* 9 (1997): 1–4. Perhaps the best source for information on animal-assisted therapy is The Delta Society, which publishes a journal for the general public, *People-Animal-Environment*, as well as one that is a scientific journal, *Anthrozous*. Their address is: Delta Society, P. O. Box 1080, Renton, WA 98057.

20. McElroy, *Animals As Teachers and Healers*, 68.
21. Sheldrake, *Dogs That Know*, xi.
22. Ornish, *Love and Survival*, 68. The emphasis is Ornish's.

Chapter Seven

1. Dean Ornish, *Love & Survival*, 29.
2. G. H. Colt, "The Magic of Touch," *Life Magazine*, August 1997, 55.
3. Ornish, 140.
4. James J. Lynch, *The Broken Heart: The Medical Consequences of Loneliness* (New York: Basic Books, 1985), 3.
5. Ornish, 13. The emphasis is Ornish's.
6. Harold Koenig, David Larson, and Michael McCullough, *Handbook of Religion and Health* (New York: Oxford University Press, 2001), 236–237. Koenig and Larson from Duke University Medical Center and McCullough from Southern Methodist have compiled this gargantuan and extraordinary 700-page survey, what one physician researcher has called "a signal achievement in the history of medicine." In it they offer a critical, comprehensive, and systematic analysis of more than 1,200 studies and 400 research reviews conducted during the twentieth century, showing how religion influences health. But although the book is primarily focused on how religious commitment, community, and faith contribute to health, or the absence of such contributes to illness, it covers a wide range of psychological, emotional, spiritual, and relational issues.
7. Ibid., 284.
8. Ibid., 205.

9. Ornish, 58. The emphasis is Ornish's.
10. Ibid., 59.
11. Ibid., 58–59.
12. Janice K. Kiecolt-Glaser, et al., "Negative behavior during marital conflict is associated with immunological down-regulation," *Psychosomatic Medicine* 55, no 5: 395–409.
13. This particular comment is reported by Dean Ornish from a personal conversation, but Dr. Spiegel's research is reported in both *The Lancet*, 1989, ii: 888-91, and in his book *Living Beyond Limits: New Hope and Help for Facing Life-Threatening Illness* (New York: New York Times Books, 1993).
14. Ornish, 3.
15. Dossey, *Healing Words*, xv, xvii, 2.
16. Ibid, 109.
17. Caryl Hirshberg and Marc Ian Barasch, *Remarkable Recovery: What Extraordinary Healings Tell Us about Getting Well and Staying Well* (New York: Riverhead Books,1995), 211.
18. James S. Goodwin, et al., "The effect of marital status on stage, treatment and survival of cancer patients," *Journal of the American Medical Association* 258, no. 21 (December 4, 1987): 3125.
19. Dossey, 109.
20. R.B. Williams, J.C. Barefoot, R.M. Califf, et al, "Prognostic Importance of Social and Economic Resources among . . . Patients with . . . Coronary Artery Disease," *Journal of the American Medical Association* 267 (1992): 520–524.
21. Daniel Goldman, "Doctors find comfort is a potent medicine," *The New York Times*, February 16, 1991, B5, B8.
22. James J. Lynch, *A Cry Unheard: New Insights into the Medical Consequences of Loneliness* (Baltimore: Bancroft Press, 2000), 81.
23. Ian C. Wilson and John C. Reece, "Simultaneous Death in Schizophrenic Twins," *Archives of General Psychiatry* 11 (1964): 377–384.
24. *Noetic Science Review* (Autumn, 1988): 9.
25. J.S. House, C. Robbins, and H.L. Metzner "The Association of Social Relationships and Activities with Mortality: Prospective Evidence from the Tucumseh Community Health Study," *American Journal of Epidemiology* 116 , no. 1 (1982):123–140.
26. D.C. McClelland, "The Effect of Motivational Arousal through Films on Salivary Immunoglobulin A," *Psychology and Health* 2 (1988): 31–52.
27. Hirshberg and Barasch, 209.

Chapter Eight

1. Interview in *Medical Self Care* (Fall 1980): 4.
2. David Hilfiker, *Healing the Wounds* (New York: Pantheon Books, 1985), 13.
3. Herbert Benson, *Timeless Healing* (New York: Fireside, 1996), 118.
4. Susan Kuner, Carol Orsborn, Linda Quigley, and Karen Stroup, *Speak the Language of Healing: Living with Breast Cancer without Going to War* (Berkeley, Calif.: Conari Press, 1999), 77, 78, 82.
5. Ibid., 84, 86.
6. Ibid., 88, 89.
7. Ibid., 89, 90.
8. Benson interview in *Medical Self Care* (1980): 4.
9. Benson, *Timeless Healing,* 120.
10. Christiane Northrup, *Women's Bodies, Women's Wisdom* (New York: Bantam, 1994), 9.
11. Hirschberg and Barasch, *Remarkable Recovery,* 281.
12. Ibid., 287.
13. Northrup, 12.
14. Robert Ader, *Psychoneuroimmunology,* (New York: Academic Press, Inc., 1981), 349.
15. *The New England Journal of Medicine* (July 13, 2000) as reported in the *Boulder Daily Camera*
16. Howard Brody, *The Placebo Response* (New York: Cliff Street Books,2000), 50.
17. Ibid., 60–61.
18. Ibid., 65.
19. Ibid., 62–63.
20. Bernard Lown, in his introduction to Norman Cousins, *The Healing Heart* (New York: Norton & Company, 1983), 13–15.
21. Abraham H. Maslow, *The Farthest Reaches of Human Nature* (New York: Viking, 1971), 35–36
22. Marianne Williamson, *A Return To Love* (New York: Harper Collins,1992), 165.
23. *Common Boundary* (Jan.–Feb.1997): 14.
24. Caroline Myss, Interview in *Common Boundary* (Sept.–Oct. 1996): 27.
25. Harold Koenig and K. I. Pargament, "Religious Coping and Health Status in Medically Ill Hospitalized Older Adults," *Journal of Nervous and Mental Disease* 186 (1998): 513–521.

26. Joan Borysenko, *Fire in the Soul* (New York: Warner Books, 1993), 38.
27. Carl Jung, in *Aion*, 71.
28. Karen Armstrong, *Buddha* (New York: Viking, 2001), 100–101.
29. *Majjhima Nikaya*, 22.
30. Armstrong, xxiv.

Chapter Nine

1. Michael Murphy, *The Future of the Body: Explorations into the Further Evolution of Human Nature* (Los Angeles: Jeremy P. Tarcher, Inc., 1992), 3; 9.
2. *Microsoft Encarta 98 Encyclopedia*, "The Four-Minute Mile," 1993–1997.
3. Ibid.
4. May Sarton, "Now I Become Myself," in *Collected Poems, 1930–1973* (New York: Norton, 1974), 156.
5. David Whyte, *Crossing the Unknown Sea* (New York: Riverhead Books, 2001), 7; 165.
6. Hirschberg and Barasch, *Remarkable Recovery*, 145;147.
7. Barasch, *The Healing Path*, 373.
8. Jean Shinoda Bolen, *Close to the Bone* (New York: Touchstone, 1996), 182.
9. Dawna Markova, *I Will Not Die an Unlived Life: Reclaiming Purpose and Passion* (Berkeley, Calif.: Conari Press, 2000), 12–13.
10. Ibid., 1.
11. Richard Katz, *Boiling Energy* (Boston: Harvard University Press, 1982), 344.
12. Bolen, 181.
13. Paracelsus, quoted in *Parabola*.3, no. 3: 34.
14. Koenig, McCullough, and Larson, *Handbook of Religion and Health*, 269.
15. Barasch, *Healing Dreams*, 18.

Chapter Ten

1. L. Robert Keck, *Sacred Quest: The Evolution and Future of the Human Soul* (West Chester, Pa.: Chrysalis Books, 2000), see chapter seven.
2. Albert Einstein, *Correspondence Einstein-Michele Besso 1903–1955* (Paris: Hermann, 1972), 42.
3. Ilya Prigogine, *The End of Certainty* (New York: The Free Press,1996), 176
4. Ibid., 165.
5. Ibid., 187.
6. Edward Lorenz, *The Essence of Chaos* (London: University College London Press, 1993), 14.

7. Margaret Wheatley, *Leadership and the New Science* (San Francisco: Berrett-Koehler Publishers,1992), 124.
8. Ibid., 136–137.
9. Erich Jantsch, *The Self-Organizing Universe* (Oxford: Pergamon Press, 1980), 7.
10. Ibid., 6.
11. Wheatley, 43.
12. Ibid., 127.
13. John Briggs and F. David Peat, *Seven Life Lessons of Chaos* (New York: Harper Collins, 1999), 5; 8.
14. Koenig, et. al., 280–281.
15. Herbert Benson, *Timeless Healing* (New York: Fireside, 1996), 49–50.
16. The Foundation for Global Community, *Timeline* (July/August 1999), 7.
17. Charles Garfield, *Peak Performers* (New York: William Morrow and Company, 1986), 176–177.
18. Ibid., 177.
19. Carl G. Jung, "Basic Postulates of Analytical Psychology," in "The Structure and Dynamics of the Psyche," in *The Collected Works of C.G.Jung* (Princeton: Princeton University Press, 1978) 8:357.
20. Murray Stein, *Transformation: Emergence of the Self* (College Station, Tx.: Texas A & M University Press, 1998), 5–6.

Conclusion

1. Sam Keen, *To Love and Be Loved* (New York: Bantam Books, 1997), 23.
2. If you don't know where the closest labyrinth to you may be, consult the website www.gracecathedral.org/veriditas and/or read and check the references in Melissa Gayle West's book, *Exploring the Labyrinth* (New York: Broadway Books, 2000) or Dr. Lauren Artress's book, *Walking a Sacred Path* (New York: Riverhead Books, 1995) or Sig Lonegren's book, *Labyrinths: Ancient Myths & Modern Uses* (Revised Edition) (New York: Sterling Publishing, 2001).
3. David Whyte, *Where Many Rivers Meet: Poems* (Langley, Wash.: Many Rivers Press, 1990), 2.

GRATITUDES

In chapter 9, I shared a dream in which I was physicist Stephen Hawking, confined to a wheelchair and unable to talk because of Lou Gehrig's disease. I knew that I needed to get across the street and have my voice heard but was in despair that I would not be able to do that. Then, somebody came along and helped me get across the street; and in the process, I was able to regain my voice and get out of the wheelchair and walk again.

This was during a particularly dark night of my soul, when I was discouraged and despairing about whether or not I would be able to afford the time to research and write this book. What felt powerfully relevant to me was my calling to speak and write about what I had learned about healing. I felt that no one could hear my feelings of despair about possibly not having my voice heard and not being able to get across the street—in other words, not to be able to finish the book and get it published.

In the dream, someone came up behind me and began to push my wheelchair across the street. Then, to my amazement, as we got about half way across the street, I regained my voice. By the time we reached the other side of the street, I was getting up out of the wheelchair and walking along beside the friend who had given me a hand.

In real life, not long thereafter, a number of friends did, indeed, provide the variety of assistance needed for me to get this book written and published. I am exceedingly grateful for and blessed by such friends. The Reverend Toni Cook and St. Paul's United Methodist Church created a "Deep-Value Research Fund"; and Kent Meager, Rob Walton, Nance Larson, Kiyoshi Murata, Paul and Marilyn Jerde, Jay and Mary Beth Coonan, and Raymond Montgomery Jr. contributed to that fund, enabling the time I needed for the research and writing. Kiyoshi also donated a website, Jeff Jerde created a beautiful design for the website, and Linda Commito gave valuable editorial assistance.

This book is also the result of the many blessings I have experienced in my relationship with the Swedenborg Foundation's publishing imprint, Chrysalis Books. I can't imagine having a better relationship with a publisher than what I have with Deborah Forman or a more skillful editor than I have in Mary Lou Bertucci, with whom I have had an absolutely delightful working relationship. I also want to thank Karen Conner for the wonderful jacket design.

A CALL *for* STORIES

If stories come to you, care for them. And learn to give them away where they are needed. Sometimes a person needs a story more than food to stay alive.

BARRY LOPEZ

My next book may be that of sharing stories of people who have had miraculous healings that involved the principles discussed in this book, particularly the awakening of inner potential and the transformation of one's deepest soul-self. If you have such a story to tell, would be willing to share it, and give me permission to use it in a book, please write it up—typewritten, double-spaced, along with your name, address, telephone number, and email—and send it to me at:

L. Robert Keck
P. O. Box 4589
Boulder, CO 80306

I celebrate your healing, and thank you for enriching my life and the lives of others who will read and benefit from it.

My blessings on all you are being and doing.

Bob Keck

INDEX

ABOUT *the* AUTHOR

L. Robert Keck is the inaugural senior fellow at the Foundation for Global Community in Palo Alto, California. He holds a master's degree in theology from Vanderbilt University and a Ph.D. in the Philosophy of Health from Union Graduate School. He has been a United Methodist minister, served on the medical school faculty of The Ohio State University, founded and managed a corporate wellness consulting firm, and was president of Boulder Graduate School. Recently completing a term as scholar-in-residence at the Graduate Theological Union, he also teaches at the University of Creation Spirituality in Oakland, California, and the Iliff School of Theology in Denver. He is the author of four books, including *Sacred Quest: The Evolution and Future of The Human Soul,* and is a highly acclaimed conference and convention keynote speaker. Check his web site for more information: www.robertkeck.com